MW01493838

PSYCHOANALYSIS MEETS PSYCHOSIS

Psychoanalysis Meets Psychosis proposes a major revision of the psychoanalytic theory of the most severe mental illnesses including schizophrenia. Freud believed that psychosis is the consequence of a biologically determined inability to attain and sustain a normal or neurotic mental organization. Michael Robbins proposes instead that psychosis is the outcome of a different developmental pathway. Conscious mind functions in two qualitatively different ways, primordial conscious mentation and reflective representational thought, and psychosis is the result of persistence of a primordial mental process, which is adaptive in infancy, in later situations in which it is neither appropriate nor adaptive.

In Part I Robbins describes how the medical model of psychosis underlies the current approach of both psychiatry and psychoanalysis, despite the fact that neuroscience has failed to confirm the model's basic organic assumption. In Part II Robbins examines two of Freud's models of psychosis that are based on the assumption of a constitutional inability to develop a normal or neurotic mind. The theories of succeeding generations of analysts have for the most part reiterated the biases of Freud's two models, so that psychoanalysis considers the psychoses beyond its scope. In Part III Robbins proposes that the psychoses are the result of disturbances in the attachment–separation phase of development, leading to maladaptive persistence of a primordial form of mental activity related to Freud's primary process. Finally, in Part IV Robbins describes a psychoanalytic approach to treatment based on his model. The book is richly illustrated with material from Robbins' clinical practice.

Psychoanalysis Meets Psychosis has the potential to undo centuries of alienation between society and psychotic persons. The book offers an understanding of severe mental illness that will be novel and inspiring not only to psychoanalysts but to all mental health professionals.

Michael Robbins is former Professor of Clinical Psychiatry at Harvard Medical School, USA. He is a member of the American and International Psychoanalytic Associations. His previous books include *Experiences of Schizophrenia* (1993), *Conceiving of Personality* (1996), *The Primordial Mind in Health and Illness: A Cross-Cultural Perspective* (2011), and *Consciousness, Language, and Self: A Psychoanalytic, Linguistic, and Anthropological Exploration of the Dual Nature of Mind* (2018).

PSYCHOANALYSIS MEETS PSYCHOSIS

Attachment, Separation, and the Undifferentiated Unintegrated Mind

Michael Robbins

Routledge
Taylor & Francis Group

LONDON AND NEW YORK

First published 2019
by Routledge
2 Park Square, Milton Park, Abingdon, Oxon OX14 4RN

and by Routledge
52 Vanderbilt Avenue, New York, NY 10017

Routledge is an imprint of the Taylor & Francis Group, an informa business

© 2019 Michael Robbins

The right of Michael Robbins to be identified as author of this work has been asserted by him in accordance with sections 77 and 78 of the Copyright, Designs and Patents Act 1988.

All rights reserved. No part of this book may be reprinted or reproduced or utilised in any form or by any electronic, mechanical, or other means, now known or hereafter invented, including photocopying and recording, or in any information storage or retrieval system, without permission in writing from the publishers.

Trademark notice: Product or corporate names may be trademarks or registered trademarks, and are used only for identification and explanation without intent to infringe.

British Library Cataloguing-in-Publication Data
A catalogue record for this book is available from the British Library

Library of Congress Cataloging-in-Publication Data
A catalog record has been requested for this book

ISBN: 978-0-367-19115-3 (hbk)
ISBN: 978-0-367-19117-7 (pbk)
ISBN: 978-0-429-20054-0 (ebk)

Typeset in Bembo
by Swales & Willis, Exeter, Devon, UK

CONTENTS

THEORISTS OF PSYCHOSIS WHOSE CONTRIBUTIONS ARE DISCUSSED IN CHAPTERS 4, 5, 6, AND 7

Chapter 4 includes the work of:

Chapter 5 includes the work of:

Chapter 6 includes the work of:

Knight, p. 52
Kernberg, p. 52

Chapter 7 includes the work of:

Klein, p. 59
Balint, p. 60
Fairbairn, p. 61
Sullivan, p. 62
Von Domarus, p. 63
Arieti, pp. 63–64
Matte-Blanco, pp. 63–64
Lombardi, p. 65

INTRODUCTION

I am hoping that your curiosity has been piqued by the title of the book, *Psychoanalysis Meets Psychosis*, and that you wonder about the rationale behind the words. The title refers to attachments, the kind of attachment or lack thereof that has characterized the relationship between psychoanalysis and psychosis, and the theory I propose in the book that psychosis is the outgrowth of a severe disturbance of attachment between mother and infant in the earliest stage of life.

The term "neurosis" was coined by William Cullen to denote a nervous system disease, about a quarter century before Freud's groundbreaking work. Freud co-opted the term and gave it psychological meaning as the cornerstone around which he constructed psychoanalysis. His theory has been modified in particulars by his successors over the past century, but its essential elements of infantile intrapsychic conflict, repression, unconscious mind, and re-emergence of the repressed in disguise remain as the psychoanalytic model of mind and its pathological aberration.

Psychosis, by contrast, has a lengthy history as a manifestation of pathology that long antedates psychoanalysis and its basic assumption that the workings of the mind are meaningful. The pathology we now think of as psychosis has been known by many dehumanizing labels over the centuries, ranging from madness, criminality, and hereditary defect, through such "scientific" labels as *dementia praecox, paraphrenia*, and finally the *schizophrenia* of the current day DSM, the bible of American psychiatry. Psychoanalytic attempts starting with Freud to grapple with this alien entity have mostly involved accepting the organic defect axiom underlying these medical-psychiatric definitions, and using the neurosis model of mind that is the core of psychoanalytic theory and practice as the context for incorporating it. The result is psychoanalytic models of psychosis as defect: incapacity to develop and sustain a normal/neurotic mental organization.

Some examples might serve to clarify that we are in a world in which psychoanalysis and psychosis are mutually irrelevant. A non-medical psychoanalyst colleague moved with her husband, an MD psychoanalyst, to an area in a Southern state distant from a big city. In addition to continuing with some of her former patients using distance technology she tried, with very limited success, to build a new psychoanalytic practice. Meanwhile, her husband is in great demand as a locum tenens, working with disturbed, most likely psychotic, patients as a medical psychiatrist in a psychiatric hospital setting, My own practice of psychoanalysis began many decades ago when psychoanalysis had an important role in at least some mental hospitals such as McLean, where I worked, and where parts of my therapy with Sara, summarized in Chapter 16, took place. A combination of the problems arising from the lack of an adequate psychoanalytic understanding of psychosis and the evolution of psychiatry as a branch of neuroscience and psychopharmacology has created a situation in which there is no place for psychoanalysis in mental hospitals, which play an essential role in the treatment of schizophrenia. As a consequence my more recent work with psychosis has been mostly limited to more functional individuals with psychotic personality disorders, examples of which are included later in the book.

There is no reason why psychiatry, which has enjoyed great success with its neuroscience-psychopharmacological model of psychosis should want to meet psychoanalysis, so this book represents my effort to help psychoanalysis meet psychosis. The purpose of this book is to introduce psychoanalysis to psychosis in a way that is internal to psychoanalysis and at the same time independent of the neurosis model and the biases that attend upon it.

The other aspect of attachment to which the book's title refers has to do with the theory I propose; namely that psychosis arises from a severe disturbance of the bond between mother and infant. But before pursuing that, I would like to pursue some of the history of the attachment problem between psychoanalysis and psychosis. Our understanding of psychosis has been distorted, even perverted, by the ages-old belief that it is the consequence of a hereditary neurodegenerative defect or human stain. Afflicted individuals are believed to have "lost" all or parts of their minds. This idea has evolved from centuries-old attitudes of alienation, rejection, and attack directed toward persons who frighten us because they are different, to the more caring veneer of contemporary medical "science." The basic assumption of the brain defect model has permeated psychoanalytic efforts to understand psychosis, as well. As a consequence, the concept of psychosis has a place in mental health analogous to that of leprosy in medicine.

The contemporary psychiatric iteration of the medical model is to be found in the *Diagnostic and Statistical Manual of the American Psychiatric Association* (DSM) that codifies committee judgments about constellations of symptoms and behaviors that constitute social deviance or abnormality, and regardless of the lack of supporting evidence labels them the consequence of organic disease. The standard treatment for these presumed physical ills, not surprisingly, is drugs. The medical beliefs that are taught to patients as psychotherapy adjunctive to the drugs are actually instructions about how to change the expression of psychosis to one that is more socially adaptive. As we will see, beneath the therapeutic intent they actually reinforce the basic psychotic process. What is astonishing is that the organic assumptions on which the medical model is based remain unproven despite decades of costly research sponsored largely by the very drug companies that serve to profit by it.

Psychoanalysis is a relative conceptual and therapeutic newcomer to the problem of psychosis. Freud practiced in his private office with persons who were for the most part functional, and did not knowingly encounter and attempt to treat psychotic persons. When he attempted to treat persons we would now consider psychotic he believed they were neurotic and applied the model he had devised to help such individuals.

Freud assumed children possess the capacity to differentiate self from other, and to experience intrapsychic conflict. He assumed that the major intrapsychic problems encountered growing up involve struggles with biologically driven instincts, and the major interpersonal problems involve relationship with authority in the person of the father. Instincts or drives shape a person's interpretation of early interpersonal experiences, producing psychological conflicts that the mind resolves in the course of normal/neurotic maturation. Developments preceding the Oedipal struggle with father are conceptualized not in interpersonal terms but as conflicts related to the three biologically endowed erogenous zones. He was preoccupied with the importance of the father and authority and the conflicts he believed impede the child's acceptance of it. His model emphasizes the importance of inhibiting impulses and fantasies that if enacted might be revolutionary and destructive to civilized order. For whatever reasons of his personality Freud as a theorist was unaware of the fundamental psychological importance of infantile attachment to and separation from mother, and indeed of the existence and importance of mental life and relationships before mind attains the capacity to experience intrapsychic conflict.

Freud's basic biological orientation and lack of experience with psychotic persons appears to have predisposed him to accept the conclusion of the psychiatry of his time as articulated by Eugen Bleuler, who was in turn influenced by Emil Kraepelin. Regardless of the absence of supporting organic evidence, they were convinced that psychosis is a dementing neurodegenerative illness that leaves the afflicted person lacking the basic mental equipment to attain and sustain a normal/neurotic personality organization.

While Freud's emphasis on biology, derived from his background in neurology, diminished gradually over the course of his career, it had a fundamental effect on his understanding of psychosis. Bleuler's belief that schizophrenia/psychosis is a degenerative dementing organic disease may well have influenced two of Freud's models of psychosis, relational and integrational, that figure most prominently in his writings, and are reflected in the writings of subsequent generations of psychoanalysts as well.

Although subsequent generations of analysts have moved away from his initial belief that his psychological theory would ultimately be reduced to its biological essence, and toward a theory that is more psychological and interpersonal, their views of psychosis remain for the most part reflections of Freud's biological orientation.

What attention Freud did pay to psychosis took the form of two hypotheses that came from the same basic assumption of neurodegenerative defect. In chronological order, the first is that psychotic persons are unable to form a relationship (the transference) and hence are beyond the scope of psychoanalysis. The second is that the psychotic person is incapable of developing and sustaining a normal/neurotic mental structure and hence has a mind that is inherently split into a regressive-degenerative psychotic part and a more mature non-psychotic part, as a consequence of an ego that is too weak to repress disruptive content and hence is incapable of guarding against regression. Influenced by Freud's first, relational, hypothesis psychoanalysts split into two camps. The first, including the vast majority, have assumed that it is not possible to form a relationship with a schizophrenic person, or else believe that intensive work with people deemed susceptible should be avoided as it encourages regression. They agree that this defect renders psychosis beyond the scope of psychoanalysis. The other camp, comprising a smaller number of analysts, devoted their clinical careers to proving it is possible to establish a relationship with a psychotic person, while for the most part failing to recognize that the basic problem of psychosis has more to do with the nature of the relationships such persons form than whether they can form relationships to begin with.

Although the proliferation of writings about psychosis by subsequent generations of analysts may convey the illusion of progress, and indeed many elaborate the nature of the psychotic process, most actually perpetuate and expand Freud's beliefs that schizophrenia is the result of an inherited defect in the capacity to attain and sustain a neurotic/normal personality organization and to develop the ordinary forms of relationship that go along with it. The psychoanalytic perspective on psychosis can be highlighted with an analogy. Suppose zoology had commenced with the study of zebras and had become identified with that species. While scientists would have been aware of the existence of other creatures, if they were deemed worthy of study at all they might be defined not as different members of the animal species requiring comprehension of their unique biology, but as deficient failures to become or sustain being zebras. The shocking truth is that persons with psychoses, the major mental affliction of humankind, have been treated like medicine once treated lepers, quarantined from ordinary human relationships. What has not been considered is the possibility that psychosis is the consequence of a developmental pathway separate and independent from that of neurosis, commencing with problems of attachment and separation, and that the condition may be treatable with an approach that is different from the methodology developed to analyze neurosis.

That is not the end of the Freud story, however. In the earliest stages of his career, prior to his relationship with Bleuler, Freud did make one effort to conceptualize psychosis as a condition different from neurosis but every bit as human and understandable. He speculated that his primary process model (1900), the mental activity of infancy and dreaming, is also the basis of psychosis. However he did not pursue this idea and he left the primary process concept in a condition of confusion and contradiction about its relationship to thought, about its fundamental normality or pathology, and about the nature of consciousness itself (Robbins, 2018).

In the pages to come, building upon Freud's theory of primary process, I articulate a psychoanalytic model in which psychosis is conceived of not as a human stain or defect but as the result of a different developmental pathway from that which eventuates in neurosis. It is based on ideas I have proposed elsewhere (2011, 2018), that mind consists of two qualitatively different conscious processes, primordial consciousness and reflective representational thought, each of which is inherently normal. Despite Freud's biological orientation and the historical taint of defect that saturates our understanding of psychosis, normality and abnormality are social judgments. It is the individually unique admixture of reflective thought and first mind or primordial consciousness, and the social context in which the result emerges, that determine the expressions of personality that elicit social judgments of normality or psychotic pathology.

Building upon contributions of Rank, Bowlby, and others, the model I propose contrasts neurosis, a condition arising in more or less separate autonomous individuals, whose manifestations are based on repressed unresolved intrapsychic conflict, with psychosis, a disorder of attachment resulting in failure to become a psychologically separate individual with the capacity to experience and sustain intrapsychic conflict. Neurotic persons function for the most part in reflective representational thought whereas psychotic persons for the most part function according to a process I call first mind or primordial conscious mentation, though the less severely impaired are successful in concealing the fact in their everyday dealings.

A psychoanalysis that embraces psychosis as a separate condition with its own line of development, standing alongside neurosis, has the potential to mitigate the stigma historically attached to afflicted individuals. It can offer a haven of understanding and growth to those who might otherwise hide themselves from treatment, or be subject to medical treatment that unwittingly perpetuates the psychotic process and hinders its sufferers from realizing their full human potential.

PART I

Not fully human

The unwitting collusion between medicine and psychoanalysis

1

NOT FULLY HUMAN

Psychiatric and psychoanalytic understandings of psychosis

Neurosis and psychosis are both mental illnesses with no specific organic cause – other than the subtle genetics that underlie ordinary personality idiosyncrasies – despite decades of costly research. Yet there is a historically based chasm of social acceptance and understanding separating them based on the belief psychosis is an organic disease whereas neurosis is not. Over the course of hundreds of years western culture has engaged in a search and destroy mission, sometimes blatant and other times more subtle, toward persons manifesting extremes of socially deviant behavior and mentation. However legitimized by medical jargon and papered over by a veneer of medical compassion it is widely accepted that such persons suffer from an organic defect or degeneracy that renders them morally and intellectually deficient, pariahs, not fully human. They are not ordinary folk like "us" who suffer from the range of personality quirks or idiosyncrasies, or suffer from an illness like diabetes or depression. The medical-psychiatric edition of this prejudice, for it is a judgment reached by committee without substantiating organic data, is the *Diagnostic and Statistical Manual of the American Psychiatric Association* (DSM). The belief dates to the dawn of modern medical psychiatry and the work of Emil Kraepelin and Eugen Bleuler. It is based on observation and description of signs, symptoms, and behavior of persons considered abnormal or socially deviant, and inferences about causation. In that model, psychosis, more or less synonymous with schizophrenia and manic-depressive illness, is considered to be a form of organic degeneracy of early adult onset. In his textbook of psychiatry Bleuler, who is responsible for the diagnosis schizophrenia, was of the opinion that such persons are racially inferior and should be sterilized to prevent species contamination.

Psychoanalysis represents an entirely different tradition, one that considers mind as a meaningful system and seeks to understand it in an accepting humanistic way. It seeks to understand the "inner" and less conscious workings of mind, dynamic and structural, the ways in which they are unusual, and their relationship to individual psychosocial development. It is no accident that Freud created psychoanalysis in the course of his attempt to understand his own mind. Its paradigmatic problem is neurosis, a variant of normal mature mind that he believed afflicts many of us and limits our potential and sense of satisfaction. Psychoanalysis defines neurosis as the symptomatic manifestation of unresolved unconscious mental conflicts. Because of this humanistic history one would expect, and most psychoanalysts believe, that it depicts the psychoses in a more humanistic way. But such is not the case.

Freud and psychoanalysis did not knowingly venture into the land of psychosis, the territory of medical psychiatry. Freud had a private practice in his office and did not work in a mental hospital. He more or less accepted the belief prevalent among his psychiatric contemporaries Kraepelin and Bleuler that psychosis is a genetically determined mental/moral deficiency caused by an underlying genetic-organic deficiency.

Freud's background in medicine and neurology meant that he was no stranger to biological reductionism and therefore open to accepting such conclusions. The term he chose to designate psychoanalysis' flagship disorder, "neurosis" was coined by the Scottish physician William Cullen in 1869 to denote a disease of the nervous system. Freud borrowed the term and re-defined it to designate those conditions characterized by symptomatology arising from repressed unconscious conflict, one pole of which is usually driven by biological drive derivatives. In the introduction to his 1895 "Project for a scientific psychology" he writes "The intention is to furnish a psychology that shall be a natural science: that is, to represent psychical processes as quantitatively determinate states of specifiable material particles" (1895, p. 294). A quarter century later he wrote:

> The deficiencies in our description would probably vanish if we were already in a position to replace the psychological terms by physiological or chemical ones. ... We may expect it [biology] to give us the most surprising information ... which will blow away the whole of our artificial structure of hypotheses.
>
> *(1920, p. 59)*

Psychoanalytic historians tend to focus on how Bleuler, who was one of Freud's earliest followers, was influenced by Freud, citing a number of psychoanalytic publications authored in the first decade of the 20th century by Bleuler alone and in conjunction with Jung, which unfortunately have not been translated into English (Falzeder, 2003), and by a series of letters exchanged between the two between 1915 and 1925 (Alexander & Selesnick, 1965). Of particular interest with regard to psychosis is the reciprocal question, how Freud may have been influenced by Bleuler.

Unlike Freud, who treated affluent patients sufficiently independent to live outside a hospital and come to his office, Bleuler practiced in a mental hospital, the Burghölzli, was its director beginning in 1898, and lived there with his family. He and Jung, who also practiced there, were colleagues and professional collaborators, as well as followers of Freud and his new discipline. Bleuler was a member of Freud's Vienna Society and helped Jung publish the *Jahrbuch*, a forerunner of what is now the *International Journal of Psychoanalysis*. Jung and Bleuler were especially interested in Freud's work on dreaming and fantasy, and in the concept of free association (1896, 1906). Bleuler published his well-known textbook in which he coined the term schizophrenia in 1911, the year Freud published his analysis of the Schreber case.

Bleuler resigned from the psychoanalytic society around that time. He was distressed by what he believed was the authoritarian religious element Freud was promoting. Of particular relevance to this book, he had a theoretical disagreement with Freud's conclusion that Schreber's illness was essentially neurotic, the consequence of repressed Oedipal conflicts over homosexuality and castration anxiety (Bleuler, 1912). He continued to admire Freud, however, and subsequently tried to nominate him for a Nobel Prize.

Although he was much more psychologically minded and humanistic than Kraepelin, Bleuler fundamentally concurred with Kraepelin that schizophrenia is a neuro-degenerative dementing disease. What he called the primary symptoms, the well-known "four A's," disturbed affect, autism, ambivalence, and disturbed associations, along with mental splitting or failure of integration, presumably reflect the degenerative organic core. Bleuler believed that what he called the secondary symptoms, delusions and hallucinations, are psychologically meaningful, susceptible of analysis using Freud's theories, but the implication is that the meaning is epiphenomenal, not related to the origins of the illness. Brill (1944) quotes Bleuler's 1906 paper on Freudian mechanisms in psychosis:

> It is impossible to know the meaning of delusions without considering the Freudian discoveries. The content of many delusions is often nothing but a poorly concealed wish-dream, which by the means offered by the particular disease (hallucinations of the various senses, delusions, paramnesias) seeks to represent the wish as fulfilled – I say seeks to represent, for even in a delirium and in a dream, a person does not always entirely forget that his wishes are confronted by obstacles. The latter become symbolized as "persecutions," just as similar experiences of healthy persons created Ormuz and Ahriman, God and the Devil.
>
> *(p. 98)*

Bleuler's basic belief, however, is reflected in his advocacy for sterilization of schizophrenics so that their hereditary dehumanizing taint not be passed on to others (Joseph, 2003, p. 160). He believed the secondary symptoms of hallucination and delusion were optional, so that it was possible to diagnose schizophrenia even in their absence. This belief is of interest with regard to the model advanced further in this book of a psychotic continuum, and the concept of psychotic personality disorder, a condition in which there are no blatantly obvious delusions or hallucinations.

Freud was conditioned to accept the opinions of Bleuler and others for two reasons. Unlike them he did not work in a mental hospital and did not knowingly have clinical contact with individuals deemed schizophrenic. And his neurological background led him to believe that his theory should be reducible to biology. The concept of fundamental organic deficiency rendering the person less than fully human runs through two of his models. First, his model of inability to form a human relationship, and second, his model that psychosis represents defect or deficiency in the mental equipment necessary to develop and maintain a normal or neurotic psyche, leading to splitting of the personality into more mature and progressively regressive or degenerative parts. He never pursued his most promising model that he derived from the phenomenon of dreaming, the primary process. He was committed to the concept of unconscious mind and the idea that the primary process was its modus operandi. He was unable to understand that the primary process is a modality of conscious mind as normal as that which underlies neurosis, and that just as ordinary thought can evolve into neurosis under suitable circumstances, so primary process consciousness can evolve into psychosis. Such an idea would lead to a model not of one human and one subhuman condition, but of two different but equally understandable mental disorders and their separate lines of development. Those who followed in Freud's footsteps formulated models related to his and failed to recognize the extent to which they elaborated his basic assumptions, and that their idiosyncratically conceptualized efforts have perpetuated the prejudices and limitations of his model.

While psychoanalysis has made a number of efforts to extend its psychological theory of mind and meaning to psychosis in general, and schizophrenia in particular, these have by and large been unsatisfactory. With a single exception, the work of Ronald Fairbairn, psychoanalysis defines the psychoses, more or less, as failures or deficiencies in the maturational capacity to attain and sustain a normal/neurotic personality organization. Psychoanalysis has not succeeded in defining a realm separate but equivalent to the neuroses that we can accept and recognize in ourselves and those around us that is not tainted with the stigma of defectiveness. It has not articulated a model of illness and treatment that can be used to help the vast majority of the world's mentally ill whose afflictions are beyond the purview of the theory of neurosis and an office psychoanalytic practice with the "worried well." The relevance of Fairbairn's (1952) contribution to psychosis is not widely recognized. In contrast to the majority of psychoanalytic theory, which is oriented around a conception of normality that holds that we are all neurotic, more or less, Fairbairn's theory of schizoid personality holds that we are all psychotic, more or less, ranging from milder forms of schizoid personality that afflict all of us, to the severe conditions like schizophrenia.

In the pages to come I elaborate the hypothesis that there are two forms of normal mental activity and that depending on the vicissitudes of attachment and separation one may evolve in the direction of neurosis, the other in the direction of psychosis, and that both conditions are fully human, meaningful, and comprehensible by psychoanalytic theory. I propose that in addition to the more extreme conditions such as schizophrenia, there is a psychotic personality organization that many of us who are perceived as respected constructive members of society suffer from. The model I propose is intended to make psychosis a problem as ordinary and socially acceptable as neurosis, and in so doing bring it under the umbrella of psychoanalytic theory and therapy.

It is the thesis of this book that psychosis, in most instances, is a particular manifestation of personality that is no better explained as the result of neural defect than any other variant. Neurotic individuals are able to negotiate the major transitions of separation and individuation reasonably successfully, and as a result are capable of experiencing intrapsychic conflict. They suffer distress and limitations resulting from difficulties consciously recognizing the nature of the conflicts and resolving them. Psychosis, by contrast, arises from failure of attachment and consequent inability to separate from the mothering person and integrate a mind of one's own. The result is inability to live independently and experience and resolve internal conflict. While genetic factors no doubt play a role in some instances, as they do in all personality variations, there is no convincing evidence that they are more than ancillary forces influencing conditions whose origins lie within the family of origin, and most specifically in the mother or caregiver–infant interaction.

Psychosis manifests itself in a variety of guises. Unlike neurosis it does not present as a complaint about internal suffering. Its manifestations tend to be external and to involve social perturbations in relationships and self-care. These may go unnoticed until they come to social attention around times in the life cycle that require new steps or transitions toward separation from family of origin and establishment of an independent identity and sense of self. The most severe manifestation, child psychosis, emerges when children cannot separate sufficiently from their primary relationship and home to begin school. During the second separation phase in the normal life cycle, in late adolescence and early adulthood, the configuration known as schizophrenia emerges when the person is unable to separate successfully from home and family of origin to make an independent life involving college, work or career, intimate relationship, and starting a family. From a social adaptation perspective the least severe form, psychotic personality, comes to light still later, when those who are apparently able to negotiate both separations but on closer examination have depended on the shaky scaffolding of a façade, perhaps even a socially successful and constructive one, are unable to form and sustain an intimate relationship and a stable work life. Currently they are labelled things like addictive personality, sociopathy, narcissistic personality, schizoid personality, or even PTSD. I call this condition psychotic personality disorder. For those who equate psychosis with schizophrenia and cite hallucinations and delusions as defining characteristics it is instructive to note that both Bleuler (1911b) and Jung (1939), who collaborated with him in the first decade of the 20th century, believed that it is what Bleuler called the primary symptoms that define psychosis/schizophrenia, and that the presence of the secondary symptoms of hallucinations and delusions is not essential to the diagnosis.

2

THE MEDICALIZATION OF MADNESS

Evolution of the equation of psychosis with degeneracy

The prevailing view of psychosis is the result of a collaborative and financially lucrative effort by a quartet comprised of psychiatry, neuroscience, and the pharmaceutical and health insurance industries. They maintain that psychosis is an organic physical illness of genetic origin, whose mental manifestations are secondary products of a chemical disruption or an electrical storm in the brain that are either meaningless or whose meaning has no relevance to treatment. However cloaked with medical caring, this view is dehumanizing and stigmatizing. Unlike our attitude toward persons afflicted with diabetes or cancer, conditions that do not primarily affect mind and behavior, or conditions that do, such as neurosis and depression, most of us would have trouble acknowledging or wanting a close relationship with someone diagnosed schizophrenic. This is a culturally determined prejudice, not an objective assessment, as many cultures, ancient, tribal, and non-western, make a special place for such persons and designate them with names that reflect reverence not revulsion, like seer.

In order to understand the reasons for this prejudice it is important to understand the history and genealogy of the current view of psychosis. The history of the concept involves a journey of at least several hundred years, from the prisons and so-called hospitals like Bedlam of early industrial England to the hospitals and clinics of contemporary society that function according to the dictates of the *Diagnostic and Statistical Manual* (DSM).

The history of denigrating social judgment about persons whose mental expressions and behaviors are disruptive to others dates back hundreds of years to long before there was a medical profession. It includes labels and associated "treatments" that to our modern ears sound degrading and horrifying. This history has included the belief that the person is subhuman or bestial, genetically defective, lacking morals and the capacity for reason, possessed by demons, criminal, and more. As medicine slowly evolved into a profession with scientific pretensions such blatantly denigrating labels have slowly been replaced by ones that we assume are more "scientific" because they are supposedly related to brain disease, and technology has been developed to map and measure neural activity.

A brief history of the evolution of mental illness from social dehumanization and rejection to medical legitimization can be divided into three parts. The first of these, which I will call Pseudoscience I, spans the 18th and 19th centuries, including the beginnings of medicine as a profession and its treatment of the mentally disturbed, and its first efforts to differentiate itself from theologically inspired efforts to exorcise the devil. Benjamin Rush, one of the signers of the Declaration of Independence, helped to found the first medical school in the United States in the late 1700s. He became interested in the treatment of mental illness during his training in London, and after returning to the United States established the first mental ward within a hospital. For this he is known as the father of American psychiatry. However, he perpetuated many of the dehumanizing views about mentally disturbed persons and their treatment he had learned from practices common in England in institutions like Bedlam, which housed and treated the insane beginning around 1500. Rush considered himself a humanist, and while he did not use practices common in England like flagellation and confinement in chains in a dungeon, he devised a number of treatments that we would now look upon as torture and physical punishment, designed to exorcise the person of the imagined diabolical, bestial, or criminal elements. These include devices that seem like precursors of ones used to simulate extreme gravity conditions for astronauts – dehydration, starvation, exsanguination, purging with calomel (mercury chloride, formerly used as a purgative, now considered a fungicide and insecticide), and blistering of skin with pitch or branding iron, near drowning, exposure to extremes of heat and cold, and more.

Jumping ahead 100 years, the second installment of the history of mental illness, which I call Pseudoscience II, includes the first half of the 20th century, ending shortly after World War II. While for the most part it was no longer believed that the mentally ill had been entered by the devil, even the most academic medical wisdom was that it is possible to get rid of the body parts that were considered to be the seat of defectiveness, criminality, and insanity, terms that were used more or less interchangeably. Organs removed with pseudoscientific rationalization included clitoris, testicles and ovaries, teeth, gallbladder, and thyroid. Other practices included inducing extreme fever with malaria, and refrigeration to lower temperature to near coma.

As the brain was increasingly viewed as the site of the illness, and it is obviously impossible to remove the brain without removing the person, attention turned to genetics, and the eugenics movement emerged. It involved compulsory sterilization of "defectives." Most states passed compulsory sterilization laws. In a 1927 judgment made by the Supreme Court (*Buck v. Bell*), the respected Justice Oliver Wendell Holmes wrote the Court's opinion, entitled "Three generations of imbeciles are enough." He stated that a Virginia state law permitting compulsory sterilization of those labelled unfit "for the protection and health of the state" was constitutional. The movement to legalize sterilization came from respectable academic institutions like Harvard, as well. These practices reflected views that became increasingly popular until their ultimate and extreme expression, Nazi Germany. They more or less disappeared around World War II, perhaps because the mass extermination of Jews as non-Aryan defectives was inescapably repugnant to civilized people.

Other practices that mostly ended shortly after I finished my own psychiatric training in the early 1960s included insulin coma designed to produce hypoglycemic shock, use of cold packs, and prefrontal lobotomy. Walter Freeman, the king of lobotomy, performed about 3,500 lobotomies, refining his technique in later years so he simply drove an ice pick into the frontal lobe through the eye socket above the upper lid. His most famous patient was John F. Kennedy's sister Rosemary, whom he lobotomized when she was 23 at the request of her father Joe, who did not like her behavior. The procedure failed and left her in need of lifelong institutional care. The use of electroconvulsive therapy (ECT) continues.

Moving to the present day we come to what I call Pseudoscience III, "medical" understanding and treatment. What we find is, in a sense, the same old wine in new bottles. In the first volume of his *Études cliniques* (1851) Benedict Morel used the term *démence précoce* to describe the characteristics of a subset of young patients that he associated with dementia. He employed the phrase frequently in his textbook *Traité des maladies mentales* which was published in 1860. In 1896 Emil Kraepelin (1919) ushered in the modern era of understanding when he published his famous text on dementia praecox, a progressive mental deterioration beginning in late adolescence and early adulthood that he believed to be an organic disease of the frontal lobes despite the absence of any detectable lesion. In 1911 Eugen Bleuler (1911b) ushered in our current understanding when he re-named Kraepelin's dementia praecox "schizophrenia." He described an illness characterized by splitting of psychic functions. He distinguished what he called primary symptoms – known to students as "the four A's," dissociation of affect from thought, fragmentation of associations, ambivalence defined as the simultaneous presence of contradictory affects and ideas or splitting, and autism or withdrawal – from secondary or accessory symptoms: delusions and hallucinations. Bleuler believed the primary symptoms were the consequence of hereditary neural degeneracy, and in his *Textbook of Psychiatry* (1911a) he recommended sterilization of schizophrenics to avoid propagating this organic taint.

> The more severely burdened should not propagate themselves. … If we do nothing but make mental and physical cripples capable of propagating themselves, and the healthy stocks have to limit the number of their children because so much has to be done for the maintenance of others, if natural selection is generally suppressed, then unless we will get new measures our race must rapidly deteriorate.
>
> *(p. 214)*

He considered secondary symptoms, delusions and hallucinations, comprehensible utilizing Freudian principles of interpretation of the unconscious meaning of dreams and fantasies.

When considering the psychiatric view of psychosis and the gulf between it and psychoanalysis it is important to keep in mind that psychiatry is largely an external descriptive discipline, based upon observable signs and symptoms, whereas psychoanalysis focuses on the inner dynamics of mind and meaning. Since Kraepelin, psychiatry, in conjunction with neuroscience, has attempted to find an internal foundation for psychosis, albeit one that is organic rather than psychological. This psychiatric model, based on phenomenological observation of behavior rather than an attempt to understand meaning, remains the predominant way most people including psychoanalysts think about psychosis.

Returning to the evolution of the psychiatric view of psychosis, concurrent with the development of psychiatry after World War II two other fields emerged: psychiatry and neuroscience, and two new industries, pharmaceutical and health care insurance. These strange bedfellows soon discovered a common interest and have informally joined forces and profited immensely by literally selling to the public the belief that mental ills are physical ills that are treatable by physical-chemical means. After the landmark belief that a "model psychosis" could be induced and studied with LSD and the creation of chlorpromazine, a drug that seemed capable of treating psychosis, the rapidly expanding pharmaceutical industry recognized that creation of new drugs to treat the symptoms of the new class of diseases created by psychiatry and the DSM might be a hugely profitable enterprise, and psychiatrists soon realized that psychopharmacology, enabling rapid treatment of a large number of patients, could be a hugely profitable enterprise. The psychiatric treatment of psychosis based on the use of drugs is discussed in Chapter 11.

How did this collaboration come about? After World War II psychiatry was looked down upon by the other medical specialties because it had no physically defined diseases in its stable, and no remarkable treatments except for some continued use of lobotomy, insulin coma, and electroshock. There was a brief romance between psychoanalysis and psychosis in the aftermath of the war, expressed in movies like *Spellbound* and novels like *I Never Promised You a Rose Garden* (Green, 1964) and *The Fifty-Minute Hour* (Lindner, 1966). Many psychiatrists, unable or unwilling to undertake psychoanalytic training, practiced their understanding of psychoanalytically informed therapy with psychotic persons, and while there were some successes the specialized training, labor intensity, and apparent cost per patient of such an enterprise led to disillusionment, and an opportunistic psychiatric profession changed conceptual and institutional horses, turned away from the idea that the mental process in psychosis and other mental ills is psychologically meaningful, and hopped aboard the new and financially lucrative medical bandwagon. The banner slogan of neuroscience, an upgrade of the various labels of subhuman defectiveness of the past but still in the same ballpark, was articulated by Sir Francis Crick, the co-discoverer of the structure of DNA, in the introduction to his 1994 book *The Astonishing Hypothesis*:

> The Astonishing Hypothesis is that "You," your joys and your sorrows, your memories and your ambitions, your sense of personal identity and free will, are in fact no more than the behavior of a vast assembly of nerve cells and their associated molecules. As Lewis Carroll's Alice might have phrased it: "You're nothing but a pack of neurons."

In its new and more respectable bottles, the old wine of insanity remains imbedded in the concept of defect, the product of meaningless firings of a genetically abnormal chemically unbalanced brain. With the blessings of science psychiatry became a branch of organic medicine and psychopharmacology.

In 1952 a committee of the American Psychiatric Association wrote the bible of psychiatry, the *Diagnostic and Statistical Manual* (DSM), naming patterns of mind and behavior they believed abnormal as diseases regardless of the fact that they failed to meet two essential criteria of a medical disease: that the designated patient complains of suffering and that there is an underlying physical abnormality. The manual has undergone five major and several minor revisions since then, and while some of these diagnostic labels like schizophrenia, depression, and bipolar disorder have remained more or less constant, others come and go as fashions have changed. The most egregious example of the denigrating or dehumanizing nature of the social judgments underlying DSM "science" is homosexuality. In the first 1952 edition homosexuality was listed among the sociopathic disorders. Needless to say, in common parlance sociopathy is more or less equated with criminality. It remained a DSM diagnosis until 1974 when it was "de-criminalized" and replaced by a vote of the membership of the American Psychiatric Association with "sexual orientation disturbance." This is but one instance of many DSM diagnoses that are thinly disguised name calling.

Chapter 2 of the now current DSM-5 describes schizophrenia as the most common and prototypical psychosis, characterized by hallucinations, delusions, disorganized speech and thought, grossly abnormal behavior, and so-called negative symptoms. It asserts that psychosis is the result of a genetically determined neurological disorder that begins at predictable developmental stages, childhood or late adolescence and early adulthood.

Contrary to the axiom of the psychiatric bible and despite extensive and expensive research spanning many decades, funded by the quartet that stands most to profit from it, it has not been proven that the DSM "disease" called schizophrenia has a specific identifiable physical substrate. Reduced volume of parts of the brain has been noted in some studies of chronic schizophrenic persons (Okasha & Madkour, 1982; Vita, Sacchetti, Calzroni, & Cazzuto, 1988) and subtle disturbances of ability to concentrate have been noted in others, but there are no consistent findings in all or even most cases, and in individual cases none are of a magnitude that distinguishes a schizophrenic person from a "normal" one.

Furthermore, other explanations for these findings are possible. For example some of the findings may be the result of chronic administration of the drugs that most patients in these studies have received. The abnormal findings may not be causes of schizophrenia at all, but results of the characteristic mental activity. Paranoid delusions characteristic of more severe psychotic conditions in particular involve irresponsible attribution of agency to external forces. These people do not engage in the mental work of representing, struggling with, and resolving psychological conflicts, reflecting about themselves in relation to reality, making difficult decisions, taking action to implement them, taking the consequences, and learning from them. However much they seem to be suffering, psychotic persons are relatively unaware of their emotions and motivations. They tend to lead passive, dependent, marginal existences. The delusional mental state may be a way of avoiding facing and coping with emotionally difficult aspects of their lives. There is research evidence to support the hypothesis that the brains of some severely psychotic persons have atrophied, like what happens to other parts of the body such as muscles and bones that are not utilized (Okasha & Madkour, 1982; Vita et al., 1988).

It is the genetic findings that most proponents of the organic hypothesis cite as evidence. These are based on identical twin studies of concordance and adoption. Joseph (2003) has made an exhaustive analysis of the original studies and concluded that there is no convincing evidence that genetic factors account for more than a small percentage of the variance among schizophrenics. Certainly no specific causal gene or combination of genes with physical abnormality has been found as is the case, for example, in Huntington's disease. In my extensive hospital experience it was infrequent to find other severely psychotic persons in the immediate family tree of a schizophrenic person. This does not rule out genetic factors as many recessive conditions jump generations, but the best that genetic research has yielded is clusters of minor abnormalities in some but not all persons diagnosed schizophrenic, clusters that are not consistent from one schizophrenic person to another. While researchers are pursuing the hypothesis that there may be many different diseases that have a superficially similar end point, all we know is that genetic factors of low level individual potency appear to enhance risk but are not determinative.

On April 2, 2013, Steven Hyman, former director of the National Institute of Mental Health, referred to the DSM in a post on the website of the Dana foundation for brain research as "an absolute scientific nightmare ... totally wrong." In an April 29, 2013 post on the National Institute of Health website his successor, Thomas Insel, said: "Unlike our definitions of ischemic heart disease, lymphoma, or AIDS, the DSM diagnoses are based on a consensus about clusters of clinical symptoms, not any objective laboratory measure ... symptoms alone rarely indicate the best choice of treatment." Allen Frances, chair of the task force that published the fourth edition of DSM, subsequently became disenchanted with its legitimacy. In 2014 he wrote that DSM diagnoses are nothing more than descriptive observations and judgments, not research-validated medical diseases.

The chasm between a psychiatry of meaningless organic disease and a psychoanalysis of meaningful mind widened in 1980 when the committee of the American Psychiatric Association charged with compiling and updating the DSM voted to eliminate neurosis as an official diagnosis, eliminating the already tenuous link between the psychiatry of material disease and the psychoanalysis of meaning.

One of the worst of the multiple and not always obvious consequences of the psychiatric take-over of psychosis is the stigmatization of the condition and those who manifest it. The stigma is particularly attached to the diagnosis schizophrenia, even though the name itself captures lack of integration, an important aspect of the psychotic process. Psychosis is not a respectable affliction like neurosis or depression that our partners or professional associates would "have." This despite the fact that many psychotic personalities are highly productive even admired human beings, as I illustrate in clinical vignettes in subsequent chapters. So when someone close to us, perhaps one of our children, is diagnosed schizophrenic it is a matter of shame and concealment. Psychoanalysis has been an unwitting co-conspirator in this unfortunate process by not conceptualizing and supporting a model for psychosis that is neither driven by these psychiatric assumptions nor free-standing as a by-path of normality like the model of neurosis.

PART II

Psychoanalytic models of psychosis

3

FREUD'S ATTEMPT TO TREAT PSYCHOSIS AS THOUGH IT WERE NEUROSIS

Both wittingly and unwittingly Freud made a number of efforts to apply the neurosis model to psychosis, a mistake that subsequent generations of psychoanalysts repeat to this day. The current iteration is that psychosis is the consequence of failure to develop the ego strength and capacity to repress necessary to sustain a normal/neurotic personality organization. Such a model implicitly assumes that there is but a single developmental pathway and psychosis is a regressive failure rather than an independent organization. Freud did not work in a mental hospital nor did he knowingly undertake the treatment of psychotic persons. Looking back on the patients whose treatments he wrote about, however, there is reason to believe he did attempt to treat some people we would now diagnose as psychotic. He applied his neurosis model to their treatment, at times even insistently and aggressively. In 1928, Ruth Mack Brunswick discovered that the Wolf Man had become overtly psychotic subsequent to his work with Freud. She used Freud's material to comment on his psychotic characteristics. Suzanne Reichard (1956) suggested that two of his so-called hysterics, Anna O (Bertha Pappenheim) who was actually treated by Breuer, and Emmy von N were in fact schizophrenic.

Because Freud did not treat Anna O, I will not comment on her case here except to say that she was regressed when Breuer treated her. Her speech was disorganized, she was mute for periods of time, she spent much time in bed "daydreaming," she had delusions she was becoming blind and deaf. When she was sitting by the bedside of her dying father she hallucinated a black snake emerging from the wall and approaching her father, as if to bite him. She wanted to drive the snake away but discovered that her right arm was "paralyzed" and as she looked at her hand the fingers changed into small snakes with skulls in place of fingernails. She had numerous somatic symptoms as well.

Emmy von N (Fanny Moser), the patient who helped Freud to discover free association, was 40 when Breuer referred her to his then young assistant Freud.

She was an aristocrat, said to be the wealthiest woman in central Europe. She had married a man old enough to be her grandfather when she was 23, and four days after the birth of their second child, when she was 26, he died of a heart attack. She was openly hostile to the child, lived a somewhat reclusive life thereafter, and was said to be "nervous" and eccentric. According to Freud her affect was inappropriate, she repeated a magic formula when upset, "Keep quiet – don't speak – don't touch me!", and she had what sounds like hallucinations, not fantasies, of gory heads on waves, trees full of mice, rats, frogs, and her bran bath full of little worms. There were numerous somatic symptoms and physical enactments – stomachaches, lip smacking, and a periodic speech problem Freud called "spastic interruptions." Her symptoms were only transiently resolved, and in her quest for relief in subsequent years she was admitted to a sanitarium and she returned to see him.

I believe that another of his patients, Ernst Lanzer, aka the Rat Man, a case Freud used in his 1909 paper to illustrate his model of neurotic repression and symptom formation, was also psychotic. The case is unique insofar as it is the only one in which Freud left notes of sessions that enable us to get a retrospective sense of the data from which his formulations came. In Chapter 9 I use his notes to illustrate the primordial conscious mental functioning characteristic of psychosis that I have written about elsewhere (Robbins, 2011, 2018). My intention in this chapter is to demonstrate that Lanzer was psychotic and to describe how Freud attempted to apply his neurosis model of repressed infantile psychosexual conflicts and their role in symptom formation. He postulated events in Lanzer's childhood that he believed would account for the symptoms and urged him to treat these hypothetical events as facts. Lanzer's relationship with his mother and his earlier development play almost no part in Freud's account.

Obsessive-compulsive thoughts or delusional/hallucinatory enactments?

Freud was preoccupied with what he called Lanzer's obsessions. These were a series of bizarre ritualistic actions engaged in with the magical belief that they would prevent his sadistic phantasies ranging from anal torture to death from actually befalling people ostensibly important to him, including his deceased father, who in the phantasy was very much alive, and the woman he was ambivalent about marrying. I use the term phantasy rather than fantasy, as Klein did, to denote the quality of reality and belief rather than imagination. The title "Rat Man" was derived from Lanzer's sadistic phantasy about a rat gnawing the anus of his lady friend and his father, and the ritualistic counteractions he devised to magically undo what for him was reality and to us are ideas that he could not differentiate from reality. The symptoms that brought Lanzer to Freud appeared in his twenties as a consequence of intense ambivalence about whether to marry the woman he believed he loved or to marry a wealthy socially well-connected woman. His father had once faced a similar dilemma and resolved it by marrying for money.

Freud recounts how Lanzer would interrupt his work and open the door to his apartment motivated by the hallucinatory conviction that his long-dead father about whom he had harbored ambivalent feelings was outside. Then he would take out his penis and look at it in the mirror. In order to prevent the reality of the anal rat invasion Lanzer elaborated another belief that was equally illogical, about payment for a pair of glasses he had ordered. Freud's construction was that this was a symbolically disguised representation of a repressed memory containing a rage-filled wish:

> His sanction to the effect that something would happen to his father in the next world is simply to be understood as an ellipse. ... "If my father was still alive and learnt of this he would chastise me again and I should fly into a rage with him once more, and this would cause his death, since my affects are omnipotent."
>
> *(1909, p. 278)*

In other words, Freud did something a neurotic person might have done but Lanzer was unable to do, namely to assume Lanzer's mentation was the symptomatic expression of a repressed forbidden angry "fuck you" wish from childhood toward his father. However Lanzer's phantasy was concrete, undifferentiated, magical, hallucinatory, and sensory-perceptual-motor enactive. It was not a represented thought.

Another of Lanzer's obsessions was precipitated by the woman he was ambivalent about, whom Freud refers to as "his lady," leaving him for a period of time to visit her aged grandmother while he was studying for examinations. The Rat Man told Freud "If you received a command to take your examination this term at the first possible opportunity, you might manage to obey it. But if you were commanded to cut your throat with a razor, what then?" Freud adds:

> He had at once become aware that this command had already been given, and was hurrying to the cupboard to fetch his razor when he thought: "No, it's not so simple as that. You must go and kill the old woman." Upon that, he had fallen to the ground, beside himself with horror.
>
> *(p. 186)*

Once again Freud postulates a repressed thoughtful conflict, and infers that what his patient *really* thought was: "'Oh, I should like to go and kill that old woman for robbing me of my love!' Thereupon followed the command: 'Kill yourself, as a punishment for these savage and murderous passions!'" (p. 186). To me it sounds as though the fantasy, implying a thoughtful conflict, might have been something like "I'm in such an undifferentiated rage at myself and her grandmother that I can't just do the constructive thing and get my exams over as quickly as possible so I can be with her." Instead there is no thought, no fantasy, only a self–other-undifferentiated magical enactment and counter-enactment. As we will see in Chapter 9 these are elements of the primordial conscious mentation that is characteristic of psychosis.

Freud's interpretive enactment of his theory of repressed unconscious and its results

There was a good deal of unacknowledged sadism and abuse in Lanzer's background, especially in stories his mother told him about her upbringing. He had no sense of guilt in telling Freud that he had a history of seducing the younger daughters of his friends by taking them on trips and entering their hotel bedrooms at night and masturbating them. In fact he seemed to believe they had enjoyed it. And during the course of his treatment Lanzer reported sadistic dreams and fantasies he had about Freud, albeit apparently with little affect. Freud attempted to teach/force his ideas about repressed rage by translating into the language of reflective representational thought the conflicts he believed Lanzer had harbored prior to repressing them. He writes:

> The unconscious, I explained [to Lanzer], was the infantile; it was that part of the self which had become separated off from it in infancy, which had not shared the later stages of its development, and which had in consequence become repressed. It was the derivatives of this repressed unconscious that were responsible for the involuntary thoughts which constituted his illness.
>
> *(1909, pp. 163–164, bracketed comments mine)*

Freud writes:

> While he was wishing Constanze the rats [the torture of having rats gnaw at her anus] he felt a rat gnawing at his own anus and had a visual image of it. I established a connection which throws a fresh light on the rats. After all, he had had worms. What had he been given against them? "Tablets." Not enemas as well? He thought he remembered that he had certainly had them too. If so, no doubt he must have objected to them strongly, since a repressed pleasure lay behind them. He agreed to this, too. Before this he must have had a period of itching in his anus.
>
> *(1909, p. 307, bracketed comments mine)*

Whatever the truth of Freud's constructions, they involved re-conceptualizing a concrete somatic-affective mental state in which Lanzer could not clearly differentiate his rage toward himself from that toward "his lady" into a thoughtful anal sadistic fantasy about which he was conflicted.

Despite his apparent certainty Freud could not entirely dispel his own doubts about the validity of his theory. Consistent with his understanding of the primary process mental state underlying dreaming, Freud had some sense that Lanzer was expressing himself in a mode qualitatively different from ordinary conflicted thought and fantasy. For example, he writes:

I refer to the omnipotence which he ascribed to his thoughts and feelings, and to his wishes, whether good or evil. ... It is, I must admit, decidedly tempting to declare that this idea was a delusion and that it oversteps the limits of obsessional neurosis ... this belief is a frank acknowledgement of a relic of the old megalomania of infancy.

(1909, pp. 232–233)

He also writes: "The omnipotence of thoughts, or, more accurately speaking, of wishes, has since been recognized as an essential element in the mental life of primitive people" (1909, p. 234). He does not note that the omnipotence of childhood is a reflection of inability to distinguish self from other.

Freud also writes about Lanzer's numerous contradictions and absence of logic, another bit of evidence that he was psychotic: "the detailed account which the patient gave me of the external events of these days and of his reactions to them was full of self-contradictions and sounded hopelessly confused" (1909, p. 169). And "I could begin straightening out the various distortions involved in his story" (p. 171). In what might be interpreted as Freud's unconscious acknowledgment of the folly of his enterprise he writes:

We are not used to feeling strong affects without their having any ideational content, and therefore, if the content is missing, we seize as a substitute upon some other content which is in some way or other suitable, much as our police, when they cannot catch the right murderer, arrest a wrong one instead. Moreover, this fact of there being a false connection is the only way of accounting for the powerlessness of logical processes to combat the tormenting idea.

(p. 175)

While Freud did not seem to appreciate that the phenomena he observed bore considerable resemblance to his description of affect-driven images in dreaming and the primary process, he suggested as much when he noted that his patient's nocturnal dreams often seemed just like his waking obsessions.

According to Freud's notes Lanzer was never really convinced that the infantile memories Freud imputed to him had once existed and had been repressed. I have already commented on Lanzer's latent hostility toward Freud, which seems to have been split or dissociated from his compliant attitude, a characteristic transferentially consistent with the passive compliant personality suggested in the material about his difficulties gaining independence from his father and establishing satisfactory adult relationships. Freud was aware of the difficulty he encountered trying to convince his patient of the validity of his repressed thought construction when he writes: "Strangely enough, his belief that he really nourished feelings of rage against his father has made no progress in spite of his seeing that there was every logical reason for supposing that he had those feelings" (1909, p. 306). Freud seemingly could not entertain the idea Lanzer might be psychotic.

Perhaps the reader wonders how Freud could possibly have overlooked his patient's delusions and hallucination, to say nothing of less obvious manifestations of psychosis, as well as his own statement that it was tempting to see Lanzer's sense of omnipotence as an indication of psychosis. Of course he was committed to "proving" the validity of his theory of neurosis. Lest we in turn be tempted to be smug, I believe the problem persists in contemporary psychoanalytic practice. On a number of occasions I have attended presentations at national psychoanalytic meetings of puzzling chronic analytic stalemates, treatments that did not seem to be going anywhere using standard methodology consisting of couch, free association, and interpretations based on the assumption the individual was neurotic and that patient and analyst were communicating in the language of reflective representational thought. I have wondered why the possibility the person was psychotic and required an entirely different understanding had not been considered. In that sense, Freud's attempt to treat Lanzer using the theory of neurosis might be looked upon as a model for subsequent generations, unintentional though it was and is.

Why did Freud fail to recognize what judging from his own comments was on the periphery of his awareness? In addition to his commitment to validating his theory of neurosis it is likely that he was influenced by the psychiatry of his day that led him to the hypothesis that schizophrenia is a condition that renders its victims incapable of forming relationships and attaining and sustaining a neurotic personality organization. In that case Lanzer would probably have been hospitalized, unable to live independently, work or study, have a close relationship, and come to Freud's office for treatment. Lanzer did not fit such a stereotype.

In subsequent chapters I examine the spectrum of severity that comprises psychosis, including the more highly functional end, psychotic personality organization, in which the characteristic mental state is concealed from all but the person's most intimate contacts by a functional façade or false self.

But that is not the end of the story of Freud's efforts to believe that psychosis is in fact an extreme version of neurosis. At the time he wrote his 1911 monograph on Daniel Paul Schreber based on his memoirs Freud was well aware Schreber was psychotic. Nonetheless he interpreted Schreber's delusions as though they were neurotic symptoms related to the Oedipus complex, based on defenses of repression and projection against repressed conflicts with his father related to homosexual desires and castration anxiety.

4

FREUD'S THREE MODELS AND THEIR OFFSPRING I

The inability to relate

In Chapter 3 I described what might be called one of Freud's models of psychosis, had he not mistakenly believed that the patients he treated were neurotic. He tried to fit his basic neurosis model of unconscious conflict, repression, and symptomatic return of the repressed to people like Emmy von N and the Rat Man without much success. He also consciously tried to apply the neurosis model to Schreber (Freud, 1911), a person he believed to be schizophrenic whose history he gleaned from an autobiography. Freud did go beyond the neurosis model in an effort to understand psychosis, however, but his efforts were brief and tentative. He articulated three models for psychosis, which I group under three headings: relationship, integration, and thought disorder. Each of these models has been elaborated by subsequent generations of theorists and practitioners though frequently without their conscious awareness of its genealogical roots and related limitations. The first two reflect how much his thinking was influenced by the psychiatry of the time, in particular the belief advanced by Kraepelin and Bleuler that psychosis is an organic dementia. The relational model of psychosexual development and libidinal cathexis that he may have taken from Bleuler's description of autism not long before (1911a, 1911b) is the model that has had the most profound influence on subsequent generations of analysts. As with any genealogy, root systems are complex and not linear. In each of these next three chapters I will describe the major theorists who appear to have been elaborating (or in the case of the relational model trying to disprove) Freud's hypotheses. In a number of instances these same theorists will appear in the root systems of one of his other models, as well, as their work drew upon various of Freud's ideas and was a hybrid, in some instances more a pastiche than an integrated harmonious one.

We now know that in postulating an initial autoerotic stage in which there is presumably no libidinal cathexis of the object world Freud was conflating psychological undifferentiation of self from the object world with the issue of actual attachment to others, which is observable in the attachment bond, and intense from the beginning of life. In his 1914 paper "On narcissism" (1914) Freud postulated an initial stage of objectless autoerotic libido preceding the development of the first object-related stage of primary narcissism. He concluded: "Paraphrenics display two fundamental characteristics: megalomania and diversion of their interest from the external world – from people and things. In consequence of the latter change, they become inaccessible to the influence of psychoanalysis and cannot be cured by our efforts" (1914, p. 74). In 1915 he elaborated the idea that in this state of what he called narcissistic neurosis schizophrenic persons are incapable of forming a transference relationship with the analyst and are therefore untreatable by psychoanalytic methodology.

In his 1916 *Introductory Lectures* Freud writes:

> Sufferers from narcissistic neuroses [i.e., people with psychosis] have no capacity for transference or only insufficient residues of it. They reject the doctor, not with hostility but with indifference. For that reason they cannot be influenced by him either; what he says leaves them cold, makes no impression on them; consequently the mechanism of cure which we carry through with other people – the revival of the pathogenic conflict and the overcoming of the resistance due to repression – cannot be operated with them. They remain as they are. ... We cannot alter this in any way.
>
> *(p. 447)*

Freud's absorption of the prevailing cultural-scientific belief that schizophrenic persons are organically defective and hence constitutionally unable to mature sufficiently to achieve and sustain a normal/neurotic personality organization is not the only reason he did not recognize the importance of mother and the phase of attachment and separation. Had he done so he might have developed an independent model of the nature and development of psychosis as an entity in its own right separate from his model of neurosis. His fundamental developmental assumption, consistent with the beliefs of the society in which he grew up, was male dominated and autocratic. Civilization itself and the maturation of its individual members depended on acceptance of male superiority, and internalization of the authority and rule of the father. Freud's theory tends to denigrate females as inferior versions of males, and to give little importance to mothers. True to his background in biology Freud postulated a developmental process based on instinct rather than relationship, in which successful resolution of the Oedipus complex, an organizational concept whose existence he discovered during the first two decades of the 20th century, by internalization of paternal authority and attainment of a mind capable of neurotic conflict, became the ultimate maturational landmark. In such a conception psychosis represents the failure to attain this neurotic organization.

In the psychosexual stage model development is driven by instinct, culminating in phallic sexuality. Mother is literally an object of instinctual discharge, not a person with whom the infant has a primary crucially determinative attachment and relationship. It is only at that point of desire for phallic instinctual discharge that relationship enters, in the form of awareness of father the law enforcer in the case of a male (if you don't give up the urge to use it you will lose it), and the potential gift-giver in the case of a female (you can have a baby instead). Freud did recognize that girls might have an initial love attachment to mother. In the first decade or so of the 20th century when psychoanalysis was discovering complexes (conflicts) he and his followers called it a mother complex, and it was seen as a liability, something pathological, to be relinquished. Freud, as well as Binswanger, Jung, Ferenczi, and Jones, members of his inner circle, all referred to the "mother complex" as a pathological entity to be resolved not by accepting the importance of mother and internalizing the caring attributes of the primary relationship but by repudiating the attachment. Here is an excerpt from letter 159J written by Jung to Freud in November, 1909, shortly after their return from the trip to America and Clark University:

> In America the mother is decidedly the dominant member of the family. American culture really is a bottomless abyss; the men have become a flock of sheep and the women play the ravening wolves – within the family circle, of course. I ask myself whether such conditions have ever existed in the world before. I really don't think they have.
>
> *(Freud & Jung, 1994)*

Of course most contemporary analysts subscribe only to parts, if any, of this idea, but it has left a residue that theories of primary attachment and relationship are in the process of rectifying. Psychosis is an example of the way the theory has not caught up with knowledge and changed, so that a separate line of development can be recognized with as much legitimacy as the development of neurosis, beginning in the undifferentiated unintegrated stage of early infant mind.

There may be yet another reason why Freud believed psychotic persons were incapable of attachment to the analyst. To understand it one must appreciate his methodology in the light of the Heisenberg principle that states that the method of observation not only affects what is observed, but changes it as well. Freud's methodology was not designed to make a relationship, rather to depend on the patient's transference eagerness to repeat existing relationship patterns and willingness to make an alliance with an analyst functioning as an observing and commenting instrument. Freud devised the iconic analytic couch because he did not like face to face contact with his patients, and however rigorously he adhered to it, he promoted a system in which the analyst acted as though he or she were an objective personally disengaged observer-commentator. This posture was taught candidates in analytic training for decades prior to the relational turn. Candidates were taught not to respond emotionally or give personal information of any kind to their analysands. This was hardly a setting designed to encourage persons who may have experienced significant rejection in the attachment phase to become engaged in a caring collaborative relationship.

The Freudian blind spot to primary attachment and its importance is not simply a relic of the early days of psychoanalysis. It is not often that Freud and **Kohut** are mentioned in the same breath, but in his own way Kohut is one of the most articulate advocates of the point of view that psychotic persons are incapable of forming therapeutic relationships, or as he conceptualized it, selfobject mergers. There is no evidence in his 1971 and 1977 books that he was aware of the work of Bowlby and other attachment theorists. In 1971 he stated that the nascent self is constituted through cathexis with narcissistic libido. By 1977 he had abandoned the libidinal cathexis model entirely and come to a belief that events prior to age two are psychologically meaningless, that the first meaningful event is a selfobject merger that normally occurs around age two, and that when this does not occur and the urge to merge is chronically frustrated then "the self is seriously damaged ... the drives become powerful constellations in their own right" (1977, p. 122). Psychologically meaningless phenomena including rage and autoerotic preoccupations, defensive operations including splitting and projection, and efforts at delusional restitution, characterize the chronically fragmented or shattered personality, borderline or schizophrenic. In other words, the regressed state that he believed constitutes psychosis does not re-trace a normal developmental pathway.

However, a small group of Freud's early followers, particularly Rank, Ferenczi, and Groddeck, did not accept his formulations and wrote about the importance of mother and attachment (Rudnytsky, 2002; Poster, 2009). Rudnytsky (2002) describes 1923, the year Groddeck published *The Book of the It*, Ferenczi wrote *Thalassa*, Rank published *The Trauma of Birth* (1924), Ferenczi and Rank co-authored *The Development of Psychoanalysis*, and Freud was diagnosed with cancer, as a turning point in the history of psychoanalysis. Ferenczi and Groddeck (1977) wrote about the importance of maternal transference and its somatic expressions. In his classic 1933 paper "On the confusion of tongues" and his 1924 book *Thalassa* Ferenczi elaborated on the critical importance of conflict between the urge to grow and the urge to regress, and the role of trauma related to confused communication early in life, but he did not explore the importance of attachment to mother. Rank was the first to propose that human development is a lifelong struggle to separate from primary attachment, and to resolve the conflict between separateness and primal unity. Rank's 1926 lecture on "The genesis of the object relation" is the landmark in what eventually became known as object relations theory. Freud commented that Rank had come close to committing anti-Oedipal heresy.

It was **Melanie Klein** (1935, 1946), in the 1930s, almost two decades later, who put together the importance of the primary attachment to mother and the origins of psychosis. She was influenced by her analyses with Ferenczi, who recognized the importance of the. maternal transference, and Abraham, who emphasized the concept of developmental stages. Whereas those who preceded her failed to recognize the significance of attachment and its vicissitudes as developmentally primary and essential, Klein's problem was that she viewed the infant member of the dyad as psychically fragmented by rage in response to the initial separation of birth, leading to the primal splitting of the virtual intact ego at birth. The initial attachment was not viewed as a positive development experience but rather as a kind of therapeutic remediation of another version of basic flaw. In this she was doubtless influenced by her work with disturbed children, and perhaps by her conflicts with her own children as well. Her contribution is elaborated on in Chapters 5 and 7.

In the two decades or so following World War II there emerged a major psychoanalytic interest in schizophrenia in particular and the psychoses in general. Freud's dictum that schizophrenia is a presumably hereditary disorder of instinctual cathexis such that it is not possible to form therapeutic relationships with afflicted persons was demonstrated over and over to be incorrect. To a greater or lesser degree the American contingent who were bent on proving Freud wrong shared an ego psychological model based on the concept of weak ego strength, inability to sustain a normal/neurotic organization, and susceptibility to regression based on failure of capacity to repress leading to uncontrolled expression of the primary process unconscious. By and large these analysts were so preoccupied with demonstrating their often extraordinary and idiosyncratic abilities to establish a relationship with schizophrenic persons that they mostly contented themselves with the idea that psychosis is a regression from relationship. In other words, psychosis was viewed like a photographic negative, a kind of failed attempt at neurosis. This aspect is elaborated on in the next chapter discussing Freud's second model.

These therapists constituted a kind of cult of personality, as what was considered important was their capacity to engage the patient, which Fromm-Reichmann, one of the best known among this elite group, described as the attribute of an exceptionally gifted therapist. As a result they were looked upon with a degree of awe, often starred in conferences where they were asked to interview difficult patients, and their particular personality styles and idiosyncrasies were slavishly imitated by students. This period of romance between psychoanalysis and schizophrenia generated movies like *Spellbound* and books like *The Fifty-Minute Hour* and *I Never Promised You a Rose Garden*.

As the test of time proved that engagement is not tantamount to cure there was massive disillusionment with psychoanalysis in general, and a counter-movement away from intensive work with psychotic persons. A psychiatry based on the ideas of Kraepelin and Bleuler that influenced Freud, namely that nature, not nurture, causes psychosis, championed by neuroscience and psychopharmacology, soon filled the vacuum. Although some analysts continued to work with severely psychotic persons, Freud's original assertion about inability to relate achieved the status of a psychoanalytic axiom. It is codified by both the International and American Psychoanalytic Associations in descriptions of the psychoanalytic educational curriculum. Work with psychotic persons does not count for credit toward graduation.

Harry Stack Sullivan (1953, 1962) was probably the first notable psychiatrist to champion work with psychotic persons. He has a unique place in the history of understanding and treating schizophrenia, even though he did not actually spend much of his career doing such work – 18 months according to Chassell (1962) and four years according to Gibson (1989). Some of his writings – the title of his 1962 book *Schizophrenia as a Human Process* and his phrase that the schizophrenic "is more simply human than otherwise" (1940) – have attained the status of slogans or banners. He was not a psychoanalyst, although he was a follower of Freud and aware of the importance of his work. He believed that it is possible to form a transference relationship with a schizophrenic person. He wrote:

> the infantile and early childhood experiences [lead to] a consideration of the *interpersonal requirements* for the successful therapy of the schizophrenic. ... The only tools that have shown results that justify any enthusiasm in regard of the treatment of schizophrenia are the *psychoanalytic* procedures and the *socio-psy-chiatric* which the writer has evolved from them. ... The achievement of this double process requires the establishment between the physician and the patient of the situation called by Freud transference.
>
> *(1931, p. 283; italics Sullivan's)*

What is generally overlooked is how "psychoanalytic" some of his ideas are, their resemblance to Freud's primary process model, and to the ideas about how problems of attachment relate to the genesis of psychosis. I describe these in Chapter 7 as part of the discussion of Freud's thought disorder model. Important as those might be, however, Sullivan's major contribution was to provide a rallying cry around the belief that schizophrenic persons are accessible to a caring human relationship.

Michael Balint (1937, 1958, 1968), worked in Great Britain at approximately the same time as Sullivan was doing his work in the United States. Balint acknowledges that he did not work with psychotic persons. However, his observations about early development and psychosis are very important. He was aware of the primary importance of mother and attachment, and he distinguished between what he called stage one, in which the infant is not psychologically separate and differentiated from mother, and a subsequent stage three, in which the child is capable of a triadic Oedipal relationship. A middle stage two, of creativity, bears some resemblance to Winnicott's later articulation of the transitional object phase.

Balint believed that psychotic persons, regressed to the first phase of what he called the basic fault, are only accessible by re-mothering and a new beginning. He writes:

> This [stage one] is *the area of the basic fault*, characterized by the number "2," which means that in it two, and only two, people are involved.

Their relationship, however, is not that obtaining between two adults. It is more primitive. A further difference between the two areas is caused by the nature of the dynamic force operating in each. In the area of the Oedipus complex the form of the force is that of a conflict. Although highly dynamic, the force originating from the basic fault has *not* the form of a conflict. As described above, it has the form of a fault, something wrong in the mind, a deficiency that must be put right.

(1958, p. 338)

Balint clearly distinguishes between neurosis, requiring a separate differentiated mind that has internalized the capacity to experience conflict, and what I call primordial consciousness or first mind, a self–object-undifferentiated and uninte-grated state. What he failed to realize is that this mental state is not "something wrong in the mind," but rather a qualitatively different mental process.

As most of the analysts influenced by and subsequent to Sullivan exerted their influence around the same time, in the two decades subsequent to World War II, no special significance is to be attributed to the order in which I mention their work.

Gertrude Schwing (1940) was a nurse who worked in Germany. Her work was discovered by Paul Federn, who worked in the same hospital, and with his encouragement she became his co-worker and eventually a psychoanalytic col-league. She based her work on what she called motherliness, providing the maternal love that she felt had been missing in the upbringing of psychotic per-sons, with the assumption they could be given a new beginning. As Eissler put it: "Like a medieval saint, she released the schizophrenics from their strait-jack-ets, and patients who had just been howling immediately quieted down when she turned toward them" (1951, p. 155). She ministered to her patients as though they were children, including kissing and grooming, things we might think of as mutual enactments of a phantasy.

Frieda Fromm-Reichmann (1950) was perhaps Sullivan's most influential pupil, and one of the first to come to mind when one thinks of engaging a schizo-phrenic person. She was also initially (1939) influenced by people like Gertrude Schwing and the idea of regressive re-mothering. She initially viewed the schizo-phrenic as delicate and advocated a position of permissive giving without confronta-tion and limit setting. While she did not give up her idea that the schizophrenic is a person of special sensitivity, often more sensitive and psychologically attuned than the average therapist, she eventually moved away from Schwing's ideas, remarking "This type of doctor-patient relationship addresses itself too much to the rejected child in the schizophrenic and too little to the grown up person" (1952, p. 106). She added that "Understanding that which has been done to the patient in his early years sooner or later must be followed up by the investigation of what, in turn, the patient has done to his environment" (p. 106). She eventually came to emphasize the importance of rage in schizophrenia (1954a, p. 417). She is known for her unfortunate attribution of psychosis to faulty mothering (the "schizophrenogenic mother"; 1948, p. 265) and for promoting the cult of personality, the belief that it takes an extraordinarily gifted therapist to work with a schizophrenic person. Her fame was spread by the best-selling novel *I Never Promised You a Rose Garden*, written by a former patient, Joanne Greenberg (alias Hannah Green). Whether or not related to having been teacher and pupil Sullivan and Fromm-Reichmann were both intimidating critical teachers according to the accounts of several of the contributors to Silver's 1989 volume, Sullivan to the point of sadism at times, and they fostered the belief that only very special gifted people like them were able to do this exalted work. Perhaps in the long run this is one of the factors that has mitigated against a more widespread acceptance of schizophrenia as falling within the scope of psychoanalysis.

Fromm-Reichmann's model of schizophrenia is actually a standard American ego psychological formulation. These ideas are discussed later in the book, as part of Freud's third model. From the perspective of therapeutic engagement she focused on interpreting the transference and thereby uncovering the early experiences that led to the parataxic distortions that along with Sullivan she believed characterize schizophrenia.

Paul Federn (1952) immigrated to the US from Germany, where he had worked in a mental hospital with Schwing, in 1938. He hypothesized that the essence of psychotic estrangement from others is what he called an ego defect in libidinal cathexis. In Germany Federn utilized a tandem approach to the treatment of schizophrenic persons, consisting of the primary therapist and a helper. While he considered himself to be the primary therapist and the nurse Gertrude Schwing his helper, it would seem that she did most of the work. The therapy consisted of treating the person like a regressed infant and providing re-mothering, a new beginning. Borrowing from Freud's concept of homosexual panic, and his own concept of weak ego boundaries, Federn believed that for a male patient the primary treatment figure should be a woman. This idea contrasts with the approach of Sullivan, who himself was homosexual, that involved working with psychotic male homosexual patients on a separate ward.

When Federn came to the United States he did not work in a mental hospital nor did he have a co-therapist like Gertrude Schwing, and his perspective on schizophrenia changed to that of an ego psychologist, as I describe in Chapter 6. When he encountered in his office practice people he believed might be on the edge of psychosis he eschewed psychoanalytic "uncovering" work including transference interpretations, or indeed interpretations of any kind, because he believed they would shake the fragile ego and promote regression. Instead he advocated ego supportive therapy including shoring up defenses, a kind of theoretical putting one's finger in the leaky dike. His ideas about love and re-mothering applied to people to whom, in his way of looking at it, the worst had already happened, and who were unable to relate in any other way, but they had no place in his practice in the United States as he had difficulty getting a medical license to practice and he did not do hospital work or have a therapeutic partner as he did in Europe.

Following on Freud's belief that psychotic individuals are beyond the scope of psychoanalysis because they are unable to develop a transference relationship **Marguerite Sechehaye** (1951b) focused on what she called the pre-transference or autistic stage of treatment of schizophrenia. What she calls the pre-transference phase of treatment is what I refer to in Chapter 13 as the first solipsistic phase. Her description of its phenology in 1956 is very similar to my own. She set out to demonstrate that it is possible to create a relationship with a person in such an extreme self–other-undifferentiated state. In her 1951 book (1951a) she illustrated her thesis with the case of Louisa Duss, to whom she gave the pseudonym Renee. While the book is titled an autobiography, it is actually a biography written by Sechehaye herself.

Sechehaye believed that gratification of infantile needs is the pathway to establishing a relationship with such a person. She writes:

> It is of no use, if the schizophrenic is at a pre-verbal stage, to interpret orally his symbols or his behaviour, or even to express to him our sympathy and desire to help him. Not all the psychotherapist's words will penetrate to the patient's field of conscious awareness; for him they will constitute but an indistinct background sound. On the other hand it is in these very regressed forms of schizophrenia that the importance of the procedures of "contact and physical care" is revealed, procedures which are directed to the "body ego" of the schizophrenic.
>
> *(1956, p. 270)*

In other words, she realized that such persons were not functioning in symbolic reflective representational thought. However, her reasoning suffers from confusion similar to that of Freud, Klein, and others about the distinction between symbolism, concreteness, and imagery. In addition she used the language of neurosis (conflict, defense, repression, ego regression) to describe mental states it is clear she believed were not neurotic. Because she believed conflicts over guilt precluded the patient from accepting gratification of oral needs directly it had to be provided indirectly, for which she used the term "symbolic realization." What she called symbols were actually concrete, for instance giving the patient an apple and suggesting it was a breast.

Symbolic realization is one example of therapeutic interventions known as re-mothering. The case of Renee illustrates the concreteness of her conception in more ways than just her therapeutic interventions. Sechehaye and her husband actually adopted Louisa and became her parents, not a kind of therapy available to everyone even leaving aside its other problems. Such interventions are rationalized by a very loose understanding of concepts of love and mothering. The idea that mother love can be turned on by a therapeutic professional like a spigot, especially toward people whose manner, self-care, and hostility make them unlikeable to say the least is questionable. In addition real love is much more than unconditional gratification. It involves helping the person become aware of his or her painful emotions such as rage; and it involves having expectations and setting limits, as well.

John Rosen (1947, 1953) was an extreme proponent of the belief that schizophrenia is the result of lack of mother love, dating literally to the oral stage. He was not a psychoanalyst but he borrowed Freud's idea that schizophrenia is related to dreaming, and believed that it is a nightmare-like state into which the person has regressed in defense against intolerable reality. His approach, which he called direct analysis, was a kind of psychic shock-therapy consisting of intensive interventions – aggressive, nurturing, seductive, and oral-interpretive – designed to break through to the patient in what he called the out-of-contact phase. He often spent hours a day with his patients, most of whom were women. It is doubtful he comprehended the notion of transference–countertransference enactment. The results of his work and that of others are summarized in the chapters on therapy.

I conclude discussion of reactions to Freud's belief that psychotic persons are unable to engage in a psychoanalytic relationship with the work of Margaret Mahler and Harold Searles. Mahler wrote about the relation of what she called the symbiotic phase of development to psychosis, and **Harold Searles** employed her concept to explain his own work, which was largely devoted to engaging these difficult persons.

In a groundbreaking series of papers and books **Margaret Mahler** (1952, 1968; Mahler, Bergman, & Pine, 1975) returned to the importance of maternal attachment and separation in the development of normal personality and psychosis that was begun a century before in the work of Rank, Ferenczi, and Groddeck. Mahler's tri-phasic developmental model (autism, symbiosis, and separation–individuation) is derived from the corresponding auto-erotic, primary narcissistic, and object stages suggested by Freud in his 1915 model of psychosexual development. Following on Freud's now discredited hypothesis of an autoerotic or autistic stage of normal development prior to the stage of primary narcissism, Mahler, Bergman, and Pine (1975) believed there is a normal autistic phase in which the infant is unrelated to the mother. This was followed, they believed, by a "pre-objectal" relationship, symbiosis (p. 48). Mahler and colleagues refer to symbiosis as "that self-object undifferentiated state" (1968, p. 8). "The essential feature of symbiosis is hallucinatory or delusional, somatopsychic omnipotent fusion with the representation of the mother, and, in particular, the delusion of a common boundary of the two actually and physically separate individuals." In other words, the normal symbiotic phase is also defined as psychotic. In so doing she followed in the footsteps of Freud and then Melanie Klein, who conflated normal development and psychosis. The concept of symbiotic relationship in the second phase derives from Freud's concept of a purified pleasure ego. "Any unpleasurable perception, external or internal, is projected beyond the common boundary of the symbiotic *milieu intérieur* (cf. Freud's concept of the 'purified pleasure ego')" (1968, p. 9). The resemblance of this presumed second stage of development to Klein's description of the paranoid-schizoid phase and phantasy is evident, but not credited.

Harold Searles believed, as did Fairbairn, that schizophrenia (1965) and borderline personality (1986) exist on a continuum of severity albeit with similar structural and dynamic features. He modelled his ideas after those of Mahler, tweaked by his awareness of their resemblance to those of Klein about evolution from a paranoid-schizoid to a depressive position. It is important to note that while Mahler wrote extensively about infant and child psychosis and schizophrenia in the context of early disturbances in the mother–infant relationship she did not write about adult schizophrenia. Other than references suggestive of the ego psychological view about weak ego and regression it is not clear how she would have applied her developmental model.

Searles accepted the American ego psychological conclusion that schizophrenia is a regression occasioned by the inability of a weak ego to repress drive derivatives. He used Mahler's work to fill the gap between adult and early childhood states and hypothesized that the point of regression is the so-called but now discredited autistic phase. "This central difficulty in schizophrenia – the impairment of integration-differentiation – seems to be most fundamentally attributable to the schizophrenic's regression to the level of early infancy" (1965, p. 320). According to Searles, the schizophrenic is unable to form the normal first stage of symbiosis that Searles, influenced by Mahler, describes. His relational approach contains the idea of a new beginning, the achievement of symbiosis with his patient.

However, Searles' ideas about symbiosis are a confused mixture of Mahler's conception, Melanie Klein's paranoid-schizoid position with its defense of projective identification, and the particular contribution of schizophrenic rage. Leaving aside the question of whether the theories of Mahler and Klein are compatible to begin with, Searles uses the concepts of each author in an idiosyncratic manner, not as they intended.

Searles describes the first relationship with a schizophrenic as one of ambivalent symbiosis, one in which both parties, therapist and patient, merge in a kind of chaos driven by schizophrenic rage. Ambivalence, however, a Kleinian concept, refers to a conflict between two differentiated states of mind, and is not characteristic of the undifferentiated, unintegrated state he describes. According to Searles, the therapist's experience of this ambivalent symbiosis is one of being driven crazy, or as I would put it, being pressured to lose his own sense of boundaries and differentiation.

Searles refers to the second stage of therapy as pre-ambivalent symbiosis, a conception that might fit Klein's notion of the unintegrated, undifferentiated paranoid-schizoid position that precedes the ambivalent depressive position in Klein's model. It is difficult for me to imagine a state prior to undifferentiated chaos. This stage, according to Searles, is characterized by mutual adoration: "a purely 'good' experience of himself and the other person, while the 'bad' elements in the relationship are maintained in a state of repression and projection onto the world outside the nest" (1965, p. 269). This second stage also resembles Klein's first stage, the paranoid-schizoid position, but now the projective identification, to use Searles' and Klein's terminology, is no longer onto the therapist but involves a rage-driven split between the "good" therapist and others, presumably the "bad" hospital staff. Certainly this phenomenon can be observed in intensive hospital-based treatment situations (Stanton & Schwartz, 1954). However, this is not an ambivalent (integrated) state like the depressive position, that reflects a differentiated integrated view of the world and a separate sense of self. Some of Searles' confusion about the second, pre-ambivalent stage arises because he based it on Mahler's idea about the all-good relationship between mother and infant that is characteristic of her idea of normal symbiosis. From observations of normal infant development, however, it does not appear that the initial symbiotic relationship with mother is sustained at the expense of perceiving either the therapist (Searles' stage one) or the hospital staff (Searles' stage two) as bad and directing hostility outward.

Follow-up studies (McGlashan & Keats, 1989) of Chestnut Lodge therapy cases suggest the possibility that many of Searles' treatment efforts never got very far. My speculation is that both of Searles' phases of therapeutic work can be encompassed by Klein's model of a paranoid-schizoid position, and the progression he describes involves collusion with the therapist and sharing the belief they have a positive relationship at the expense of projective identification of rage into the patient's relationships with others. In other words, there is a reorganization of the psychosis that gives the illusion/collusion of stability to the patient–therapist relationship. It may be more stable, but it is a chronic state that can never progress toward the realistic differentiation of self from other and integration of conflicting and ambivalent elements into the patient's psyche that is necessary for real separation, individuation, and eventually, termination.

The analysts who reacted against Freud's pronouncement that schizophrenia is outside the scope of psychoanalysis because afflicted persons cannot form a working relationship focused on proving he was incorrect. In at least some instances they seem to have believed that therapy of schizophrenia consists entirely of forming a relationship. They seem to have believed that schizophrenia is the manifestation of regression to an infantile state in which the person is unable to form and sustain a normal/neurotic organization. This approach is based on the assumption that once a relationship is formed the person will have achieved a normal/neurotic personality organization.

As important as engagement is, in order for therapy to be successful it is necessary to have a theoretical model of psychosis as a separate entity, not a regressive disorganized failure of the mind to be capable of attaining a neurotic organization. Freud's second model that I present in the next two chapters elaborates the idea that originated from Freud's conception of psychoanalysis as a theory and practice based on neurosis. In such a model there is but a single line of development, and the psychotic person represents a failure to develop and sustain a normal/neurotic personality organization based on the "ego strength" to experience intrapsychic conflict and use mature defenses (repression).

5
FREUD'S THREE MODELS AND THEIR OFFSPRING IIA

The inability to integrate mind and become neurotic: The European Kleinian iteration

Freud's integration model of schizophrenia is based on the idea that one part of the personality is fighting the undertow of a split-off regressive part in an effort to achieve and maintain a normal/neurotic personality organization. As is the case with the relationship model, it was also likely influenced by the psychiatry of his time. Freud's colleague Bleuler named the condition schizophrenia because of its primary characteristic of splitting, which he also referred to as ambivalence. He believed that this, and the other so-called primary symptoms of schizophrenia – affect disturbance, autism, and association aberration – are reflections of neural degeneration. Bleuler believed hallucinations and delusions are secondary symptoms of the regression, and Freud writes "My explanation of hallucinations in hysteria and paranoia and of visions in mentally normal subjects is that they are in fact regressions – that is, thoughts transformed into images" (1900, p. 544). He notes that the same reduction in censorship in sleep that triggers the primary process and dreaming can also occur under pathological conditions in waking life, leading to a state of "hallucinatory regression." He goes on to assert: "To this state of things we give the name of psychosis" (1900, p. 568). The less mature mental activity, which he called the primary process, is discussed in Chapter 7; for now the focus is on the problem of integration.

Elsewhere Freud more specifically refers to a split in the psychic apparatus:

> what occurs in all such cases is a *split* in the mind. Two mental attitudes have been formed instead of a single one – one, the normal one, which takes account of reality, and another which under the influence of the instincts detaches the ego from reality. The two exist alongside each other. The issue depends upon their relative strength. If the second is or becomes the stronger, the necessary condition for a psychosis is present.
>
> *(Freud, 1940, p. 202)*

The two mental attitudes to which Freud referred became the basis for a growing rift between the two child analysts who vied to represent psychoanalysis during Freud's terminal years in the decade prior to World War II – his daughter Anna and Melanie Klein, emigre to London. Anna developed her father's structural model and elaborated what later came to be known in the United States as ego psychology, emphasizing the defense mechanisms, principally repression. Had she written about psychosis it would have been depicted as the result of regressive failure of the ego and repression. Whereas Anna Freud studied the normal/neurotic ego Klein focused on the regressive part and chose to study what she called the paranoid-schizoid position and the process she called phantasy as it reflected itself in the play of disturbed children. Klein postulated two mental positions, in developmental sequence and at times in conflict with one another. Had these women collaborated rather than engaging in a personalized acrimonious struggle culminating in the so-called Controversial Discussions (King & Steiner, 1991), they might have developed a model integrating the primary and secondary processes of Freud and the two positions of Klein. They might have appreciated the similarities between phantasy, characteristic of the paranoid-schizoid position, and the primary process, and the similarities between the depressive position and the secondary process mind in conflict and utilizing mature defenses. As it unfolded, Anna Freud's work had its major impact on American ego psychology, whose contribution to psychosis is detailed in the next chapter, whereas Melanie Klein's analytic offspring articulated the theories of schizoid processes and psychotic and non-psychotic aspects of personality that I next describe. Both articulate the concept of a mind that is unable to attain and sustain a normal/neurotic organization because it is split.

Melanie Klein (1932, 1935, 1937, 1946) postulated a normal neonatal conflict between love and hate, reflective of a psychotic core in all of us. She believed rage at the frustration of extra-uterine life drives defensive ego splitting and projective identification in order to preserve the sense of a good self. She called this the paranoid-schizoid position. In other words, although her conceptual language was one of psychosis, she seems to have believed that infants are capable of experiencing intrapsychic conflict, an essential feature of the neurotic mind that distinguishes it from the absence of integration of the psychotic mind. She postulated a second stage developing later in infancy, the depressive position. This is characterized by a more advanced or reflective form of intrapsychic conflict and integration that enables more realistic whole-object relationships and tolerance of ambivalence and conflict. Like Freud, who believed that the capacity to repress primary process (psychotic) mentation is an essential aspect of maturation and development of a normal/neurotic mind, she conflated normal development with a process of healing from a postulated normal infantile psychotic state.

Klein called the mental process characteristic of the paranoid-schizoid position phantasy. It is sensory-perceptual-somatic-motor, a gastrointestinal urogenital body-mind. It is concrete yet also imagistic (in Kleinian terminology, symbolic equation). It is undifferentiated and unintegrated with regard to inner and outer reality, which is to say that boundaries between self and object are created by instinct-driven imagery rather than reality. In the quest for the ideal physical state of satiation unwanted affects (rage) and related body parts constitute the image of the other person. This self–other-undifferentiated process creates a kind of hallucinatory-delusional sense of actualization, the world not as it is, but as it is phantasized. The infant experiences oral impulse-driven total body tropism toward the part-object breast image of mother that is experienced as nourishment. Through the undifferentiated process of projective identification the infant experiences ridding itself of unwanted parts and putting them inside another person, or incorporating concrete "good" aspects of the other person into the self-image.

In Chapter 7 on the thought disorder model there is a more detailed description of Klein's model of phantasy, its unacknowledged similarity to Freud's primary process, and its reiteration of some of the confusions that limit Freud's model. And yet, her model of early infancy is based on the assumption of the capacity to experience intrapsychic conflict and initiate defensive processes. For purposes of elaborating the integration model of psychosis what is important to know is that in the course of her work with psychotic persons, child and adult, Klein (1932) was the first to introduce the defensive concepts of splitting of the ego and schizoid personality. She wrote about it in 1935 and 1940, and finally in her 1946 paper on schizoid mechanisms.

Ronald Fairbairn (1940, 1941) constructed a model of mind around Klein's schizoid concept that is strikingly different from Freud's model of neurosis. Freud's model is built around neurosis, and the idea that normality and neurosis are related and we are all neurotic, more or less. It is based on a linear developmental path of construction defined as structure formation, with potential for regression. Structures emerge from instinct-driven primary process chaos as mind develops defenses to master intrapsychic conflicts and paternal authority is internalized eventuating in the attainment of an integrated intact ego organization. Fairbairn's model, in contrast, is built around psychosis (schizoid) and the idea that we are all psychotic, more or less. In his model of development structuralization is paradoxically equivalent to destruction, a splitting of the intact ego of birth, a schizoid process in response to lack of maternal caring. As the infant experiences inevitable failures of caring he or she withdraws from the pain of the real world and lives increasingly in a schizoid inner world, what he called endopsychic structures constructed using defenses of splitting and repression. Through projective identification this inner world is not differentiated from the "real" external world resulting in the pathological enactments characteristic of the schizoid personality. In other words, conflict resolution in Fairbairn's cosmology is not growth-promoting as in Freud's model; it is a destructive process of withdrawing from the real world into a world of enacted phantasy.

In Klein's paranoid-schizoid cosmology splitting is the infant's way of trying to preserve a good enough sense of self in the face of innate overwhelming rage at the trauma of birth separation. Some have characterized her hypothesis of innate rage in religious terms as a kind of original sin. Fairbairn, in contrast, believed rage is an understandable response to the failures of caring in the infantile environment, and the purpose of splitting is to maintain the sense of a good *object*, so that the infant does not have to experience helplessness and hopelessness in a world of bad, or at least not quite good enough objects. Fairbairn's father was a minister, and his religious upbringing led to the famous comment that "It is better to be a sinner in a world ruled by God than a good person in a world ruled by the Devil" (1943, p. 67). The location of the "sin" is very different in each theory. I have found this irrational belief in a good loving parent or other, evidence to the contrary notwithstanding, to be a predominant feature of the psyches of persons who have experienced severe abuse, not only psychotic individuals but victims of domestic abuse and some who have been imprisoned and tortured for long periods of time. Jacob, whose personal essay is included later in the book, is a striking example. Despite compelling evidence to the contrary, for many years he refused to believe that his mother had abused him and had not loved him.

Just as Freud believed we all have neurotic elements of our personalities Fairbairn believed all of us suffer from at least mild schizoid conditions and he postulated a continuum ranging from schizoid personality of varying degrees of severity through what he called psychopathic personality ("a high percentage of fanatics, agitators, criminals, revolutionaries, and other disruptive elements" (1940, p. 6)) and finally to schizophrenia. He also believed that literary, artistic, and scientific pursuits often attract schizoid personalities, a notion I elaborate in later chapters when discussing the fate of primordial consciousness.

Fairbairn's theory of endopsychic structure is elaborated on in Chapter 7 on Freud's third, thought disorder, model.

Donald Winnicott (1945, 1960) wrote about schizoid personality in 1945, not long after Klein and Fairbairn, and in 1960 he elaborated on the aspect of splitting that he referred to as the true and false selves. Whether he was influenced by Helene Deutsch's concept of the as-if personality (1942) is not clear. His labels are widely but often incorrectly believed to imply a normal and pathological self. However, he believed, as did Fairbairn, that the schizoid personality, comprising true and false self as a kind of unit, is more or less the neurotic norm; we are all that way to some extent. The surface functional and often seemingly normal false self is conformist and defensive, protecting against the possibility of attacks on the spontaneous emotional true self or emotional core. In that sense it is not entirely unlike the brittle ego of ego psychology protecting against regression to primary process chaos.

As with Fairbairn, and Klein before them, it is pathology of earliest attachment that is determinative. The neurotic false self is constructed to protect against anxiety. When the infant is rejected and impinged upon and not allowed a period of omnipotent control it defends by introjecting environmental demands and creating a compliant false self in order to protect the true self from undergoing further attack and disintegrating.

Psychosis, according to Winnicott, results from inability to separate from the maternal person even sufficiently to form a protective false-self shield. It occurs in situations where the mother is unable to respond to the infant's true self, and instead continues to infantilize the child and is unable to separate from him or her. Reciprocally, the infant is unable to relinquish an undifferentiated state of primary omnipotence and recognize separate objects and instead clings to omnipotent delusions and attempts to possess and control the object by insistence on their reality.

Wilfred Bion's (1957, 1959, 1962) understanding of psychosis derived from his World War I experiences of traumatic psychosis or what we would now call PTSD. He found the framework to account for it in Klein's work on phantasy, splitting, and projective identification. Like Freud he related psychosis to dreaming. However he maintained that there are two kinds of dreaming, normal and psychotic, and these relate respectively to what he described (1957) as the psychotic and non-psychotic parts of the personality. He postulated what he called the alpha function of mind, that is associated with the process of dreaming, and metabolizes the raw elements of sensation and perception into mature thought. In the absence of alpha function the mind cannot think and instead works according to what Klein described as the paranoid-schizoid position and phantasy. He writes that the dream

> can be employed for two dissimilar purposes. One is concerned with the transformation of stimuli received from the world of external reality and internal psychic reality so that they can be stored (memory) in a form making them accessible to recall (attention) and synthesis with each other. The other … is the use of the visual images of the dream for purposes of control and ejection of unwanted … emotional experience … . a vehicle for the evacuatory process. The dream itself is then felt to be an act of evacuation in much the same way as the visual hallucination is felt to be a positive act of expulsion through the eyes.

In this case: "The fact that the dream is being employed in an excretory function contributes to the patient's feeling that he is unable to dream" (1962, p. 67). He made confusing assertions such as: "If the patient cannot transform his emotional experiences into alpha-elements, he cannot dream … the patient who cannot dream cannot go to sleep and cannot wake up" (1962, p. 7). I believe he meant that as a consequence of deficient alpha functioning the psychotic individual does not possess the neurotic organization necessary to think and reflect and hence be aware that he or she is, in a sense, dreaming all the time. I think Bion's hypothesis of a specific alpha function that is involved forming mental representations from raw sensory-perceptual-motor stimuli can stand on its own independent of whether one accepts his idea that there are two kinds of dreaming, a normal one that accomplishes this process and a pathological one more like Klein's paranoid-schizoid position. The primary process that underlies dreaming is a process of imagery and actualization and not a representation-making process but that does not make it pathological.

Bion (1957) postulated a psychotic part of the personality with four essential features:

> These are: a preponderance of destructive impulses so great that even the impulse to love is suffused by them and turned to sadism; a hatred of reality, internal and external, which is extended to all that makes for awareness of it; a dread of imminent annihilation; and finally, a premature and precipitate formation of object relations.
>
> *(1957, p. 266)*

He explains:

> Where the non-psychotic part of the personality resorts to repression as a means of cutting off certain trends in the mind both from consciousness and from other forms of manifestation and activity, the psychotic part of the personality has attempted to rid itself of the apparatus on which the psyche depends to carry out the repressions; the unconscious would seem to be replaced by the world of dream furniture.
>
> *(1957, p. 269)*

He adds:

> Since contact with reality is never entirely lost, the phenomena which we are accustomed to associate with the neuroses are never absent and serve to complicate the analysis, when sufficient progress has been made, by their presence amidst psychotic material. On this fact, that the ego retains contact with reality, depends the existence of a non-psychotic personality parallel with, but obscured by, the psychotic personality.
>
> *(1957, p. 266)*

Finally:

> The sadistic attacks on the ego and on the matrix of thought, together with projective identification of the fragments, make it certain that from this point on there is an ever-widening divergence between the psychotic and non-psychotic parts of the personality until at last the gulf between them is felt to be unbridgeable.
>
> *(1957, p. 268)*

Each of these interesting and different systems shares the idea of a linear developmental pathway leading to a normal/neurotic personality organization, and the related idea that failure to achieve and sustain this goal involves a split-off regressive psychotic part of the personality. On the other side of the Atlantic the same integration model based on similar assumptions developed in a different direction because the focus was on the psychology of the ego and the defenses – the "strong" and potentially normal part of the personality, and not on the regressive or psychotic part.

6

FREUD'S THREE MODELS AND THEIR OFFSPRING IIB

The inability to be neurotic: The American ego psychology iteration of the integration model and Kernberg's transatlantic rapprochement

A number of analysts including some of Freud's inner circle of ring-bearers, and others influenced by Anna Freud and the more conservative developments in London, immigrated to America around the outbreak of World War II and established themselves as a theoretically coherent group initially based in New York City. They based their work on Freud's structural and economic model of psychosexual development and designated themselves ego psychologists. I have no idea whether they were consciously attempting to distinguish themselves from the emphasis on "id psychology" of the Kleinian group many of them split from. Their influence extended to the mental hospitals where others were attempting to refute Freud's belief that schizophrenic persons are unable to form relationships. Most notable of these was Chestnut Lodge in the person of Frieda Fromm-Reichmann and Harold Searles, and the Menninger Clinic and Austen Riggs in the person of Robert Knight and Otto Will.

The ideas of Melanie Klein and her associates, which focused on the psychotic process itself, did not take hold in the United States for another quarter century. In the mid-1960s Otto Kernberg came to the United States from Chile where he learned Kleinian theory, and came under the influence of the North American ego psychology. His efforts to integrate these two schools of thought led to his important work on borderline personality organization.

The ego psychological perspective on psychosis is that a presumed genetically "weak ego" is unable to regulate and repress the strong drive derivatives that arise in adolescence and young adulthood, leading to regressive emergence of uncontrolled primary process mentation and behavior. In this frame of reference schizophrenia and the psychoses are seen as adult onset regressions.

The work of **Paul Federn** (1952), one of the first of the American ego psychologists to take an interest in psychosis, was described in the discussion of Freud's first relationship model in the context of his support of the re-mothering therapy of his nurse pupil-turned-colleague Gertrude Schwing in a German hospital in the years prior to World War II. He immigrated to the US in 1938 and became a mainstay of the New York group of ego psychologists. His interest apparently shifted from hospital treatment of schizophrenia to out-patient work with the group that in Europe were called schizoid personalities, and he called latent schizophrenic.

Federn emphasized the concept of ego boundaries, and their loss during psychotic regression. His concept of latent schizophrenia denotes a person with a superficial neurotic organization but weak ego boundaries, who, when treated with standard neurotic psychoanalytic treatment including couch, free association, and interpretation of negative transference, is vulnerable to regress and lose the capacity to distinguish inner from outer reality. For this potentially psychotic group of patients he advocated positive supportive therapy designed to shore up repression and keep the demons at bay, as it were.

Other than Federn, the best known of the New York ego psychologists of psychosis were **Ernest Hartmann** (1953) and **Arlow and Brenner** (1964, 1969). Hartmann's ideas were standard ego psychology. He characterized the regressive state as one dominated by primitive defense mechanisms and the primary process, a conceptual combination I discuss subsequently in the context of the work of Kernberg. Arlow and Brenner emphasized the conflict of a weak ego with reality, and pointed out that the conflicts of a psychotic person tend to involve aggression in contrast to neurotic conflicts that they believed involve sexuality (1964, pp. 144–178).

Moving to the mental hospital contingent of ego psychologists, **Frieda Fromm-Reichmann** is best known for her association with Harry Stack Sullivan and her skill in engaging schizophrenic patients. What is not so well known is that while her writings are primarily about engaging the psychotic person in a therapeutic relationship she appears to have employed a basically standard neurosis-informed ego psychological model to the work itself. The ego weakness she attributed to deficient mothering, and she originated the unfortunate phrase "schizophrenogenic mother" (1948, p. 265). She viewed schizophrenia as the result of failure of repression and regression to a dream-like state, although she did not refer to Freud's concept of primary process. She utilized the transference to identify her patients' parataxic distortions, a term she learned from Sullivan whose significance is discussed in the chapter on Freud's thought disorder model. She attempted through classical neurosis-based techniques of free association and interpretation of transference to uncover the childhood origins of what was repressed. The paradox, it seems to me, is that at the same time she attributed the schizophrenic state to failure of repression she utilized techniques based on the idea that the important content is repressed. She placed "therapeutic emphasis primarily on the investigation of the anxiety aroused by unearthing repressed material and of the anxiety operating in the relationship with the therapist who helps patients to resolve repressive processes" (Fromm-Reichmann, 1954b, p. 715). She wrote modern trends in the intensive psychoanalytically oriented treatment of mental disturbances have been to put the investigation of the unknown and the known genetic and dynamic causes of a patient's anxieties into the centre of psychotherapeutic endeavour. His ways of expressing anxiety and of warding it off by his symptomatology at large are scrutinized, and among them especially his security operations with his defences against the psychiatrist, who undertakes to bring the patient's anxieties to the fore. Through the scrutiny of a patient's security operations with the psychiatrist, his defences against the other people of his present and previous environment can also be spotted .

(Fromm-Reichmann, 1952, p. 101)

Working at the Menninger Clinic **Robert Knight** (1953) introduced the concept of borderline states. Much like Federn, he described these as conditions of ego weakness in which secondary process thinking is disrupted by eruptions of the primary process. He identified persons in a borderline state by such things as peculiarities of word usage, inappropriate affect, contamination of idioms, and most important, the fact that the emerging thought disorder is ego syntonic; unremarkable to the person, who is unable to reflect on it.

In summary, the ego psychological elaboration of Freud's failure of integration model of psychosis portrays it as the result of a failure to achieve and maintain neurotic organization due to defective structure (ego). The differences between neurosis and psychosis include weak ego, strong drives with an emphasis on aggression rather than sexuality, primitive defenses, and regression to primary process function. Instances of undifferentiation are conceived of as projective identification, and instances of lack of integration as denial. In this regard the formulation of the ego psychologists was similar to that of Melanie Klein, whose work they seemed unaware of until Kernberg came along. She also conceived of the paranoid-schizoid position as a defensive operation, although a primary not a regressive one. In contrast, Freud conceived of the primary process as the first mental operation and not a secondary line of defense. One implication of the ego psychological position is that schizophrenia is an adult onset disorder, not the inappropriate perpetuation of a primary mental activity. I question the validity of this assumption in subsequent chapters.

Otto Kernberg (1966, 1967) is responsible for introducing Kleinian ideas, that had either gone largely unrecognized or else dismissed as bizarre, to North American psychoanalysis. He made these theoretical vegetables palatable by attempting to integrate them with the classical steak and potatoes structural theory and ego psychology then in vogue. Kernberg writes:

Unfortunately, some basic assumptions of Melanie Klein, to which she tended to adhere in a rather dogmatic way and which have rightly been questioned by most authors in this field – the lack of consideration of structural factors in her writings; her disregard for epigenetic development;

and, finally, her rather peculiar language – have made her observations difficult for most people to accept .

(1967, p. 677)

He took the concept of schizoid personality or character from the Klein group, designating a stable configuration and amalgamated it with the concept of borderline state from Knight and ego psychology, designating an unstable way-station between neurosis and psychosis, and from these parents birthed the concept of borderline personality organization, a stable cyclothymic configuration of personality, meaning that the emotional cycles are part of a stable configuration and not periodic regressions. From Klein he took her major contributions of the paranoid-schizoid positions, splitting of good from bad object images in response to rage, and projective identification, He rejected Klein's notion of innate neonatal rage in favor of an ego psychological orientation that the genesis of borderline personality is pathological infant–caregiver interactions. From the ego psychological perspective he developed a highly complex abstract puzzle-like model of normal and pathological development of psychic structure through introjection of what he called "building blocks."

The borderline personality is said to suffer from ego weakness and vulnerability to regression to primary process functioning and what Kernberg called primitive defenses of splitting, and projective identification, primitive idealization, split omnipotence and devaluation, and denial. He writes:

> In my attempt to analyze borderline personality organization, I shall first apply the kind of structural analysis which considers the ego as an overall structure which integrates substructures and functions, and then analyze the specific structural derivatives of internalized object relationships which are relevant to this form of psychopathology.
>
> *(1967, p. 659)*

And: "*This defensive division of the ego, in which what was at first a simple defect in integration is then used actively for other purposes, is in essence the mechanism of splitting*" (1967, p. 662, italics his).

The extent to which Kernberg copied Klein is further evident from his formulation of one type of narcissistic personality that appears to be modelled after the transition between Klein's paranoid-schizoid and depressive positions, a point when self–object differentiation is at times sustained and at other times relinquished. In Kernberg's model of narcissistic personality differentiated object relations entailing awareness of dependent feelings are defended against by self–self relationships in which a "grandiose self" relates to a projectively idealized object. The model is similar to Klein's "manic" relation to the object of dependency and her theoretical description of the normal infant's struggles at the interface of the depressive position and the preceding paranoid-schizoid position.

Finally, Kernberg distinguishes between the severe psychoses, which entail regressive loss of self–object differentiation, and borderline personality, characterized by stable defense mechanisms of splitting and projective identification.

Kernberg was responsible for my first exposure to Kleinian theory, as he was for many other analysts of my generation. His theory of borderline and narcissistic personalities is a very detailed and complex edifice combining theoretical apples and oranges that I find difficult to follow in detail. Can Klein and ego psychology be cobbled together as he tried to do? Whatever the answer, there is no question in my mind that Kernberg was responsible for a major shift and a new era of integration between North American and European psychoanalysis, at the same time that he reiterated Freud's basic model of psychosis as a split between a part that strives to be normal and an undertow regressive part.

Kernberg was not entirely alone in the effort to create a model for psychosis that attempted to integrate the European and American contribution. In his work on psychosis (1965) and borderline personality (1986) Harold Searles incorporated Klein's concept of projective identification with the ego psychological idea of ego weakness and regression. He also included the work of Margaret Mahler on separation–individuation,

Finally, we turn to Freud's third model; thought disorder, which came first chronologically in his work, and is the most generative. I have saved it until last because he put it aside after his 1900 work on dreaming, did not use it as the basis for a separate model of psychosis, and turned instead to more conservative ideas, but most importantly, turned away from psychosis entirely. Psychotic persons differ from normal and neurotic people not because they cannot relate, or because they are deficient in the strength to experience intrapsychic conflict and defense and become neurotic, but because they relate in a qualitatively different way to others that does not involve the psychic differentiation and integration necessary to experience such conflict. This form of relationship can be elucidated with a version of Freud's thought disorder model, but in contrast to his understanding, the process is not unconscious, it is conscious in a different way. It results from the persistence of a form of mentation and relationship characteristic of early life that under ordinary circumstances selectively supports adult phenomena that are normal and even creative, but under circumstances of pathology in the attachment phase persists in social settings in which it is inappropriate that we label abnormal and psychotic.

7

FREUD'S THREE MODELS AND THEIR OFFSPRING III

Thought disorder: The primary process

Freud's models of psychosis as inability to form a relationship and as failure to achieve sufficient maturity or ego strength to repress and to have a normal/neurotic organization reflect his commitment to two fundamental ideas. One relates to his neurology background in general, and to his acceptance of the psychiatric opinion prevalent during the years when he developed psychoanalysis, that psychosis is the result of a neurodegenerative defect. The other is his commitment to an authoritarian model of psychosexual and structural development in which the central character is the father and the basic issue is learning to experience and resolve conflict with father and to repress it in the service of civilized growth. The notion of significant pathology comprehensible and treatable by psychoanalysis based on the importance of the attachment to mother and pathology of that phase of development is an idea whose time was not to come for half a century, despite frequent references in the classical literature, especially by ego psychologists to the presence of "pre-Oedipal factors."

In his seminal work on dreaming (1900) Freud formulated the basis for a different model of psychosis, one that I elaborate in subsequent chapters that is psychological not organic, and is separate from the neurotic model that has dominated psychoanalysis. He believed that the primary process is the mental operation of infancy and schizophrenia as well as dreaming. The primary process model is the historically fundamental contribution to our understanding of psychosis, its genealogical Adam and Eve, so to speak. In prior chapters I indicated why Freud seemed to have preferred less revolutionary models more consistent with the ethos of his time, and those who followed him have been similarly conservative. At the same time we need to recognize the revolutionary nature of his discovery and its implications for a psychoanalysis that includes psychosis within its scope, it is also important to understand why, in the form he presented it, the primary process conceptualization of psychosis is not adequate to the task.

In his classic, *The Interpretation of Dreams* (1900), Freud proposed two basic mental processes, the primary process, which he believed to be unconscious, and the secondary process of ordinary conscious thought. Freud seems not to have realized the revolutionary nature of his discovery, that he was conceptualizing a normal form of conscious mental activity that is qualitatively different from reflective representational thought (Robbins, 2008, 2011, 2015, 2018). He vacillated between describing the primary process as invisible to direct conscious awareness as an object of reflective contemplation (unconscious) and as an arcane variant of ordinary symbolic thought, and he vacillated as to whether the process is normal or abnormal.

Freud's prototypical data for existence of a primary mental process is the phenomenology of dreaming. Freud described dreaming as the royal road to the aspect of mind that is unconscious or invisible. In other words, he believed that its mental structure or fabric, which he described as the primary process, is unconscious because we are not aware of it. That is, we cannot know it as part of reflective thought. We have to wake up and think or reflect about it before we know we were dreaming. Possibly another reason Freud labelled the process unconscious is that his prototypical mental activity, dreaming, occurs in a state of *physiological* unconsciousness in which the mind is periodically active but the motor system is paralyzed. It is important to distinguish this state from psychological unconsciousness, which Freud attempted to do by proposing an ambiguous state he called pre-consciousness.

Freud concluded that dreams are the sensory-perceptual actualizations of a mind momentarily unfettered by waking conscious awareness of social reality or by the potential consequences of uncontrolled action were the motor system not immobilized. He believed this state that he called unconsciousness was one in which, lacking reflection and reality checking, wishes become transformed into psychic realities. Therefore he called the governing motivation the pleasure principle. The process is characterized by displacement, condensation, and absence of contradiction. It creates sensory-perceptual identity or a sense of reality related to hallucination and delusion in waking life. In other words, a major feature of the primary process is absence of differentiation between mind and world. The primary process creates a narrative sequence by affective (instinctual) association of images rather than by reality-governed logic and temporal causality. In contrasting the primary process with wakeful consciousness he states: "The primary process endeavors to bring about a discharge of excitation in order that … it may establish a 'perceptual identity.' The secondary process, however, has abandoned this intention and taken on another in its place – the establishment of a 'thought identity'" (1900, p. 602). He adds that the subjective experience of the dreamer is not one of thought but "a complete hallucinatory cathexis of the perceptual systems" (p. 548). And the "dream-work proper diverges further from our picture of waking thought than has been supposed … it is completely different from it qualitatively and for that reason not immediately comparable with it" (1900, p. 507). He elaborates on the differences between dreaming and reflective representational thought: "One is the fact that the thought is represented as an immediate situation with the 'perhaps' omitted, and the other is the fact that the thought is transformed into visual images and speech" (p. 534).

After describing the primary process Freud made the fateful and questionable leap of reason that "These are the characteristics we may expect to find in processes belonging to the system *Ucs.*" (1915, p. 187). While Freud believed that dreaming, the prototype of the primary process, occurred in a state of psychic regression (sleep) it is important in relation to how some have thought about it subsequently that he did not believe that the primary process involves mechanisms of defense. He believed it is primary.

Freud called the mental process primary because he believed it is the ontologically first process, the mind of infancy prior to awareness of reality, and primary to the mind's capacity to initiate defensive activity. He wrote that

> the infant ... probably hallucinates the fulfilment of its internal needs; it betrays its unpleasure when there is an increase of stimulus and an absence of satisfaction, by the motor discharge of screaming and beating about with its arms and legs, and it then experiences the satisfaction it has hallucinated.
>
> *(1911, p. 218fn)*

In the process of growth and adaptation based on the reality principle, the secondary system or process, conscious reflective thought, develops. Many since Freud have questioned Freud's assumption that infant mind is unconscious and unrealistic, citing evidence that infants adapt to reality in a different way utilizing the conscious processes available to them. By equating consciousness with waking reflective representational thought Freud was able to reason that the primary process is unconscious. Other conclusions follow from this path of reasoning. For example such things as we cannot observe its presence directly, and that symptoms mask something deeper that must be inferred. In order to account for this masking he introduced the concept of dynamic repression, which, though it has an important place in the theory of neurosis, has been over-applied to account for phenomena that are immediately and directly evident if we know how to understand them as manifestations of an alternative (primordial) expression of conscious mind.

Freud seemed not to have been fully able to appreciate the profundity of his discovery of a qualitatively different mental process and its role in mental life. Instead of fully embracing that conclusion and its implications for mind he retreated in various writings and contradicted himself by making the more conservative argument that the primary process is just an arcane version of reflective symbolic thought. In a number of places he articulated his belief that the structure of dreams is qualitatively similar to that of thought, implying that it is not necessary to postulate a qualitatively distinctive mental process to comprehend them. He did not make the obvious conclusion that dreaming is the outcome of a variant of consciousness mind not an absence of it. He writes: "dreams appear to engage in making symbolic representations of the body, we now know that those representations are the product of certain unconscious phantasies" (1900, p. 612).

Without realizing he was implying dreaming is a conscious activity he used the analogy of different languages to describe the difference between dreams and waking thoughts. In *The Interpretation of Dreams* (1900) we read that:

> The dream-thoughts and the dream-content are presented to us like two versions of the same subject-matter in two different languages. Or, more properly, the dream-content seems like a transcript of the dream-thoughts into another mode of expression, whose characters and syntactic laws it is our business to discover by comparing the original and the translation. The dream-thoughts are immediately comprehensible, as soon as we have learnt them. The dream-content, on the other hand, is expressed as it were in a pictographic script, the characters of which have to be transposed individually into the language of the dream-thoughts.
>
> *(1900, p. 277)*

He notes that "the productions of the dream-work, which, it must be remembered, are not made with the intention of being understood, present no greater difficulties to their translators than do the ancient hieroglyphic scripts to those who seek to read them," and "the keys are generally known and laid down by firmly established linguistic usage" (1900, pp. 341–342). In summary, at the same time that Freud maintained that language is used by the primary process concretely and literally as a thing of action (for example the use of expletives) in a primary process qualitatively different from logical symbolic thought, he also believed that the language of dreaming is an arcane form of symbolism that can be decoded by the same associative language principles that apply to ordinary language.

Freud did consider another possibility in his effort to resolve the ambiguity and confusion, namely that dreaming in particular and the primary process in general might be conscious albeit in a different way from reflective symbolic thought. Once again his attempt to do so was fraught with confusion and complexity. In proposing another mental process, *preconscious*, he suggested the possibility of concrete evanescent affect-driven imagery different from constant abstract representation. He writes: "A very great part of this preconscious originates in the unconscious, has the character of its derivatives and is subjected to a censorship before it can become conscious. Another part of the *Pcs.* is capable of becoming conscious without any censorship" (1915, p. 190). System pcs is characterized as an intermediate censor that partakes of both systems at different times. It seems confusing to describe dreaming both as a primary process function and as a preconscious one. But perhaps the concept of preconscious was Freud's embryonic effort to describe another form of consciousness with characteristics such as evanescent imagery, different from the stable mental representations characteristic of reflective symbolic thought.

Freud linked schizophrenia to dreaming and the primary process in a number of his writings, even though he did not build upon his idea. He believed that dreaming is inherently psychotic in the sense of creating a subjectively wishful view of the world that he labeled hallucinatory and delusional. He wrote that: "A dream, then, is a psychosis with all the absurdities, delusions and illusions of a psychosis" (1940, p. 172). In 1915 he wrote "In schizophrenia *words* are subjected to the same process as that which makes the dream-images out of latent dream-thoughts – to what we have called the primary psychical process" (p. 198). He writes that "we are working towards the explanation of the psychoses when we endeavour to elucidate the mystery of dreams" (1900, p. 66).

Freud did not try to reconcile how and why the same process could be the underpinning of normal infant mind, dreaming, and psychotic mind. One is left with the confusing idea that infuses Klein's writings as well, that we are all normally psychotic in infancy, and that normal development is a kind of therapeutic process. That belief is reflected in the various efforts over the years to promote therapies based on the idea of re-parenting or new beginnings.

Freud was not the only one in his time who believed that dreaming and psychosis are related. Jung wrote: "The psychological mechanisms of dreams and hysteria are most closely related to those of dementia praecox" (1906, p. 78). In his classic (1911b) text on dementia praecox Bleuler remarked on the similarity between the mental activity of the schizophrenic and that of the dreamer, and stated that schizophrenic thinking, especially its delusional aspect, operates by rules that distinguish it from waking thought.

Melanie Klein (1935, 1946) articulated another form of mental activity, the unintegrated and undifferentiated paranoid-schizoid position and its characteristic process of phantasy. While the description bears much resemblance to Freud's primary process she (and most of her followers) do not acknowledge their theoretical roots. In fact most of the theorists whose work is described in this chapter formulated models that in substance resemble the primary process but are couched in idiosyncratic conceptual terminology, without crediting Freud.

Whereas Freud did not knowingly work with psychotic persons, and dreaming served as his basic data from which he extrapolated his theory of unconscious mind and of psychosis, Klein worked with psychotic adults and very disturbed children who expressed themselves in action (play) in which non-reflective language plays an obvious role. While Klein did not emphasize the idea that the process she described is unconscious, in 1946 she conjoined her concept of phantasy, the mental process of the paranoid-schizoid position, with the adjective "unconscious." Most of the references to phantasy of Susan Isaacs, as well as those of Hannah Segal, Klein's most important explicators, are similarly coupled with the adjective "unconscious."

Isaacs (1948) offers a particularly eloquent description of phantasy as a somatic process different from and antecedent to conceptual thought. It is concrete and enactive rather than symbolic and reflective, sensory-perceptual-somatic-motor, undifferentiated and unintegrated in the sense implied by projective identification.

It creates a hallucinatory-delusional sense of actualization. The mind of phantasy is somatic; gastrointestinal and urogenital; based on the belief that what is "good" can be ingested and what is "bad" can be excreted or eliminated. Need is experienced and enacted orally as somatic tropism toward the mother (breast) that is undifferentiated from a state of satisfaction (goodness), and frustration elicits somatic-psychic excretory responses that are equally undifferentiated from parts of the object (badness). States of incipient and actual satisfaction are experienced as an omnipotent (undifferentiated) hallucinatory/delusional belief that Klein named the "good" breast, while states of frustration and rage are projectively identified in the other as belief in a destroyed/destroying (persecutory) "bad" breast. In contrast to Klein and most Kleinians, Isaacs acknowledges that:

> The earliest and most rudimentary phantasies, bound up with sensory experience, and being affective interpretations of bodily sensations, are naturally characterized by those qualities that Freud described as belonging to the "primary process": lack of co-ordination of impulse, lack of sense of time, of contradiction, and of negation. Furthermore, at this level, there is no discrimination of external reality. Experience is governed by "all or none" responses and the absence of satisfaction is felt as a positive evil. Loss, dissatisfaction or deprivation are felt in sensation to be positive, painful experiences.
>
> *(1948, p. 87)*

One of the difficulties distinguishing the presence of two different normal mental processes and their developmental origins and consequences, is that Freud's description of the primary process and Klein's of the paranoid-schizoid position and phantasy imply that normal development is pathological, or to put it differently, that we are all psychotic as infants, but outgrow it and become normal if we are fortunate. Klein (1946) perpetuated Freud's confusion when she gave the pathological name paranoid-schizoid position to the mental process she described and she used the term "manic" to describe some of its operations, leaving the reader to wonder if she is expressing phenomena that are normal, pathological, or somehow both. Another source of confusion in Klein's writings relates to the capacity to integrate and bear intrapsychic conflict. While she writes that neurotic integration in the sense of toleration for ambivalence and related replacement of part-object with whole-object relationships, she also believed that the capacity for intrapsychic conflict and defense mechanisms, principally splitting and projective identification, is present from birth.

Michael Balint (1958), another analysand of Ferenczi, did not work with psychotic persons. Nevertheless, writing more or less contemporaneously with Klein, he was one of the first to write about the positive importance of attachment to mother and postulated that pathology of attachment is the "basic fault" in schizophrenia. He distinguished neurosis, involving the capacity for a three-person (Oedipal) relationship and the experience of intrapsychic conflict, from psychosis, involving an undifferentiated primary (mother–infant) attachment and the inability to experience conflict. He writes: "the basic fault has *not* the form of a conflict. As described above, it has the form of a fault, something wrong in the mind, a deficiency that must be put right" (1958, p. 338).

Ronald Fairbairn's theory of thought disorder (1941, 1943, 1944, 1952, 1963) bears some similarity to Freud's model of the primary process, although he does not mention the primary process in his writings. It is a theory of undifferentiation, splitting, and failure of integration. However, unlike the primary process the thought disorder is an intrapsychic adaptation to unsatisfactory attachment relationships rather than a primary way that mind works and one of two natural processes. Like Freud he uses dreaming as a model. He notes that each of the figures in a dream represents an unintegrated aspect of the dreamer's psyche. He believed unintegrated or part-object relationships result from failure of self–object differentiation in the primary relationships, and of psychological awareness of separation of self from other. As he put it, there is a tendency for the outer world to derive its meaning from the inner world. However, he believed this undifferentiation of inner from outer reality is defensive (projective identification) and secondary rather than the result of primary failure of differentiation. He wrote about role playing in the schizoid personality as a product of splitting and a failure to separate from a mother who does not value her child as a separate person. The major consequence of internal mastery of disappointing relationships is schizoid withdrawal and depression, attitudes of isolation, omnipotence or grandiosity, and self-preoccupation, followed by distortion of subsequent relationships by projective identification. The details constitute Fairbairn's schizoid and depressive positions, as well as the neuroses. The thought disorder in Fairbairn's theory is the result of splitting and projective identification, whereas Freud considered the primary process a normal way the infant mind works that the psychotic person is vulnerable to regress to because of a presumably genetically determined structural weakness.

Fairbairn's thought disorder is a function of structuralization in response to disappointing primary relationships, an effort to maintain the sense of a world controlled by good objects by creating an internally structured world of pathological conflict that draws the person's mind increasingly away from external reality. Structuralization consists of horizontal splitting (repression) and vertical splitting (fragmentation). Fairbairn seemed to believe that repression, which requires sufficient integration to enable intrapsychic conflict, and splitting, which implies a personality that is fragmented and unintegrated, could co-exist. In contrast to Freud's purified pleasure ego and Klein's all-good self the purpose of splitting is to preserve the sense of a good object, not a good sense of self. The result is his three self- subsystems: the unconscious libidinal and antilibidinal selves and the conscious central self. What is repressed are not wishes or drives, but bad objects, or as we would now say, representations of these unsatisfying objects and the parts of the ego that seek relationships with them. These libidinal and antilibidinal configurations are projected into salient relationships leading to pathological enactments and a world that is increasingly withdrawn and internal and at the same time confused with or undifferentiated from the external world.

It is not widely appreciated that **Harry Stack Sullivan** (1931, 1933, 1940, 1953, 1954, 1962), one of the founders of the Washington School of Psychiatry, and a person who, as I have noted, is best known for demonstrating that it is possible to relate to schizophrenic persons, proposed a thought disorder model for schizophrenia not all that different from Freud's primary process. His model, however, is couched in unrelated terminology, and it is not clear if he was even aware of the primary process concept when he formulated it. He named the thought disorder parataxic distortion. He proposed a three stage model of normal development – prototaxic, parataxic, and syntaxic (1953, p. 18, editor's note). Mentation in the earliest prototaxic stage is immediate, unintegrated or momentary, without a sense of time or causality, and holistic or cosmic insofar as it does not differentiate inner from outer reality. The subsequent parataxic phase is differentiated but not integrated. And the syntactic phase is one of mature differentiation and integration. The resemblance to the primary process and development of secondary process thinking is apparent.

Sullivan anticipated attachment theory and speculated that intense anxiety in relation to an anxious mother in the oral phase led to splitting or dissociation of self-systems that he called "selective inattention." What we would now call the split-off good object, and he called the good breast, from the non-anxious mother, promotes formation of a "good me" self that is presented to the outside world. The bad-breast-self related to the anxious mother causes anxiety and dissociative development of a repressed or suppressed "bad me." During adolescence, under pressure to establish intimacy involving what he called "lust dynamics," when rejections cause serious blows to the good me self-esteem system, anxiety becomes intolerable panic. Then the schizophrenic forms a "not me" self, consisting of parataxic distortions that are delusional and have no relation to causality or reality.

Sullivan believed that schizophrenia is a regression to the parataxic stage in which experience is differentiated into entities but not integrated into a logical or realistic sequence, hence there can be no consensually or socially validated reality. Given the propensity toward selective inattention and splitting or dissociation of self-systems the schizophrenic person presents a delusional not-self. In 1962 Sullivan described schizophrenia as "a serious disorder of the integrating systems" (p. 278) and he added:

> It is equally clear that the "retreat" from the personal realities of others, the "seclusiveness" and the inaccessibility to easy personal contacts that are so classically schizophrenic are but the avoidance of accentuated conflict between the systems which integrate or "strive" to integrate the sufferer into mutually incongruous interpersonal relations.
>
> *(1962, p. 281)*

As well as resembling Freud's primary process model, Sullivan's system resembles Freud's second model of schizophrenia insofar as it is based on the idea of failure to achieve and maintain a normal/neurotic self based on secondary process mentation and the capacity to experience intrapsychic conflict.

Proceeding chronologically, I do not know if **Eilhard Von Domarus** (1925, 1944) was familiar with Sullivan's work, much less Freud's, but writing about schizophrenia he introduced the concept of paralogical thinking, a concept that bears striking resemblance to Sullivan's concept of parataxic thinking. He described this thought disorder as predicate identity, a confusing concept that more or less means inability to differentiate, leading to the putting together of two things that are according to reality logic unrelated because they share a common characteristic. What is confusing is that instead of using "subject" to mean subject as in ordinary discourse, distinct from object, he utilizes Vygotsky's definitions of subject, which refers to object, or predicate: "Vygotsky calls the subject of a sentence that about which something is said, and the predicate that which expresses what is said about the subject; subject and predicate are for him psychological, not grammatical terms" (1944, p. 111fn). Predicate identity means that two elements are treated by the schizophrenic subject as though they are identical (not *are associated*) because they share a quality that fits the person's wishful belief. "The paralogical thinker finds identity of subjects whenever and wherever he finds identity of predicates" (Von Domarus, 1944, p. 113).

Von Domarus cites the example of a patient who believed that Jesus, cigar boxes, and sex are identical. They shared the quality of being encircled (halo, cigar band, holding). The delusional belief of a schizophrenic that an unrelated woman is her mother, for instance, may result from making an identity of the predicate fact that both that person and the patient's mother are women. I read of a patient who maintained that men are grass. A detailed analysis revealed that the subject of belief was death, and the predicates "men" and "grass" were treated as identical because they share the characteristic of dying. If expressed in symbolic representational thought, inserting the word *like*, the statement becomes "men are *like* grass." The syllogism "men die, grass dies, therefore men are *like* grass" might even become poetic, as it is in one of the most moving parts of the Brahms *German Requiem*. A schizophrenic might say "Johnny is a weed," failing to differentiate and making the concrete paralogical assertion "Johnny is growing fast, weeds grow fast, therefore Johnny is a weed." Expressed in symbolic thought one might simply say "Johnny is *growing like* a weed." Werner and Kaplan (1963), who used the concept of syncretism to describe the schizophrenic's fusion of contradictory thoughts, report an example from the work of Tuczek of a patient who used the term "the sent" to denote the color white. The underlying process was that snow is white, and snow is sent from God. The meaning of many otherwise arcane schizophrenic associations can be grasped if one can determine the idiosyncratic predicate quality that aggregates them.

The most recent two proponents of Freud's primary process vintage in new conceptual bottles, **Silvano Arieti** and **Ignacio Matte-Blanco** did so around the same time, the mid-1970s, both introducing the idea of two kinds of logic. Arieti (1955, 1967) contrasted what he called paleologic, characterized by the concept of adualism, with ordinary Aristotelian logic. He claims to have derived his ideas from Von Domarus' concept of paralogic and predicate identity. Arieti describes four characteristics of Aristotelian logic (presumably thought) as the law of identity, where A cannot be B; the law of contradiction, where A cannot be both A and B at the same time; the law of excluded middle, where A must either be A or not be A and there cannot be a fusion or shape changing between them, and finally, the law of sufficient reason which requires a shared logical cause for every event. In contrast he describes paleologic, where A can be B, can be both, can change shape from one to the other, and where causes are concrete and subjective. He describes in paleologic a kind of immediacy that disregards distinctions between time past, present, and future, in which things are concrete and literal, and where there is identity rather than the more differentiated process of identification. He tells us about the schizophrenic that: "As long as he interprets reality with Aristotelian logic, he is aware of the unbearable truth ... new logic ... will permit him to see reality as he wants to" (1967, p. 229). And: "The content of the hallucination ... represents or refers to a crucial part of the patient's personal predicament" (1967, p. 273). He named the central feature of paleologic "Adualism ... lack of the ability to distinguish between the two realities, that of the mind and that of the external world" (1967, p. 278) and related it to Federn's concept of lack of ego boundaries. While concreteness and immediacy are described as characteristic of paleologic, its major feature, adualism, described in many different ways, is none other than inability to differentiate. What Arieti describes as paleologic, then, is Freud's primary process reconceptualized, which he makes but a single fleeting reference to in his book.

Finally, we turn to another logician, **Ignacio Matte-Blanco** (1959, 1975, 1988) and his theory of bi-logic, symmetrical and asymmetrical or heteromodal. Asymmetric logic is the equivalent of what Freud called the secondary process and Arieti called Aristotelian logic. His description of symmetric logic is of an unconscious process like Freud's primary process, whose influence on his work he does not reference. As with Freud's description of symptom formation he believed its presence must be inferred by its effects on asymmetric logic, even though the process he described is directly observable.

The characteristics of symmetrical logic, according to Matte-Blanco, include absence of contradiction and negation, displacement and condensation, timelessness. undifferentiation of external and psychical reality, replacement of logical connection and causal-temporal logic with contiguity of events, and replacement of similarity with identity. Matte-Blanco seems to accept the idea that symmetrical logic is unconscious in the sense of being invisible, a kind of mental void whose presence is only to be inferred by observing how it distorts thought (asymmetrical logic). Mental processes become observable in his theory in the form of structures involving interactions between the two logics. Dreaming is one such structure, that he called Tridim. In a Tridim (three dimensional) structure the presence of symmetrical logic is concealed by the kinds of splits to which Fairbairn alluded when he wrote about different characteristics of the dreamer being expressed by different characters in the dream, and by the fact that the dreamer and the dream characters are not actually differentiated. Multiple meanings must be fit into three dimensions. He writes:

> (a) One can see in it the presence of symmetrical logic in that two [or more] different persons are implicitly treated as only one; i.e. the original person and the person on to whom displacement takes place are really the same person in different "incarnations," just as happens in a symmetrized class or set. (b) Classical logic is present in the fact that one sees the appearances of two [or more] quite different and separated persons: no identification. It is only by means of the analysis of the associations that one can discover the (secret) identity of the two [or more]. It is, therefore, a dissimulated bi-logical structure. ... In the Tridim structure one can, at first sight, detect only the heterogenic-dividing mode, while the indivisible mode is dissimulated, precisely by means of splitting-displacement, which makes one appear as two. ... In condensation we see that a given person who appears as "normally" three-dimensional has the features of several different persons. It is as though these persons have all been catapulted and compressed into only one. ... This suggests that a being which is isomorphic to a space of more than three dimensions is made to appear as three-dimensional. The traces of a number of dimensions higher than three, however, are suggested in the different features of different three-dimensional persons
>
> *(1988, pp. 48–49)*

To my mind this is an excessively complex way to refer, once again, to the phenomena of undifferentiation and dis-integration.

More recently (2015) **Riccardo Lombardi** has attempted to amalgamate the work of Matte-Blanco and Bion, proposing a concept of formless infinity to denote what Matte-Blanco called symmetrical logic, and supplementing it with Bion's concept of psychotic and non-psychotic parts of the personality.

None of the analysts whose work I have quoted traces his or her theoretical genealogy to Freud's primary process model despite the fact he said it first, and perhaps better. Therefore his model of the primary process deserves to be the foundation of understanding of the psychotic thought disorder. However, it suffers from confusions with regard to its relationship with reflective representational thought, and with regard to its relationship to consciousness. Freud was also not clear whether in itself it is normal or pathological, and that confusion is reflected in the idea that the normal infant is also psychotic. Those who have re-presented a similar idea using idiosyncratic terminology have perpetuated similar confusion.

There is an additional problem with Arieti and Matte-Blanco that might ironically be described as failure of conceptual differentiation, involving their respective postulations of two kinds of logic. Dictionary sources generally use similar terminology to define logic, including such terms as reasoning, rationality, good judgment, validation, causality, systematic, scientific, and the like. There is no mention of more than one kind of logic, and certainly none whose characteristics as so markedly at odds as those of Arieti and Matte-Blanco.

I have reviewed Freud's three models of psychosis – inability to form relationship, inability to form and sustain a neurotic organization related to failure of integration, and thought disorder – and the genealogical pathways of their theoretical offspring. Whether he did not carry any of these lines of investigation very far because of the prevailing ethos that schizophrenia is a degenerative brain disease, because of his emphasis on the civilizing role of paternal authority and his curious neglect of the primary significance of the mother–infant bond, because he practiced in his office rather than a mental hospital, or some combination thereof, we can only speculate.

Before proposing a model for psychosis that involves a line of development separate from and independent of that of neurosis, I would like to summarize the problems with Freud's three models and their genealogical reincarnations. The relationship model and the failure of integration model both accept the psychiatric conception of psychosis as a presumed inherent neurological defect resulting in a basic split in the personality and a related failure to become fully human, full humanity being a condition equated with the "ability" to be neurotic. The model that is based on the assumption that psychotic persons cannot form a relationship has been proven incorrect as we know that psychotic persons are capable of forming relationships with skilled therapists. The failure of integration model defines psychosis in relation to normality and neurosis as a kind of negative or failure, an adult onset illness resulting from inability to achieve and sustain a normal/neurotic form of organization, resulting in the dissociated presence of non-psychotic and psychotic elements of personality. The classical psychoanalytic model of mind, following Freud, is based on linear development of a neurotic organization of mind, capable of experiencing intrapsychic conflict and initiating defense. In this model psychosis is conceived of as a genetically determined *forme fruste*, an aberrant incomplete development that renders the person deficient both mentally and in the capacity to relate to others in a fully human sense.

What sets Fairbairn's contribution apart from the others that bears some relationship to the model of mind and psychosis that I will be developing is that it is not based on the capacity to be neurotic as maturational norm, and the associated idea we are all neurotic, more or less. Fairbairn's contrasting model is based on psychosis and the idea that we are all psychotic (schizoid), more or less. And the deficiency it postulates does not originate in the afflicted person as it does in Freud's model and that of those who have elaborated it, but in his or her earliest attachment relationship. Fairbairn reversed Freud's conception of development as structure building toward the capacity to experience and resolve neurotic conflict. He proposed a model of structuralization as destructive splitting, psychosis of greater or lesser severity. Just as Freud had no separate place for psychosis, Fairbairn's model has no place for neurosis; there are only degrees of psychotic pathology. In Part III I construct a model in which psychosis and neurosis represent end points of separate lines of development, without prejudice that one is more "normal" and the other pathological.

Freud's thought disorder model is his potentially most fruitful contribution to understanding psychosis. While he did not use the term "thought disorder" to refer to the primary process in psychosis, it is implied in his belief psychosis is a regressive process. Similar thinking underlies the models of those who followed in his footsteps. It is important to understand that regression is a misnomer. As we shall see in chapters to come, it is not a kind of disintegration of thought that characterizes psychosis but a different equally normal and important mental activity that is employed in contextually inappropriate situations. Moreover, looking at psychosis as a thought disorder is but one manifestation of the problem inherent in Freud's other models, namely that psychosis is a defect or a failure to attain and sustain a neurotic organization.

PART III

A new beginning

Distinguishing psychosis from neurosis

CLINICAL PREFACE TO CHAPTERS 8, 10, AND 13

Clinical illustrations of psychosis and its treatment are interspersed throughout the book. Chapters 8, 10, and 13 describe the model I propose for psychosis and its psychoanalytic treatment. I have chosen to illustrate them with clinical material from four patients whose problems I would describe as psychotic personality disorder, a condition where there is some capacity for independent living and relating via a more or less effective false self. In the course of intensive long term psychoanalytic therapy these individuals to varying degrees resolved their own psychotic problems.

The material is unusual, for it comprises excerpts from essays about the understandings they had achieved that they were kind enough to contribute to my 2018 book on the subject of language aberration. While the topic of these essays was neither the nature of the psychotic process nor its therapy, there is sufficient relevant material on these topics to merit the inclusion of excerpts from these essays. I chose not to include material from a schizophrenic person in these three chapters, but the reader will find detailed accounts in Chapter 16 of my work with Sara, a chronic paranoid schizophrenic woman. In my 2011 and 2018 books I wrote about Caroline, a schizophrenic woman, and in my 1993 book on schizophrenia I recounted five other cases, three successful and two failures, from start to finish. So as not to interrupt the flow in these subsequent chapters I present introductions to the four patients below. They can be referenced later if needed. More detailed accounts of each of these people as well as the original essays can be found in the 2018 book.

Each individual was in intensive psychotherapy 3–4 times per week for at least two decades. Each one made major changes including much more use of reflective representational thought, as evidenced by the introspective essays they gave me as well as by major changes in feelings of well-being and significant improvements in work and relationships.

These brief biographies all illustrate primordial consciousness, the mental activity that characterizes psychosis. Primordial conscious mentation also underlies such normal phenomena as dreaming, early infant mentation, parent–infant bonding, creativity, belief systems, the predominant mental activity in non-western tribal-spiritual cultures, and more. Here are some of the salient characteristics of first mind or primordial consciousness.

- Psychological undifferentiation of self and other.
- Absence of psychic integration, as unrepresented aspects of self are perceived externally as characteristics of others and the world.
- Concreteness of language and somatization rather than mental representation and the capacity for symbolization.
- Mental images linked by predominant affects rather than by logic and represented emotions.
- An "it is" sense of living in the moment, in which there is no psychological sense of time or separation of past, present, and future.
- The mental state of unquestioned belief or conviction, without capacity for reflection, introspection, fantasy, "as if."

Jane

Jane was an unmarried professor in her early 40s when she was referred to me in the throes of a severe regressive episode in which she isolated herself in her apartment, did not bathe, eat, or take out trash, and engaged in physical self-mutilation. She had hoarded pills and was on the verge of killing herself. We worked together for many years, during which the quality of her life and self-care improved greatly, and except for subtle remnants, her thought disorder disappeared. While she developed friends and sources of satisfaction she was never seriously motivated to try to form an intimate relationship.

Jane was paranoid about me at first, convinced I had a knife in my drawer and was about to kill her. I had to leave the office door open to convince her that she could leave if necessary. Among her delusions was the belief that if she shot herself in the head a beautiful flower garden would grow there. She harbored an even stranger idea since a vow she could remember making in early adolescence, that she literally had no body, would henceforth have no feelings, and did not care about or need anyone else. She could actually look in the mirror and not see anything except her head, and she had a science fiction-like quasi-belief that she was a disembodied head.

If you are expecting from this description to hear about a dilapidated schizophrenic you will be surprised to learn that Jane had a successful false self, and was an accomplished academic, a respected teacher and internationally recognized authority on adolescent behavior. As we eventually discovered, consistent with her delusions, she did not believe any of what she taught others applied to her. She had no intimate relationships, and none of her acquaintances suspected that she had significant problems. For many years none of her friends could understand why she was in therapy.

Jane's childhood was extremely traumatic. Her mother rejected her at birth and refused to believe Jane was her baby, not even remembering her name. She treated Jane with a combination of neglect and abuse the extent of which Jane was hardly aware of as she internalized many of her mother's destructive attitudes which seemed to her normal. She believed she had had a loving relationship with her father but in the course of some years of therapy, through the medium of the transference and analysis of various body sensations, gestures, and beliefs she came to realize that her father had regularly sexually assaulted her. When she was in graduate school Jane was hospitalized with suicidal ideation, hallucinations, and delusions. She managed to get herself out of the hospital by reconstituting her false self and pretending she was well, to complete her graduate degree and become a successful academic.

Jacob

Jacob was almost 60 years of age when he was referred to me in search of another in a long series of "psychoanalyses." He was a married father of three teenage sons and a manager in a technology corporation. He complained of a sense of alienation from a world that he perceived as hostile and dangerous, as well as a literal sense of coldness that required him to wear an outdoor coat in the consulting room. Not long after we met he took early retirement and for many years remained unemployed and reclusively preoccupied with relationships with women, first his wife, and subsequent to their divorce, a series of others. He had a long history of choosing and seducing women who did not seem to have an independent identity and were masochistic. He achieved control over them, attacked and subjugated them verbally and sexually, and created an undifferentiated universe in which they behaved like figments of his hostile imagination, which, as we gradually learned, replicated in reverse his unresolved relationship with his sadistic assaultive mother.

Despite his years of therapy prior to seeing me, Jacob was entirely unaware of the fact that he seemed to know only one way to interact, in which one person tries to psychologically annihilate the other with vicious argumentation, attack, and criticism. He perceived himself as the victim, and it rapidly became evident he experienced me as trying to destroy his identity. He was full of images in which I was suffocating or strangling him and he was being forced to "suck up" to me. There was a period of time he believed I was crazy, and was overcome by literal images of me as a monster attacking him. His behavior promoted and belied these terrifying images, as his conception of the "rule" of free association was one in which he had unrestrained license to vent his vicious hostility toward me and grandiose beliefs about himself. In this state he seemed to believe he was perfect, and he alternated between blaming and attacking others in his life and "analyzing" and viciously attacking me with a seemingly endless litany of my flaws and mistakes.

Jacob had had been in what he believed was a psychoanalysis with an analyst who had an international reputation for success treating psychotic persons. He used the couch so that he did not need to have actual face to face contact, and he literally told the analyst that he was not to speak. The analyst eventually informed Jacob that he could not see him anymore because Jacob's relentless attacks were stirring up personal issues of his own that disqualified him from being able to be of further help. Jacob was crushed and uncomprehending when I told him that I did not think psychoanalysis, as he understood it, was the best form of treatment for him and that he needed face to face contact and active dialogue. It was as though I were telling him I thought he wasn't good enough to be admitted to Harvard or Oxford. His behavior with me and apparently with others consisted of critical attacks accompanied by grandiosity. He believed he was always "right," an expert on the behavior of others. He falsified and inflated his own intellectual credentials in the process. He acted like he had no need or use for me and yet if I were so much as a few seconds late for an appointment he would get very upset.

Jacob was obsessively paralyzed by powerful urges to kill persons close to him, associated with vivid sadistic imagery involving assault and mutilation. He told me he had barely been able to restrain himself from pushing one of his children out of the carriage in an amusement park roller coaster when they were small. In the course of our work his homicidal urges were at times quite direct and had a laser-like focus on me. For example he had the urge to throw acid in my face when I greeted him, or throw me downstairs as we said hello on the landing outside my office. Having had much experience with homicidal persons in hospital settings I often sensed he was actually close to acting.

Jacob's beliefs, images, and related actions were concrete and deeply somatically rooted. He was severely hypochondriacal, preoccupied with one after another real or imagined physical ailments that he was convinced were about to kill him, and visits to doctors with whom he enacted these scenarios. He was preoccupied with his bowels and had encopresis, and with his penis and its state of health and functional capacity to erect and ejaculate, around which his only sense of power seemed to revolve. He was driven to masturbate on a daily basis and have intercourse whenever possible, both of which were sadomasochistic acts. His goal with women seemed to be to excite them to a state of orgastic frenzy he interpreted as loss of control and "craziness." He was addicted to pornography, and one of his favorite activities was masturbating to an image of a naked woman seated on his head with legs spread apart. He had a recurrent transient sensation that he had a woman's breast, so real that he made gestures with his hands to wipe it away. He made reflexive grimaces which he came to realize were efforts to imitate his mother's facial expressions, which he had literally practiced in front of a mirror during his childhood.

Jacob's mind worked in images. These tended to be stereotypic and repetitive, dissociated from affect, whose meaning, while obvious to me, he had neither language for nor emotional awareness of. When we talked he often felt, almost to the point of belief, that he had a knife in his pocket. One of his repetitive images was of me literally sitting in shit. Another involved sadistically abusing my daughter. While these arose at meaningful places in our interaction he had no thoughtful reflective emotional language with which to describe and understand them. In contrast, for more abstract matters he had an unusually large vocabulary. With increasing self-awareness his significant aphasia for mature thought and emotion became a source of intense feelings of impotence and frustration.

Jacob's problems revolved around his relationship with his mother, though he was for a long time unaware of it. He was convinced that he loved his mother and that she had loved him, but a repetitive vivid set of images from various times in his childhood, articulated in photographic detail and clarity, told me another story. As a small child she told him about her episiotomy and how his birth had almost killed her. She undressed him in public, dressed him like a girl, and physically controlled, invaded, and manipulated his body, primarily his anus, with her fingers and other devices. Although there seemed little evidence historical or current that he was not healthy, she conveyed her belief that he had a serious disease, something terribly wrong with him inside that she had to root out and expunge or else he would die. She kept him in the house and the bathroom, bedroom, and bed with her much of the time during the day on the pretext that he was ill, and regularly brought doctors in to diagnose and treat him for what seem mostly to have been imaginary ailments. Mother was inappropriately seductive as well, taking him to bed with her, and displaying herself to him in varying degrees of undress that excited him as a child to want to get under her skirts and inside her body through holes he believed existed in her body including one between her breasts. She forbade him from leaving their property to play with other children.

The combination of fear and seduction crippled him. Indeed when other boys were oriented to get out and play with peers Jacob's preoccupation seemed to be to get back into his mother in a way that we eventually discovered involved a combination of narcotizing his thought process and sadistic destructive urges. When father came home from work mother would recite all of Jacob's badness and transgressions during the day, and father would beat him with a belt while mother looked on, wringing her hands in apparent dismay and crying. Jacob repeatedly presented some of these images of being attacked, rejected, and humiliated by his mother without apparent affect. I came to realize that he had no emotional awareness of their meaning, as when I shared my understanding of their emotional meaning he attacked me for failure to understand him and claimed that his relationship with his mother had been loving.

In his later adolescent years Jacob was haunted by powerful images of taking a knife and stabbing his mother to death, inhibited by reciprocal terrifying images of being apprehended and executed. While these images might seem inconsistent with his belief that he loved her, like his images she was invading and attacking him they were unconnected with any emotional awareness of rage. He experienced them as mysterious troubling obsessions. Having a knife became an important image in his adult life that he often had when talking to me, coming to signify the rage of which he had no emotional representation. He also concretely confused the knife with his penis in intercourse, and it was associated with the urge to erect and ejaculate frequently and get it into women while believing he was controlling them.

Not long after his younger brother was born, around age five or six, in a rare show of defiance, Jacob packed some things and told father he was going to run away. The result of this disguised plea for caring was that father opened the door for him and said "go ahead." Not long thereafter, around age seven, he was playing ball with other boys in the street in defiance of mother's prohibition. The ball bounced in front of an oncoming car and Jacob, in a combination of what he retrospectively realized was a sense of omnipotence and a wish to kill himself, dived in front of it, was hit and hospitalized for some days with a severe head injury.

Jacob was unusually gifted, especially in mathematics and science, and he did well at college for a time, until he became frightened he was going to kill someone, told his father, and was hospitalized. After a short hospitalization he returned to school, completed his studies, and began graduate school, but he became paralyzed and self-destructive trying to actualize the delusion that he could solve the mathematical problem of dividing by zero. Many years into our work he realized that he had been actualizing mother's "rule" that he had to make everything he did into a form of self-destruction. Despite his crippling problems Jacob was able to do well enough in the world of math-physics related technology to become a relatively high level manager in a well-known electronics corporation. He eventually married a masochistic woman who tried to care for him and their children in the face of his constant, vicious, verbal attacks on her and verbal abuse of them. Jacob was in therapy of one kind or another almost continuously subsequent to his psychotic episode in college, mostly with psychoanalysts, seemingly without benefit.

Jacob's therapeutic efforts were characterized by finding therapists who, like the women he seduced, tended to placate him and comply with his various wishes rather than confront him with feedback he might attack. In our relationship he talked non-stop, complaining or attacking. Efforts to give feedback were perceived as lethal assaults on his identity by a crazy man or monster, as evidences of my anger at him, or as evidence of how wrong or mistaken I was. He regularly distorted things I had said to him to fit this paradigm. He had a grandiose self supported in his daily interactions with falsifications of his credentials and knowledge, and he acted like he knew it all about everything, including human behavior. His language was solipsistic insofar as when he did change in ways I could see reflected our work, he talked as though the insights had been totally his own. Eventually I realized in his undifferentiated way he did not recognize I was a separate person. Despite the life and death seriousness of our work, the last thing he would ever do was to admit to anyone other than his wife that he was in therapy, the dependent aspect of which to him meant contemptible weakness. He never indicated any need for me even though he was obsessively punctual for our appointments and attacked me on the rare occasions I was even a minute late.

Beneath his grandiose omnipotent façade, however, was the truth Jacob fought for years against knowing; that he believed he was defective, that he felt powerless, frightened and enraged, and that he did not feel he could survive without a woman who loved him unconditionally. He could not maintain an emotionally laden train of thought about himself, identify and bear his feelings; and at a reflexive somatic level he literally believed he was excrement or a disease.

Lisabeth

Lisabeth was an attractive, intelligent, unmarried graduate student in her early 40s when she consulted me complaining of intense anxiety bordering on panic, difficulty concentrating on her studies, and wanting to separate herself from a sadomasochistic lesbian relationship in which she acted as surrogate parent. Many years previously she had been in a therapy that focused on a similar relationship that had concluded with her being told she should learn to accept that she was a lesbian.

Lisabeth regularly had diarrhea in the waiting room bathroom prior to our sessions and she could barely sit still during our sessions. She avoided eye contact because it or any reference to a relationship with me literally sent a feeling of shock through her body. She believed she had a penis. Although she was able to end the mutually imprisoning lesbian relationship it gradually became apparent she was developing a similar all-consuming possessively destructive attachment to me. She would shadow or stalk me between appointments, staring up at the window of my office, or she would drive by my house and sometimes lurk in the neighborhood hoping for a glimpse of me through the window. Not long after we began to meet she told me she had vivid sexual fantasies about me when she was alone in her apartment yet any reference to feelings during our sessions sent the same shock through her body. On those instances when she sighted me outside the office, which was near her school, she would flee in the other direction so I would not see her. She was terrified of any suggestion we might develop a relationship. When I asked her how she was feeling about me she angrily admonished me "don't you ever do that again!"

For much of our many years together we worked to identify and gradually resolve the intense possessive relationship she formed with me, as a transference surrogate for her mother. She could not bear the idea that we were separate people and that I had a life and loves of my own that did not include her. We discovered her waiting room diarrhea was somatization of the almost literal belief she was excrement, and the related belief that the life she lacked was in me. When we were apart she experienced a cataclysmic sense of personal annihilation, which she was convinced was because I didn't care about her and she was gone from my mind. I had no needs because I "had it all." Even the idea that I needed a fee for my work was difficult to accept. What superficially resembled idealization was in fact an intense concrete rage-filled envy and drive to reduce me to a thing and take my autonomy away.

Our work was complicated by the fact that she interpreted everything I said not as an effort to help but as criticism, exposing her inferiority, all her problems, what was wrong with her. She lacked of sense of personal direction and manifested an aversion to do feeling-based work necessary to become a separate self. She was more comfortable maintaining a perverse sense of identity as my disturbed therapy patient and was not able to integrate that with her manifest feeling of inferiority being my patient rather than my peer, so that she could have experienced a conflict. While most people feel better when they feel better, she felt worse, both because she had been taught that it was wrong, a sign of selfishness, to feel good about herself. So she reflexively attached such nascent feelings. She also realized if she felt "too good" about herself it would lead to an end to her therapy. The word "termination" elicited a catalysmic body-mind world is coming to an end reaction that we discovered meant execution, the end of her world as she understood it. Her reaction was so intense, physical, and disruptive that it was a long time before the word termination could even be mentioned and its usual meaning talked about. She was convinced that when she could not see me I no longer remembered her. During one summer separation she literally experienced her arms as having been amputated. These responses indicated her undifferentiation from me and her difficulty continuing to care and hold me and a separate sense of body-self in mind when we separated, and the catastrophic psychological consequences if she couldn't literally be with me and believe that she possessed me.

One might conclude from this description that Lisabeth led a regressed disorganized life. Far from it. As our work continued she finished graduate school and launched a career in human relations field in which she was in charge of a large organization, respected and admired for her organizational and human relations skills and her innovative creativity. However, none of this was integrated with her emotional life, which was a secret she shared only with me. As a consequence she lived for a long time in a state of paranoid terror that the people with whom she worked would find out the "truth" about what a worthless piece of shit she was convinced she was.

Lisabeth's parents had divorced when she was five and he remarried and had other children. Her mother led her to believe her father and the woman he married were evil at the same time she attempted to prevent him from having contact with her. Mother managed to convince Lisbeth that she no longer existed for him and that he had replaced her with his "new" family. Father appears to have made little effort to oppose his ex-wife's will. Mother never formed another relationship and Lisabeth, her older brother, and her mother formed an undifferentiated interdependent triad that under mother's direction developed its own private beliefs and meanings, walled off from outside influence. Mother's surface charm made many people like and even admire her. From this model Lisabeth must have learned the splitting that led to develop her own false self. Mother boasted to her children of her knowledge and became something of an omniscient deity, and Lisabeth became her mother's most effective propaganda minister, discouraging anyone who might begin to raise critical questions, as she did with me during our early years when I would try to clarify some of the implications of things she told me. LIsabeth quoted the professional jargon mother used to interpret to her children the disqualifying problems of anyone Lisabeth might begin to show interest in.

Mother showed disapproving doubts whenever Lisabeth indicated strong feelings about people and strong interests with comments such as "why do you have a need to feel that way?" Lisabeth was led to believe that there was something wrong with being attracted to or caring about anyone outside the family and she learned to reflexively attack her feelings, leading to a habit of fleeing from anyone who began to arouse them. As a result she did not allow herself to have strong emotions and she had no names for her feelings, manifesting instead the intense anxiety that resulted from her attacks on their somatic precursors. She regularly "consulted" with mother about potential friends in an unconscious effort to reinforce their isolating bond.

As she grew Lisabeth developed her own false self social façade, like that of her mother, as well as athletic skills and adventurousness based on what subsequently turned out to be dangerous risk taking based on not valuing taking care of her body, and a belief, which was based on fact, that she could do many physical and mechanical things better than most men. As she was attractive and intelligent, despite believing she was ugly, she received much attention and interest from men, from whom she uniformly fled in fear. Until some time had passed in our therapy she continued to idolize both her mother and her brother. Despite increasing accomplishments and involvement with others she continued to treat them as her best and only friends. When I met her in her 40s she still spent most of her non-working time with her mother and brother. The two earlier lesbian relationships, one of which she came to see me to free herself from, seemed to be displaced enactments of her undifferentiated attachment to her mother.

As a baby and small child Lisabeth was raised largely by a nanny while mother worked full time. Later her grandmother moved in to take care of her. She could not recall being held and actually remembered a sense of repulsion at being close to her mother's body. As a child Lisabeth for the most part avoided contacts with other children and preferred to spend time in nature. She had occasional tantrum-like episodes that led mother to take her to a psychologist who, apparently taking mother's cue, decided Lisabeth was angry because her father had left her and her mother, leaving Lisabeth without a father and mother with the terrible burden of raising two children. Lisabeth was apparently a depressed and isolated child who literally hid out in parts of her house or wandered out into the fields and woods near where they lived. She spent much of her time in the inanimate natural world, with small animals and insects, which she seemed to identify with, and liked to "capture" and take care of.

Charles

Charles was in his late twenties when he consulted me. He lived a withdrawn reclusive existence, supported by a family fortune he had inherited from his father who committed suicide in Charles' early teens. He was immobilized by a sense of despair and hopelessness in a world he believed to be hostile and dangerous, and seriously contemplated suicide. He had graduated from a college that demanded little of its students academically. He spent much of his time in the basement of his apartment, taking apart, cleaning, and rebuilding his precious motorcycle. This ability turned out to be a precursor of one of the strengths that he was able to develop over the years, a remarkable capacity to build or repair almost anything in the non-human sphere, from houses and furniture to sophisticated electrical and electronic gear. Not long after he began seeing me he got drunk one night and held a shotgun to his head, but at the last minute he decided to call me and ask for help.

Our relationship was characterized by prolonged silences during which he would breathe audibly and rhythmically through his mouth in an almost snorting manner that reminded me of a steam engine, while darting glances at me and then looking away. When I asked him to share his thoughts he would claim his mind was blank. Although over a long period of time we gradually discovered his modus operandi was a process of withholding and shutting down that he experienced as annihilating others, it turned out that indeed he did not have many formed thoughts. His experience consisted almost entirely of somatic tension and turmoil, sensations in various parts of his body along with sadomasochistic images like chopping wood or chopping himself to pieces, that for a long time he had no words to express. In the hypnotic mind-deadening atmosphere created by his withdrawal, unarticulated hostility, and somatization, I had to struggle to remain awake and focused. I gradually realized that he was unconsciosly trying to destroy my mind and make me withdraw into a mindless sleep-like state similar to what he had done during his early years in response to his mother's assaults. Very gradually his sense of undifferentiation from a world he experienced as a terrible place filled with hostile people emerged, and even more slowly awareness of enormous rage that was directed in an undifferentiated way toward his own mind and toward others. He was convinced that my efforts to pay attention to him and encourage him to talk were attacks or criticisms.

Charles' childhood had been spent in relative isolation in the country home of his wealthy upper class parents and their servants. His mother was an out of control probably psychotic alcoholic whose daily routine consisted of getting drunk and verbally and sometimes physically assaulting Charles' father when he was present. At night father would lock himself in his bedroom or retreat to another house on the family estate, leaving Charles and his brother alone with mother, who prowled the halls, banging on the locked door of father's bedroom when he was there, and then alternately invading the bedrooms of Charles or his older brother, which had no locks. She would crawl into bed with Charles and rain name-calling assaults down on him while telling him how special he was and pleading for his love. He would try his best not to move, to withdraw and shut down his mind, like an animal playing dead, and eventually she would roll over facing away from him and fall into a drunken stupor, often with her nightgown hiked up so that Charles was confronted with her naked rear end. In the morning the kitchen and bathroom would stink of vomit and diarrhea, and while mother slept it off Charles would try his best to clean up the mess, get her some breakfast, and get ready for school.

Father was in his own way as reclusive and withdrawn as Charles turned out to be. He commuted to work where he was the CEO of the successful multi-generational family business and when at home and not locked in his bedroom he spent much time in his own separate house on the family estate, characteristically walking off in the evening during mother's tirades and leaving Charles and his brother to their mother's mercy. He did make some efforts to get good schooling for his son and encourage him in that area as well as in sports, but they felt mechanical for Charles and his father had no emotional bond. Charles was passive, and while he tried to comply with father's expectations the world mystified and terrified him. He came to depend on being the special focus of his mother's world, anticipating her nightly assaults, and as we eventually realized, constructing a delusion amalgamating the belief she would change the next time he saw her and all the problems would somehow be taken away, with the idea that by withholding in the face of the pleas she made while abusing him that he love her, he was somehow getting revenge on her. Charles barely got by at school. His withdrawal and problems reading and writing were understood by school personnel to be the product of a learning disability.

Around the time Charles entered puberty father was hospitalized at a psychiatric retreat known for treating wealthy alcoholics. It is not clear what treatment he got, if any. He was eventually discharged and, it seemed in retrospect, came home to die. He took to his bed where he would spend the days more or less immobilized and alone. Soon thereafter Charles was sent to boarding school. In Charles' early adolescence father shot himself in the head with a pistol, leaving Charles feeling utterly hopeless and alone with his mother.

During the many difficult years of our work Charles gradually gained the ability to think and to use language to describe his thoughts, abilities he was convinced he did not have prior to therapy. He was able gradually to transform his somatic experiences and visual images into thoughts and feelings that were differentiated from his percepts of the external world. He became aware of his emotions, principally an enormous rage and overwhelming despair, feelings he had difficulty owning and tended to believe I was inflicting on him. Charles' split mind consisted of overwhelming rage, hatred, fear, and despair along with the belief that that he deserved restitution or compensation from the world/me in the form of a mothering figure who would transform reality so that all the hurts of his childhood would never have happened. Much as he complained about being the victim of his mother's sadism and his father's failure to rescue him he kept reliving the somatic state of diffuse unrepresented rage and fear of his encounters with mother, especially at night in bed and in his relationship with me. He began to date, and picked large-breasted women who were withdrawn and preoccupied with acting out their own unresolved childhood hurts and angers. Charles kept the details of hese relationships secret from me and as time passed we learned this was an enactment of cllinging to the special relationship he believed he had had with his mother that had excluded his father. We gradually came to realize he was sexually aggressive, discharging his anger with a penis that we came to realize was a weapon, while at the same time having fantasies of obtaining nurturance. While he treated women in a withdrawn and emotionally absent manner like his father had treated others he was not overtly sadistic.

8

TWO CONSCIOUS MENTAL PROCESSES

The role of primordial consciousness in psychosis and other human phenomena

Psychosis is a manifestation of a process that is qualitatively different from neurosis. It is not an inability to relate to others or a failure to develop and sustain a normal/neurotic personality organization. It is the result of pathology of early attachment, and while it may have its genetic neural predispositions like any variation of personality, it is not the manifestation of a fundamental defect in the brain. The disturbance in the attachment phase of development leads to perpetuation of a distorted version of primordial conscious mentation under circumstances in which it is maladaptive, as the requirements of socialized growth call for reflective representational thought.

Misconceptions of psychosis as an adult onset disorder of genetic origin

Some of the reasons for the failure to recognize the significance of attachment and separation in the origin of psychosis, including Freud's cultural and probably personally based devaluation of the importance of women and mothers, and his office-based preoccupation with neurosis and the relatively mature and self-sufficient persons who manifest it, have been discussed earlier in the book. Another is the misconception that schizophrenia is an adult onset illness. The origins of this belief have been traced to the psychiatry of the late 19th and early 20th centuries, and specifically to the organic notion of dementia praecox, that schizophrenia is an adult onset illness in which the brains of otherwise normal persons begin to degenerate in late adolescence and early adulthood. This belief is a cornerstone of the ego psychology model of psychosis as the result of a weak ego, upsurge of drives in late adolescence and early adulthood, and subsequent regression.

While genetic factors no doubt play a role in some instances of psychosis, decades of extensive research have failed to reveal any convincing causal links or indeed any consistent associated organic abnormalities (Robbins, 1993, 2011). There is no evidence that genetic-organic factors play any greater role in psychosis than they do in determining ordinary variations of personality. It is even possible that if genetic predispositions exist in some instances, rather than being defects or deficiencies they might be unusual traits like synesthesia and lucid dreaming. Under appropriate circumstances of nurturance such innate traits might alternatively develop into unusual creative abilities (Robbins, 2011). The link between schizophrenia and creativity has been noted by many, and is especially evident in the positions accorded persons westerners might call psychotic, such as shaman or seer, whose mental processes might actually be assets in the context of non-western and tribal cultures. I have found in my own practice that psychotic patients often have or develop unusual artistic ability in the course of successful treatment. Among the case examples in this book Sara, in Chapter 16, and Charles are examples.

As the family therapy literature of the 1950s revealed (Robbins, 1993), the psychotic disturbance is evident in childhood, and is part of a family equilibrium that all members depend on and believe is normal, that is a product of denial. The therapy of Rachel (Robbins, 1993), a young woman who was hospitalized during college, was complicated by such a belief. Her parents would not acknowledge the existence of any pre-morbid disturbance or any family problems whatsoever during half a year of regular social work interviews following her hospitalization for florid psychosis and diagnosis of schizophrenia. Even more striking, her parents were convinced that there was nothing currently abnormal about her, despite feedback from hospital staff about her catatonic posturing and her obvious habit of talking to her hallucinated voices. Her father remarked to me "Any of us would act the way she does if we had to be in a place like this, with all these crazy people!" Eventually they admitted having observed similar behavior in Rachel as far back as her early teens, but even then they managed to discount its pathological implications. Father, for example, insisted her hallucinating was no different from his habit of talking to himself.

After a year or so of therapy Rachel had stopped hallucinating and was working with me on conflicts she had about separating from her family and becoming her own independent person. Despite Rachel's evident progress in therapy, and family meetings in the course of which Rachel, her sister, and her mother became more assertive, her father's seductive view that she did not need treatment and that she should come home to live with him escalated and eventually prevailed. She left the hospital and treatment to go home to the distant city where they lived. Over the next two years she wrote me a series of letters, at first expressing sorrow and regret she had ended our relationship, but gradually becoming bizarre and delusional until she eventually ceased writing entirely. The last I heard her mother had gotten a divorce, but my former patient was leading a disabled life at home.

A similar story is to be found in the gripping family biography written by Elizabeth Swados (1991) entitled *The Four of Us*, centered around the chronic schizophrenia of her older brother Lincoln. Everyone in the Swados family was aware of the facts of Lincoln's disturbance from the time he was quite young, but they construed it not as illness but as the expression of an exceptionally gifted and creative individual. They encouraged Lincoln's psychosis by blaming others such as school personnel who were disturbed and concerned about his behavior. Swados concludes her remarkable account with the statement that: "The easiest way to understand his schizophrenia was to believe it didn't exist. ... My true beliefs centered around my esteem for my brother's gifts. He was a difficult genius who would prove himself to his opponents" (p. 30). Attempts at treatment were disrupted by these family dynamics and he eventually committed suicide. Families that deny often interpret the bizarre thinking of the psychotic person as creativity. While primordial conscious mentation is also involved in creativity, in this instance, although Lincoln was no doubt bright, there is no evidence he was creative.

Walker and Lewine (1990) conducted a double blind study in which experienced clinicians were shown home movies taken during the childhood of five persons who subsequently were diagnosed schizophrenic to determine if they could distinguish the child at risk from normal siblings. They were able to do so in four of the five instances. What was particularly intriguing about their report was an incidental comment about the "pilot" patient they studied to determine whether their project was feasible. Viewers of home movies had no difficulty picking him as the abnormal sibling. His parents, however, not only stoutly denied that there had been anything abnormal about him as a child, but they asserted that he had been the best adjusted of their children!

One way to interpret the denial in this family constellation is that it is very difficult for a psychotic person to separate from the family because the psychotic behavior is not only viewed as normal and expectable, but is encouraged as part of a system it is of everyone's advantage to maintain. The entire family functions as an undifferentiated unit and members fill functions for one another.

Characteristics of reflective representational thought

In my 2011 book *The Primordial Mind in Health and Illness* and my 2018 book *Consciousness, Language, and Self,* I describe the mental process of primordial consciousness as one of two qualitatively distinctive processes, both of which are normal, that in varying combinations play a major role in everyday mental life. The mental process and its language that we in western or individual-centric cultures generally think of when we think of conscious mind is reflective, representational, symbolic thought. Freud called it the secondary process, in reference to its ontological appearance in later infancy and childhood as a function of socialization. Its development is an essential ingredient of the process of separation and individuation from the primary relationship. The relationship characteristic of the attachment phase is mediated by first mind: primordial conscious mentation, initially manifest in the mother–infant relationship of late intra-uterine life and infancy, and in dreaming.

For purposes of contrast, in order to highlight the uniqueness of primordial conscious mentation I first describe the salient characteristics of reflective representational thought. The thoughtful mind is aware of its separateness from other minds, the fact that it is but one mind among many. It is capable of distinguishing its own emotions and ideas from those of others and appreciating that those of others are valid as well. It is capable of differentiating what is going on within the bounds of a conceptualized self, the intrapsychic world, from what is going on in the external world, and therefore appreciating a reality outside and independent of the self. It is capable of going beyond undifferentiated solipsism and taking itself as an object of reflection and self-examination. It is based upon constant representations of emotion-saturated ideas and of other people that can be abstracted and used symbolically because they are differentiated from the surrounding world. It is not concrete and stimulus-bound. The mind of reflective awareness can identify specific emotions and not be reflexively driven by their affective and somatic precursors. It is capable of distinguishing aspects of mind that need to be contemplated and controlled from those one may choose to enact. It is capable of integrating (holding in mind) emotionally conflicting and ambivalent ideas in order to develop a consistent separate self-position in the world.

Most important, the thoughtful mind is Cartesian. It is capable of introspection, or what linguists call recursion. That is, "cogito, ergo sum." The mind can reflect or think about itself; it can be an object of its own inquiry and not just a subjectivity that is stimulus–response-bound and caught in the present moment. The thoughtful mind is capable of questioning and introspection, appreciation of the passage of time, remembering, and projecting itself into an imagined future. In short, the thoughtful mind considers multiple perspectives rather than being concretely bound to an immediate stimulus and committed to a single belief or truth and the reflexively driven actions that would follow from it. The thoughtful mind is reasonable; more or less logical and rational.

Characteristics of primordial consciousness or first mind

I call the other ontologically primary mental process *primordial consciousness* or *first mind*. This section describes the characteristics of the mental process. Examples from the writings of patients will be found in the next section.

Primordial conscious mental activity, whose similarity to Freud's concept of the primary process is elaborated in earlier chapters, is not the same as reflective representational thought. That does not mean it is unconscious, as Freud believed. And the fact that it is the ontologically first mental operation does not mean it is inferior to thought, in the sense of being immature or pathological.

Freud's belief that the primary process is unconscious probably came from two sources, first because the phenomenological activity from which he derived it, dreaming, happens in a state of sleep or altered consciousness in which, for most of us who are not capable of lucid dreaming, reflective thought is absent.

Second is that he equated consciousness with the capacity to reflect rather than be immersed in the moment, a feature that the primary process and primordial consciousness lacks. Actually a person totally immersed in the moment can be intensely conscious; the consciousness is simply different.

Primordial conscious mental activity is immediate and stimulus-bound and hence is not recursive or reflective. Although the person using it is perfectly capable of making formal sensory-perceptual distinctions between self and world, and of testing reality in a concrete operational sense, from a psychological standpoint the language of primordial mind does not distinguish aspects of one's own feelings, ideas, and self from those of others and from the cosmos; or inner from outer reality. Jacob, for example, was a skilled driver but on the road he functioned in primordial consciousness, unaware of the distinction between his rage-filled inner life and the actions of other drivers. As a consequence he was in a constant state of road rage, ready to attack other drivers whom he believed were attacking him, and close to collisions because of his vengeful and provocative behavior. Under normal developmental circumstances cognitive operations adaptive to reality are intact, yet the psychological sense is one of a solipsistic syncretic world. Infants have no trouble adapting to reality yet they perceive it in the undifferentiated unintegrated state of primordial consciousness.

Primordial consciousness is also stimulus-bound. It is driven by somatic sensations and fleeting affects rather than emotions that can be labelled and thought about. It forms equally evanescent mental images or pictures rather than constant representations of ideas, memories, and related emotions. It is neither abstract nor symbolic. It is a state of motor action, body expression, and sensation. Its narrative consists of images linked by affect tones and somatic sensations rather than logical sequences of emotionally meaningful association. As it is immediate and not reflective or recursive it does not support recognition of time passage or sequences related to memory. It does not distinguish between past, present, and future as different entities. The absence of memory and time sense may not be readily apparent as formal abstract memory for events, with dates and images, may be present, as well as the capacity for immediate recognition of something known and familiar when it is concretely sensory-perceptually re-presented. However, formal memory of events and concrete recognition of something familiar are very different from the representational remembering that constitutes personal memory. It is a language of here and now rather than reflection, cogitation, and thinking about thinking. Emotions, perceptions, and ideas that relate to past history are repeated as though happening in an undifferentiated present. Viewed from the lens of reflective representational thought primordial conscious mentation appears to be inconsistent, disorganized, irrational, unrealistic, impulsive, at times contradictory, and "unconscious," but it is in fact merely the expression of a qualitatively different form of consciousness, and in its proper place and context can be adaptive, constructive, and productive.

One of the major features of primordial consciousness is syncretism. It is holistic. There is no separation between self and other. Sensations and perceptions are not psychologically differentiated in terms inner self and external world, so what from the perspective of reflective thought might be viewed as intrapsychic elements of the mind or self are instead perceived as originating in others and in the external world. Of course the person is formally aware that there is another person; it is simply that the characteristics perceived to be in the other person are objectively ones belonging to the subject. The process is socio-centric rather than self-centric, and to the extent the minds of others work the same way, and values and orientations are shared, its characteristic undifferentiation supports a fundamental sense of unity with others and with the cosmos rather than a sense of separateness and individuality. It is the basis of powerful ideologies and belief systems. Because the world is animated with one's own mental content without reflective awareness, there is no realistic objectivity. When the beliefs are expressed in a context that is socially inappropriate the person can seem grandiose or even delusional. In contrast, the recursive, reflective objectification and "reality" testing that are part of a reflective representational consciousness that distinguishes self from other and from world necessitates a certain skepticism or questioning of the general reality and accuracy of one's ideas. Such awareness of context and relativity are associated with acceptance of the fundamental impossibility of truly knowing another and of attaining certainty about the difference between the real world and one's subjective experience of it.

Heinz Werner described this holistic or syncretic mentality quite clearly in 1948. He writes of an initial "unity of world and ego. The world is separated only slightly from the ego; it is predominantly configured in terms of the emotional needs of the self (egomorphism)" (1948, p. 361). He says:

> in different types of primitive mentality psychological functions are more intimately fused, that is, more syncretic, than in the advanced mentality. ... In advanced forms of mental activity we observe thought processes which are quite detached from the concrete sensori-motor perceptual and affective sphere. In the primitive mentality, however, thought processes always appear as more or less perfectly fused with functions of a sensori-motor and affective type. It is this absence of a strict separation of thought proper from perception, emotion and motor action which determines the significance of so-called concrete and affective thinking ... characteristic examples of syncretic activity.
>
> *(1948, p. 213)*

In the syncretic state "the object is represented not explicitly, but implicitly by means of motor-affective behaviour" (1948, p. 250). He writes: "In the young child, however, there is a relatively close connection between perception and imagery" (1948, p. 389). He adds: "For the child the reality of the dream and of the waking world are relatively undifferentiated. At this stage waking reality often exhibits some of the characteristics of the dream" (1948, p. 391).

It is an expression of prejudice based on western privileging of reflective representational thought to dismiss the phenomenology of primordial consciousness as irrational, disorganized, unrealistic, and even psychotic. Primordial conscious mentation is not, of itself, accompanied by any cognitive sensory-perceptual failure or inability to navigate in the world, as for example blindness or deafness. As a matter of fact, infantile perception and functional response to "reality" are quite accurate and functionally adaptive, and whatever meaning infants assign to the perceptions is another matter. In my previous (2011, 2018) books I discussed and illustrated how some non-western cultures, especially tribal cultures, are socio-centric rather than separate individual-centric, and organize and cohere around primordial conscious mentation. How expressions of primordial consciousness are perceived and the consequences of its use depend upon the congruence or lack thereof with the interpersonal, social, and cultural context of the individual; that is, whether the context does or does not normalize and support such mental activity. Primordial consciousness is simply a different way of organizing self and cosmos, one that can be constructive and creative, or disturbed and pathological, depending both on the context in which it is used, and on its relationship to reflective representational thought. In this book I focus on its pathological expression in psychosis. Its fundamental normal manifestations are dreaming, from which Freud abstracted his theory, and mother–infant attachment and early relationship. A number of other "normal" manifestations are described in previous books (2011, 2018).

Clinical illustrations of primordial consciousness

In the preface to this section I presented biographical descriptions of four persons with psychotic personality disorders, each of whom I worked with for many years. These biographies illustrate many of the features of primordial consciousness. Jacob, Jane, Lisabeth, and Charles kindly wrote essays for my 2018 book expressing the understanding they had reached about their aberrant use of language. While they were not asked to write about psychosis, its origins and its treatment, many of their statements are apropos. I excerpt quotations illustrating primordial conscious mentation, and on the false self that distinguishes psychotic personalities from persons who are schizophrenic. I illustrate the chapters devoted to attachment and separation, and to therapy, with additional quotes. While I have preserved the words of these people I have taken the liberty to rearrange sentences and paragraphs in an effort to provide coherent descriptions of the particular phenomenon they are designed to illustrate.

Jane writes about her somatic behavioral enactments in lieu of representational language, and about her psychological undifferentiation from me:

> Before I met you, I knew that my gestures and body movements were noteworthy, though they were more a matter of concern to me, rather than a source of information about myself. I was concerned myself about my hand turning, or wrist turning. It seemed to me to be like the movements of autistic children and I wondered how that fit with my talking so

late. About my attention to your gestures. My response to you was exactly what I accused you of. I pounced on any observation of your movement and attributed a BIG meaning, usually sexual and a matter of your self-preoccupation. It wasn't just that I thought that your touching your tie was a substitute for masturbation; it was that I thought it outrageous that you would do it and think it OK.

Jacob writes about his inability to represent emotion, his imagistic mentation in lieu of thinking, and his behavioral and somatic enactments. I described his psychological undifferentiation from others including me in the transference, in the preceding chapter.

Something of which I have become increasingly aware is that my feelings were not buried, only to be later discovered; in fact they were not there. I do remember sitting across from Dr. Robbins keeping warm with a very heavy coat. I had not the words to describe my tragic aloneness, only the somatic feeling of coldness. Primary among these undeveloped feelings were my vulnerability, impotence, and rage. Certainly there were images which described these at most inchoate feelings, such as when my mother undressed me at the age of six, soaking wet from a rain storm, in front of our next door neighbor. Or when my mother had no second thought of pushing her finger into my rectum in search of some hidden demon of somatic defectiveness. My dark feeling of doom was described by the fear that I was going to die from some deadly disease. This sense of impending death was one of my mother's most favorite dramas. Or my own image of escaping the world and destroying myself, when I ran in front of a car and was hit, resulting in a fractured skull and concussion. And finally my image of a knife, with which I fantasized I would kill my mother, and over and over used to express my hostility to Dr. Robbins. As a teenager, well before I ever met Dr. Robbins, I began having images of holding a knife in my hand and stabbing my mother. Each time that image would occur in my mind, I would have another image of being tried in a court for that murderous crime. These images haunted me. Later the violent images included people beyond my mother, and eventually forced me to leave college in my second year. What was most important was the total absence of feelings connected to these murderous images.

There were many images I used for rage. Prominent among them was the image of fecal matter. I had the image of myself as a brown (shitty) little Jewish boy and as shit hurled both toward others and myself. Many times I would express rage by losing control of my bowels. Having been abused so many times by my mother in my rectal area, it was no surprise that I chose this portion of my anatomy. Closely associated was my sense of impotence in the relationship with my mother. This was communicated by my memory of an image as a little boy about seven standing on a chair, soaking wet after a rain storm, with my mother removing my clothes in front of the next door neighbor. It took years of therapy with Dr. Robbins to translate this image into words, eventually developing into the constellation of real feelings: impotence, rage, shame, and fear related to being identity-less.

My deep feelings of being subservient to my mother were portrayed by the sexual image of sucking in oral sex. This image meant "eating up," "being lost," or merging with my partner, an act of subsuming one of our identities. As mentioned earlier, sexual intercourse itself was more an image of aggression, than an affectionate act of love. Thus sex and the potency of my penis became an image of power, violently attacking myself through masturbation, as well as assaulting sexual partners. In short my penis became a sword of destruction. My life was filled with images of destruction, both to myself and the outside world. I really could not understand the comments that Dr. Robbins made concerning the violence of my sexual "feelings." I thought I was a real nice guy with ordinary desires. In fact, sex was not an expression of love, it was an image of violence. These images were the fractured pieces of a pseudo language, a "language" before the development of a language, before the development of feelings to support a language. Many times Dr. Robbins would ask, "What feelings do you have?" And my response was always empty, because I really had no feelings.

Here is what Jane had to say about her mental process, especially her psychological undifferentiation from others, her inability to represent emotions, and her somatization:

Mother think is the thought process adopted full-bore from my mother's brainwashing: When I began therapy I was unaware that I believed love and caring meant emotional fusion: that each person is the absolute centerpiece of the other's universe, never parting. Nor was I aware that I had no identity of my own but was defined by my perceived fusion with another. In therapy I acted out of this belief system by trying to possess Dr. Robbins and would become enraged when I could not. I would dehumanize him by complaining that he "had it all," led a "perfect" life, and enjoyed "all the love he needed." He floated on a cloud being worshiped and served by others, having no problems or difficulties. I would tell him that he did not care about me and was a fraud. I kept a journal and sometimes during separations or when there were other indications that he had a life of his own and "didn't care," I would write fantasies about ways to torture or kill him. In reality, of course, becoming fused with and trying to possess him was a form of destruction of us both. I was unaware that in mother think neither of us is a separate person. In "mother think" a separation means a devastating loss: death, suffocation, no life without the other. Since I was wedded to the delusion that love and caring were fusion with another, when Dr. Robbins would talk about an impending separation I became terrified. I would become enraged, attacking him verbally for his supposed desertion of me and removal of my identity. His actual absence meant he did not care, got rid of me, never thought about me. I could not bear the idea that he was a separate person, independent, and autonomous; could love multiple people. I had been taught otherwise. When he would go on summer vacation I would feel as if a limb had been amputated [actually she literally felt her arms were amputated]. It is clear now that I believed I was fused with him and could not survive. In his absence it was I who tried to destroy the relationship in ways described previously. It is not surprising that when the word termination surfaced in relation to ending therapy – the ultimate separation – it felt as if it was the end of the world. Metaphorically a trap door would open and I would feel as if I would fall into nothingness. At the same time there were occasions when I tried to prove I could be "independent" (the geographic definition) by getting rid of Dr. Robbins before he could "terminate" ("get rid of me").

The principal human afflictions were having feelings, being autonomous, thinking differently, and caring about anyone. Early on [speaking of how she felt about me early in the course of therapy], even a hint of real caring and I would try to physically distance myself from my feelings by sucking in my breath and turning my head to the side, away from myself, or I would delegitimize my feelings by engaging in delusions that "proved" he was terrible and unworthy. When I think about this now I can see that I was sick in a different sense. I was having strong feelings and given how I had been instructed, strong feelings were a sickness. I think now that I saw the "therapist" as a stand-in for my mother so he/she would either get rid of my feelings or tell me they were unacceptable. When angry in mother think, my feelings are diffuse with no understanding of the cause coupled with a powerful wish to eliminate the feeling. In separate think I am able to identify why I am angry and at whom or what. It is reality based and acceptable.

Charles begins discussion of his primordial conscious mentation with his struggle to conceptualize the overwhelmingly painful events of his childhood: he writes about the absence of reflective thought, the somatization of experience, the inability to represent emotions or to differentiate self from other or to have a differentiated sense of time past, present, and future.

My ongoing struggle as an adult has been to find the words to speak about these events and, primarily, to construct a mental space adequate enough to hold my feeling in the form of thought and memory of past events. My emotional responses to childhood events have an ever present quality to them. I have felt them as if they were in the moment and am prone to having emotional reactions to current events based on them. The possibility for my having an experience that was "new" did not exist for me for a long time. Unarticulated and undefined feelings have held a numbing sway over the course of my life. One of my most painful realizations has been that I have spent most of my life trying to annihilate myself and in so doing turned to hating myself and other people; others who could care for me and for whom I could care. It has been extremely difficult for me to find direct expression in words for the intensity of rageful feelings. As physical sensation I am aware of them as a rawness of the surface of my skin, as a churning acidic sensation in my gut and at times intestinal cramping and diarrhea. As a suppression of the feelings I have experienced labored breathing, tightness of my throat, and constipation. As a young boy I remember having a sensation in the inside of my wrists and ankles that felt like itching deep under my skin. I would bite and scratch at these areas to try to stop the sensation. Although I never had the thought of slitting my wrists I have often thought after becoming aware of how angry I have been that the idea was there in some rudimentary bodily form. While experiencing inner moments of rage I have on occasions experienced an almost involuntary clenching of my facial muscles that drag the corners of my mouth downward, forming a forlorn infuriated grimace. When it has happened it has been an extremely disturbing experience. On the one hand I knew I was doing this, while on the other hand I felt as if it was something I could not control.

Dreaming and primordial consciousness

Freud derived his model of the primary process from dreaming. Dreaming is the initial and quintessential expression of primordial consciousness mentation. It is also its purest form of expression as it occurs in a state of physiological unconsciousness under circumstances (sleep) when motor paralysis prevents action. Except for those unusual individuals who possess the capacity for lucid dreaming there is no competition from waking thought. It is misleading, however, to conclude, as did Freud, that because dreaming occurs in a physiologically unconscious state that the activity is psychologically unconscious. From a psychological perspective dreaming is a conscious activity, although the absence of thoughtful reflective capacity makes it impossible to think *about*. The recognition that there was something to think about and the struggle to cast the images and sequences into reflective representational thought occurs after the transition to reflective wakeful thought. This is where Bion got confused in his belief that the psychotic person is unable to dream. What I think he meant is that such a person is unable to function in reflective representational thought sufficiently to distinguish waking thought from dreaming mentation.

In dreaming there is no differentiation between internal and external or between reality and fantasy. Aspects of self are imaged as separate characters and interactions in what Matte-Blanco referred to as a Tridim structure. All the characters and actions are undifferentiated aspects of the dreamer's mind. The image sequence in a dream narrative is driven by affects, not rationality and logic, so that from the perspective of waking reflective thought it seems fragmented and disorganized. It would lead to unchecked enactment as does primordial consciousness in waking life were it not for the fact that the motor system is paralyzed. Dreams are characterized by non-symbolic (concrete) evanescent images and sequences determined by the predominant affect(s) associated with them. Such imagery has been mistaken for symbolism because on awakening the dreamer moves into the realm of reflective representational thought, re-casts the dream images into the abstract language of symbolism, and uses the recursive memory function that is lacking in the dream itself. If one is not clear about the distinction between the dream proper and its waking rendition it is easy to make the fallacious assumption that has dominated much of the psychoanalytic literature that dreaming is recursive and contains symbolic references to a deeper layer of meaning.

Attachment and the commencement of psychic life

Attachment between mother and the commencement of psychic life begin in the embryonic third trimester of pregnancy (Robbins, 2018). The evidence for an embryonic cognitive-affective core of being as well as rudimentary communication in the language of primordial consciousness includes the neurological substrate of dreaming, the REM state, that has been recorded as early as the seventh month of gestation, even before rapid eye movements commence (Schwab et al., 2009). Some toddlers are able to indicate shortly after they begin to speak and well before they have attained the capacity for reflective representational thought that they have dreams, as Freud documented in his daughter Anna's sleep-talking about strawberries at 19 months of age. At the beginning of the third trimester of intra-uterine life the fetal brain not only becomes capable of REM sleep but also of the neurological capacity for communication, the capacity to hear mother's vocalizations and other ambient sounds. That is also the time of the quickening and mother's awareness she carries a separate presence within her. In 1940 at a meeting of the British Society Winnicott gave us the felicitious phrase: "There is no such thing as an infant, meaning, of course, that whenever one finds an infant one finds maternal care, and without maternal care there would be no infant" (1960, pp. 586–587).

At this embryonic time of life and subsequently during early infancy primordial consciousness is the mental process by which infant and mother attach or bond, and broadcast and receive signals. It is the medium through which conscious communication develops. From this matrix reflective representational thought eventually emerges through a combination of socialization and neural maturation, myelination of critical aspects of brain (Paus et al., 1999).

Mothers speak "motherese" with their fetuses and infants, beginning with vocalizations, often private, to the fetus. At first the dyadic interaction is musical or prosodic. Maternal sounds and the words and sentences that accompany them elicit physical/neurological fetal responses. I have summarized research (2018) demonstrating that at birth the infant demonstrates a selective tropism toward mother's voice, and in addition to its prosody, has learned and can selectively respond to particular content meaning that was conveyed prior to birth. After birth both parties contribute gestures, facial expressions, and musical sounds to the attachment experience.

New parents are often surprised to find themselves in reflexively synchronized vocal-facial-gestural-expressive interactions with their infants, interactions that they might not want adults outside the family to witness lest they be thought to have lost their minds. In fact they have "changed" their minds and lost or more accurately relinquished reflective representational thought for the primordial mentation that is more contextually appropriate and adaptive. This language, colloquially known as "baby talk," has been called "motherese" (Durkin, Rutter, & Tucker, 1982; Fernald & Simon, 1984; Fernald & Kuhl, 1987; Grieser & Kuhl, 1988), or IDL (infant directed language). The mental process that accompanies it has the qualities of primordial consciousness – undifferentiation of self and other, and concrete affect-driven enactment.

In these initial interactions mother is teaching her infant the language with which to express primordial consciousness and the beginnings of mature communication. While the potential for primordial consciousness continues throughout life, there is research evidence that it is a unique form of interaction that is the major form of language learning during the first year or so of life, and gradually concludes as it is no longer adaptive by age five to seven. One bit of evidence that it is a separate language even though it employs vocabulary common to reflective representational thought is that after the age of five to seven it is no longer possible to learn a second language without an accent. During those first years primordial consciousness and the secure enough attachment to mother that supports it is the foundation for learning the qualitatively different mental process and language of separation, reflective representational thought. This developmental process is enabled not only by the security of the primary attachment but also by maturation of the brain, and facilitated as the processes of socialization and education promote separation–individuation. Words and language have unique significance depending on which conscious process they are expressing (Robbins, 2018).

Primordial consciousness, the mother tongue, is not transformed into reflective representational symbolic thought although under normal circumstances, at least in western culture, the latter gradually predominates as it is culturally adaptive. First mind is a separate entity in the human repertory, to be called upon as needed, for example in parenting, and not a transient developmental stage like baby teeth. Its potential remains throughout life even though, in some settings that strongly favor reflective representational logical thought, its phenomenological manifestations are scarce. Rather, maturation of the brain and social development enable acquisition of reflective symbolic consciousness, and the two forms of consciousness coexist in potential and in varying proportions depending both on the idiosyncrasies of each individual's development and the mores of the cultural, interpersonal, and social surroundings.

Chapter 10 is devoted to an exposition of development in western culture. It details the issues of attachment, normal and pathological, and separation–individuation that determine whether there is a normal maturational transition from primordial consciousness to representational thought, or whether primordial conscious mentation persists in situations where it is no longer adaptive and appropriate and the outcome is psychosis.

9

RETURN TO THE RAT MAN

Psychosis as a manifestation of primordial consciousness

In Chapter 3 I presented details from Freud's account of his treatment of Ernst Lanzer, aka the "Rat Man." to illustrate the thesis that Freud did attempt to treat psychotic persons under the misunderstanding that their pathology fit his neurosis model. Now that I have presented the model of primordial consciousness that is the basis of psychotic mentation I should like to return to his case material and highlight how clearly it demonstrates that model. The reader might want to review Chapter 3 before proceeding.

Lanzer was paralyzed by a sadomasochistic belief system that was concrete, involved body parts, and consisted of magical omnipotent ideas. His obsessive thoughts were not differentiated from impulsive affect-driven motor actions and counter-actions or prohibitions designed to undo them. He believed concretely and literally that the doing or refraining from doing of one action cancelled the doing or undoing of another one. His most prominent symptoms took the form of the anal sadistic *phantasies* (not *fantasies*) about his father and his fiancée that I recounted in Chapter 3, things that were not products of his mind but events that he believed were happening or that he had to initiate counter-acts or thoughts to prevent. While his symptomatic thoughts and actions, which Freud called obsessions, might superficially resemble conflict and defense over rage, they were more like delusions insofar as they involved affect-driven beliefs or convictions. The beliefs were not differentiated from actions, doing and undoing, did not differentiate intrapsychic from external reality and therefore had an omnipotent quality. They involved fragmentation or undifferentiation insofar as two conflicting ideas could not be held in mind simultaneously.

Lanzer had the omnipotent belief that his mind was causing or preventing real happenings, so that he had the power to alter the fates of others important to him. In this holistic undifferentiated mental state "He thought that a wish of his had actually kept his cousin alive on two occasions" (1909, p. 298). Lanzer lamented that if his cousin were actually ill then he would no longer have to worry about how his thoughts were keeping him healthy. Words and ideas were treated as concrete things of action that could alter reality, not representations of ideas and related emotions that he might communicate. Another example of undifferentiated omnipotent belief was his neologism "glejsamen" which he used when masturbating in the belief that it would prevent his sadistic fantasies from being realized. The neologism condensed words from a prayer, the name of a place his father had visited, and the name of a woman friend. Sex and aggression, masturbation and murder, phantasy and action, living and dying were holistic undifferentiated entities in a world devoid of contradiction: "the detailed account which the patient gave me of the external events of these days and of his reactions to them was full of self-contradictions and sounded hopelessly confused" (1909, p. 169). He had no conception of the passage of time or of the distinction between intrapsychic and external reality, for his dead father was very much alive for him in a hallucinated reality, which he flashed his penis at late at night. Further examples from Freud's account of that holistic, undifferentiated, fluid, somatic-affective process include persons morphing into one another because they have the same name, and the Rat Man's obsession about bodies concretely contaminating one another. In his notes Freud himself called this "displacement," apparently without realizing it was a term he had developed to describe the primary process in dreaming.

The evidence suggests Lanzer was functioning according to a mental process that is concrete rather than symbolic, somatic and behaviorally enactive rather than reflective, self–object-undifferentiated, driven by affect rather than represented emotion, and neither logical nor realistic. The improvement that Lanzer did show during his work with Freud might be related to the fact that Freud educated him to use a thoughtful language with which to comprehend his experience and in particular helped him to represent and articulate his anger.

10

PSYCHOSIS AS A DISORDER OF ATTACHMENT AND SEPARATION– INDIVIDUATION

A normal/neurotic person has developed the awareness of self and other as separate individuals including the ability to distinguish his or her inner life from that of others, and is able to experience and resolve emotional conflicts in an integrated internal manner using a combination of repression, inhibition, and selective action. He or she is able to live independently although in the instance of neurosis the internal resolution may limit satisfaction and success. Psychosis, in contrast, is a condition arising from pathology of attachment, leading to inability to achieve self–other differentiation from the primary caregiver, and inability to integrate a separate self that is capable of thoughtful representation of experience and reflective self-awareness. As a consequence of inability to recognize and resolve conflict internally, the psychotic person lives in a place where an undifferentiated world/self becomes the stage for destructive enactments.

It is very difficult for a psychotic person to move from the world of primordial conscious mentation to that of reflective representational thought, and in so doing to separate from the family of origin. Primordial conscious mental activity is normal in a family that functions as an undifferentiated unit and members fulfill functions for other members so that those persons need not integrate aspects of their minds and feelings sufficiently to function as separate selves. Efforts at physical separation pose a problem, for in the western world of school, work, relationships, and social expectations, such mentation and associated behavior are clearly bizarre and maladaptive.

Psychosis and pathology of separation: The stages of separation

Psychosis usually comes to social attention at one of three nodal points in the life cycle in which maturation requires a step toward separation and individuation. The first is when children cannot separate sufficiently from their primary relationship and home to begin school. The second is when adolescents or young adults cannot successfully leave home to begin advanced education or work. Finally, there are adults who have formally left home and live on their own and function more or less independently but are unable to form and sustain a close relationship and begin families of their own, and/or to form a stable productive work life, or in the case of women, deal with issues of pregnancy and childbirth.

Failure of the first separation produces child psychosis, a condition I have not had personal experience with and hence is beyond the scope of this book. Failure of the second separation produces the signs and symptoms of schizophrenia and other severe mental ills. Schizophrenia is not the only manifestation of the psychosis characteristic of this second stage. Leaving aside manic-depressive illness, with which I have had less experience and there is evidence to believe may have a significant genetic component, the perpetrators of school shooting tragedies, a contemporary social phenomenon, are most likely psychotic as well. These crimes are typical of separation stage two psychosis, and are mosly committed by young men in their late teens or early 20s who are about to graduate or have recently graduated high school. My mentor in my early days in psychoanalytic training, Elvin Semrad, was wont to say that schizophrenia is an alternative to suicide or homicide. In my experience the predominant emotion underlying schizophrenia is rage, and while some do not like to acknowledge it, there is a substantial percentage of both homicide and suicide among persons so diagnosed as well (Wallace, Mullen, & Burgess, 2004).

Failure at the third stage of separation reveals a psychotic personality organization that has been mostly concealed from the social world of the sufferer with a false self organization. In fact this social façade may be extremely effective, and from an external vantage point the person may seem unusually gifted and accomplished. This condition usually goes under such names as borderline, schizoid, sociopathic or narcissistic personality, severe drug addiction, or unexpected suicide. I lump these conditions under the rubric of psychotic personality disorder because in intimate personal settings such as a close relationship or a psychoanalytic treatment situation the person functions in the mentation of primordial consciousness. The characteristic elements of failure of self-care, bizarre mentation, and destructive behavior only come to attention as failures to make and sustain a close relationship, or major disruptions of career and life that from an external vantage point are entirely unexpected. They are the consequences of removal of a cloak of social invisibility conferred by a combination of false self organization and an environment sufficiently removed from the person's inner life as to be unaware of its presence.

Of course these stages of emergence of florid psychosis are not as separate and distinct as I have made them seem for heuristic purposes. Individuals who have not separated psychologically and use a destructively distorted version of primordial consciousness when reflective representational thought would be more appropriate will encounter problems of social discordance and simply be perceived by some as "unusual" throughout their lives. Two of the persons with psychotic personality disorders who wrote essays from which I have quoted, Jane and Jacob, were hospitalized in late adolescence and manifested delusions and hallucinations. With nothing more than a bit of social support, however, they were able to recoup and make what seemed to be independent existences based on false selves, Jacob's quite grandiose and based on denial he had any problems, Jane's leading to widely acclaimed professional accomplishments. Eventually problems of adjustment and unhappiness forced both of them to enter treatment.

Relationship between schizophrenia and psychotic personality disorder: The false self

While the possibility of genetic predisposition cannot be ruled out, evidence available now suggests that the difference between schizophrenia and psychotic personality organization relates to the severity of psychological trauma during the attachment phase and the ability or lack thereof to move beyond the second separation phase and establish at least the trappings of an independent life. This, in turn, requires the ability to erect and sustain a socially adaptive façade or false self. The false self in some instances is actually socially successful and productive. This is why it comes as such a shock, for example, when a well-known successful person commits suicide, or is found to be a drug or alcohol addict.

The false self is a form of compliance with perceived social expectations out of fear of exposure. The person retains sufficient sense of reality at a dissociated emotionally abstracted level to intuit and conform to ordinary social expectations unless stressed by interpersonal closeness. It is a misnomer to call it false, because rather than being an isolated normal part that has resisted regression, it is an integral part of the psychotic adaptive process. While it may employ many of the person's abilities, it is not rooted in awareness and fulfillment of the person's true emotional needs and desires. As a result, in the course of successful treatment it does not prove to be a solid "normal" foundation that can be built upon, but a wrong turn in the road of life that, however socially successful, was not satisfying. Despite the impressive abilities and accomplishments that are sometimes produced by the false self, they often have little bearing on the person's ultimate identity after successful treatment, as it was not rooted in the core emotional self, but in compliance. Jane's relinquishment of a very successful academic career in favor of other pursuits, and Lisabeth's ultimate turning to an artistic field and leaving aside her remarkable success in a social leadership role, are examples.

Clinical illustrations of false self

Here is what Jacob has to say about his false self:

> I thought I was a real nice guy with ordinary desires. An important hindrance to my understanding the depth of my involvement with images as a pseudo language, was my investment in grandiosity. This allowed me to

escape my emptiness and anger directed at myself and others including destruction of my ability to be a professional mathematician, my undifferentiated anger at the world. Moving away from this grandiosity, seeing myself as I really am, has taken many hours of work.

Actually for many years Jacob enacted hatred of me for what we eventually realized was "exposing" the falsity of his belief he was a caring person, and a myriad of other deceptions about his status and accomplishments he practiced on women in the course of seducing them. It was not that he was consciously lying; he firmly believed these things.

Lisabeth comments on her false self:

> I grew up in a world of words – not meaningful words; words as a way to tell me how and what to think. Words were also used as a form of presentation, disconnected from thought and emotion – yet spoken articulately using correct grammar and a sizeable vocabulary. This "educated" (but emotionally disconnected) use of language was considered one of several requirements for success – not a success grounded in self-motivation, passion, and caring, but achieved by developing a well-designed cover which, along with refined speaking, included appropriate use of other social conventions (proper handshakes, manners, and so forth). I learned my lesson well. Underneath I sought a non-thinking state of deadness. I appeared on the outside to be self-possessed, articulate, competent, caring, and intelligent. I fooled myself into thinking I was separate and independent by moving out-of-state after college and over the years becoming increasingly successful professionally. This was my face to the outside world. I had an operational side that spoke as if I understood individuation and all that goes with it. My hidden quest for fusion with another was invisible to me and others because I never became close enough to anyone in a non-possessive relationship for my belief system to be questioned or apparent. It took me years to understand that dependent and independent did not mean remaining emotionally fused with someone while putting on a public face that made it look as if I was independent because I was geographically separate, could live on my own, and was successful at my work.

Lisabeth's false self had no emotional energy behind it and was based on dissociation and hiding from her core self-denigration. She lived in a state of paranoid terror based on failure of differentiation from others, that the people around her who actually valued and admired her would find out who she "really" was.

Jane was considered an international expert in some of the very areas of knowledge about mind and behavior that we worked on. The astonishing thing we slowly realized is that she didn't believe a word she wrote or lectured when it came to understanding her own mind. From her sense of emotionally abstracted alienation and what we eventually deduced was a state of arrogance and grandiosity Jane compliantly adapted to what she intuited others wanted from her. She believed herself to be a science fiction-like disembodied head trying to adapt to life on an alien planet. Here is what she had to say about her false self:

> I had an extensive and well-educated vocabulary when it came to body and emotions and could use them in writing or as I talked to someone else. Their meaning, though, was not fundamentally grounded in my own past or current experience. My use of language in writing became more and more sophisticated, with language being more of an art form, I find this division between "personal" and "professional" use of language frustrating. Until you began showing interest in my gestures, I never thought of them as having meaning, only as showing my pathology which was being betrayed even as I tried so hard to pass as normal.

In his essay on language Charles did not mention aspects of his being that might be called false self. In retrospect I think this is because he didn't "have one" until some years of treatment. While I did not think of him as schizophrenic – he had no obvious hallucinations or delusions – when I met him he had barely managed to graduate from a second line college that did not give grades, and was isolated to his apartment, where he spent his time in bed or taking apart and putting together his motorcycle. He did not have to work because he was supported by inherited family wealth, and he did not have a close relationship. During the early years of our relationship he was able to go to art school and begin to realize some of his potential, and he began to construct installations that were, in essence, small universes that turned out to have a kind of hypnotic fascination for viewers because of their repetitive quality. His work was displayed in two museums, and brought him a considerable measure of acclaim. But after several years he reluctantly relinquished this activity as he realized that the process of creation, which occurred in a darkened studio, and the work itself with its repetitive quality, represented a regressive re-enactment of unresolved childhood issues. It became apparent to him that however acclaimed his artistic accomplishments, they were more the products of a sense of merger with his mother and related phantasies of restitution than of caring and self-esteem. After several years more he began to resume art, but in a completely different medium and from a total different psychic place involving thoughtful representation of things that he was beginning to care about, and reflective awareness of what he was doing. In retrospect I believe his first artistic period, which ironically brought him more public acclaim than his later work, was his false self.

Good enough attachment and development of the two mental processes: Rank and Bowlby

In order to understand the problems that arise in the attachment phase it is useful to understand the nature of good enough attachment that leads to the ability to separate and develop a satisfying individual identity.

Otto Rank (1926, 1938) was the first to propose that human development is a lifelong struggle to separate from primary attachment, and to resolve the conflict between separateness and primal unity. Rank's 1926 lecture titled "The genesis of the object relation" is the landmark in what eventually became known as object relations theory (Rank, 1926, pp. 140–149). In a 1938 lecture, Rank said:

> Life in itself is a mere succession of separations. Beginning with birth, going through several weaning periods and the development of the individual personality, and finally culminating in death – which represents the final separation. At birth, the individual experiences the first shock of separation, which throughout his life he strives to overcome. In the process of adaptation, man persistently separates from his old self, or at least from those segments of his old self that are now outlived.
>
> *(Rank, 1938, p. 270)*

While Rank was aware of the critical impact of separation, he did not write about the nature of the attachment itself. In his classic paper "On the confusion of tongues" (1932) and his book *Thalassa* (1924), **Sandor Ferenczi** elaborated on the importance of conflict between the urge to grow and the urge to regress, and the role of trauma related to confused communication early in life. Like Rank, he did not explore the importance of attachment to mother.

Rank, Groddeck, and Ferenczi wrote about the importance of mother and attachment in development and personality formation during the first decade of the 20th century. Their critical contributions were mostly marginalized. Half a century later the banner was taken up by Bowlby and Mahler. Mahler's work (1952, 1968; Mahler, Bergman, & Pine, 1975) is summarized in Chapter 4 on Freud's relational model of psychosis. **John Bowlby** (1969) studied the nature of attachment and the vicissitudes of separation. He wrote that attachment communication includes "facial expression, posture, and tone of voice" (1969, p. 120). In other words, he remarked on its somatic-enactive quality, one of the elements of primordial consciousness. Two years later, inspired by the work of Bowlby, James and Joyce Robertson (Robertson, 1971) made a now classic film series showing the nuanced subtle interactions of gesture, facial expression, and prosody between infants and their mothers during stages of attachment, separation, and reunion.

As I described in Chapter 8, mothers reflexively begin to interact with their infants during the last trimester of pregnancy when the manifestations of quickening or movement unrelated to maternal volition provide inescapable evidence of a new and separate life within. At first mothers use the music of their voices, spoken words and sounds, to communicate with this new presence. The words begin to have meaning to the fetus and ultimately to the infant. After birth the maternal repertory expands to include gestures and facial expressions as well. Mothers modify their prosody to regulate the child's arousal and attention. At this stage, while cognitively aware of a separate being, psychologically the infant is an undifferentiated part of the maternal self.

Conscious psychic life, in the sense of awareness without reflective capacity, commences around the end of the second or the beginning of the third trimester of embryonic life, from a matrix including the neural capacity for REM sleep, the coming on line of the auditory system, and the crucial catalytic force of the maternal voice. The fetus awakens, so to speak, and enters the mental-social world of being through interaction with maternal sounds, including heartbeat, intestinal and respiratory noises, and of most importance to this discussion, the musical prosody of mother's voice as she talks to her unborn child as well as to others, using language and other forms of vocalization. Intrauterine responses to mother's voice are described by Condon and Sander (1974). The fact that learning takes place in utero is demonstrated by the infant's recognition of mother's voice and preference of it to others (Kolata, 1984; Mehler & Christophe, 2000). Infants respond to the mother tongue of the caregiver by gradually developing the musicality or prosody that will later accompany their own phrases and sentences, and babble in sentence-like musicality long before the time during the first or second year when they acquire the actual words and syntax to accompany the music. Development of the language of primordial consciousness in utero includes not only the reflexive learning of prosody but also the beginnings of meaning of the words and sentences within the system of consciousness that prevails at that time. Kolata (1984) discovered that infants who were read Doctor Seuss' *The Cat in the Hat* twice a day beginning in the last six weeks of gestation sucked preferentially after birth when mother read that story in contrast to when she read another one. Partanen et al. (2013) repeatedly exposed fetuses during the last trimester to particular nonsense combinations of syllables and discovered that as infants they recognized and preferentially responded to them in contrast to others.

In other words, contrary to the universal grammar belief of the Chomsky group at MIT, this primary interaction between mother and infant is not simply a vehicle for the gradual linear emergence of the language instinct but is the essential substrate of a separate mental process, primordial consciousness, of which language is an expression. Reflective representational thought does not develop until later infancy and childhood as the brain matures. Other evidence for the uniqueness of primordial consciousness comes from studies of children adopted by parents who speak different languages than that of the birth mother, and by studies of second language acquisition. Learning through prosody and presumably primordial consciousness peaks somewhere between three months and one year of age and then gradually declines, and by age five to seven ceases (Werker & Tees, 1984; Best & McRoberts, 2003; Rivera-Gaxiola, Silvia-Pereyra, & Kuhl, 2005; Tsao, Liu, & Kuhl, 2006). Even if a child is adopted during preverbal infancy into a family that speaks a very different language, the child can learn the language of its birth mother much more quickly than a person who did not have such an infantile exposure, and with appropriate accent

(Choi, Cutler, & Broersma, 2017). Children who have been exposed to foreign languages during the first few months of life learn those languages much more rapidly and with appropriate prosody or accent later in life than those who have not had such exposure. Sometime around ages five to seven it is no longer possible to learn a foreign language with its native accent. It can be inferred that there is a distinction between the primordial mother tongue language and the language of reflective representational thought. Even after reflective representational thought comes to predominate, first language is only dormant, ready to emerge in things like parenting behaviour, belief systems, creativity, and other socially appropriate circumstances.

The early development of language, especially words used to designate oneself and others, provides a laboratory for understanding primordial consciousness and the gradual preferential acquisition of reflective representational thought when maturation and separation from mother proceed normally. The use of pronouns does not mean the same thing in the language of primordial consciousness as it does in the language of reflective representational thought. Viewed from the perspective of reflective representational thought, the first person pronoun "I" implies self-awareness or self-consciousness. However in the language of primordial consciousness "I" simply implies agency, activity, doing or being. From a similar perspective one assumes the use of second or third person pronouns refers to a differentiated separate person. However, in the undifferentiated language of primordial consciousness such pronouns denote aspects of the speaker's intrapsychic self of which he or she is unaware that are believed to exist in the other person.

Self-reference in speech is a first step in development of reflection and recursion. These first references conform to the principles of primordial conscious mentation. According to Sharpless (1985), first person pronouns that appear in speech prior to about 19–22 months tend to be stereotypic, by which she means concrete and contextual rather than truly representational. Second person pronoun use is very limited and probably still reflects the primordial conscious state of fusion or undifferentiation between self and other. In other words, the first "I" involves a sense of agency or action, not reflective awareness that the bearer is a self with an internal mind. Beginning at about 23–25 months children begin to appreciate that they have a self, and the process of reflective representational consciousness commences, including the capacity for introspection or recursion. The child begins to refer to his or her activities and to states of personal want, need, like, and dislike (Greenspan & Shanker, 2005). Instinctively recognizing that their infants have not yet mastered the self–object differentiation characteristic of pronoun use parents often refer to their infants by name ("Jane wants, Jane feels") rather than "you want." Perhaps learning from how some adults address them some children continue to use a third person designation in referring to themselves for a considerable period (Church, 1966). For the first two years the child talks mostly about the environment, concretely labelling objects and commenting on activities.

In the first part of the third year children become increasingly self-descriptive (Church, 1966). There is a transition from the primordial conscious language of agency, being and doing in the world, to the language of reflective representational thought and related awareness of the differentiated other, as manifest by the "show and tell" that is such an important aspect of early development. The child has become aware of being a separate self and needs to reinforce the fact by calling attention to its accomplishments. Labelling of one's body parts also begins around this time. These developments coincide with the Piagetian transition from sensorimotor thinking to development of object permanence and they signify the commencement of development of reflective thought characterized by continuous mental representations. Persistence of the language of primordial consciousness is one of the characteristics of pathology of attachment and ultimate psychosis. I return to this shortly.

The maternal task is to recognize, respond to and assign language to infantile affects and somatic expressions, to recognize and meet needs in order to minimize pain and distress, and interactively enhance positive experiences and affects. Good enough mothering, attuned and responsive to the actual characteristics and needs of the infant, leads to the development of a shared primordial consciousness and its language based on caring, the beginnings of an accurate sense of self, and an inner sense of security and predictability. From such a base the infant can begin to learn the thought process and language of separation, reflective representational thought, and not only tolerate but enjoy the awareness of being alone and being the agent of one's life in a world of others who are unpredictable in the sense of being autonomous and therefore capable of hurt as well as satisfaction.

Pathology of attachment, maladaptive persistence of primordial consciousness, failure to separate, and development of psychosis

Mary Ainsworth (1982; Ainsworth et al., 1978) devised a way to study some of Bowlby's propositions with 12–18-month-old infants called the "strange situation" experiment. It consisted of one-way screen observation of infants with and without their mothers and/or a stranger in a variety of combinations. She classified infant attachment behavior into four affect-driven categories, and her classifications are consistent with the hypothesis that infants function according to the characteristics of primordial consciousness mentation. The categories are: secure, ambivalent/resistant, anxious/avoidant, and disorganized/disoriented. Mothers of ambivalent/resistant infants were themselves insensitive and unpredictable, but not overtly rejecting. Their infants were anxious and passive at home, and in the strange situation preoccupied with mother and her whereabouts while also being anxious and confused. Mothers of anxious/avoidant infants were rejecting of their infants' attachment behavior, and their infants were anxious and angry, intolerant of separations. In the strange situation they insisted on exploration and tended to ignore mother. The other category, disorganized/disoriented, was elaborated by Ainsworth's student and collaborator, Mary Main. Mothers of disorganized/disoriented infants were frightening, and their infants, caught in an approach–avoidance conflict, manifested disorganized and disruptive behavior that included their language. Main comments on one such peculiarity of language relevant to primordial consciousness, namely the presence of contradictions in their speech (Hesse & Main, 2000, p. 1117).

Lyons-Ruth (2003), and the Boston Change Process Study Group (BCPSG) (2007) also formulated a model of disorganized attachment. They concluded that if caregivers behave in ways that are rejecting and attacking, and distort the meaning of infant initiatives by responding to them with dissonant or inappropriate affects, their infants will manifest in new learning situations with others the kind of maladaptive and self-destructive responses that might have been adaptive responses to the rejection, attack, and confusion of their mothers' behavior. These infants do not experience the caring, psychological holding, and attention necessary to identify and integrate into a separate sense of self their responses to maternal mistreatment. Instead, the somatic-affective precursors of rage, fear, and insecurity that are generated are experienced in primordial conscious mentation and lead to lack of integration of a sense of self, and undifferentiated confusion between the sense of self and other.

Mothers who are not attuned and responsive to infant signals and who do not have their own issues sufficiently differentiated from those of their infants will misperceive and mistakenly respond (or fail to respond) in ways that combine distortion, hostility, and rejection. Starting in utero some mothers sing negative affect tones to their fetuses and subsequently to their infants, songs of discomfort, anger, and rejection, much of it in privacy where no one else can hear. Fetal needs may be perceived as hostile attacks draining mother's body. Mothers who function in a primordial conscious state that has been distorted by their own attachment experience do not differentiate themselves accurately from others and may attribute to the fetus malevolent threatening qualities and affects not differentiated and integrated into themselves.

The children of such mothers are unable to make the normal transition that involves separation from mother and requires transition from primordial conscious mentation to the mentation of reflective representational thought, and the accompanying secure differentiation of a separate self from mother and from others. Primordial conscious mentation persists in situations where it is not contextually appropriate because the sense of self and world has been so severely traumatized and distorted that the child lacks a sufficiently secure sense to separate from mother and develop the capacity for independent differentiating thought. Moreover, any efforts in the direction of separation (differentiation) from mother subject the child to a state of helpless dependency. Nascent efforts to represent and articulate emotions of fear and rage as part of the true self will be ignored, rejected, or attacked by such mothers. The state of separateness is literally unthinkable. Remaining in the unseparated undifferentiated mental state of primordial consciousness and hence psychotic becomes an adaptive solution, a kind of false security based on psychological failure to grow.

In psychosis, second and third person pronouns that seem to imply sharing with a separate person may actually be expressing the undifferentiated state of self, and the belief that others possess the content the subject is not fully aware is in his or her mind. In reality they are "I" or "me" conceptions disguised as sharing. They are unaware that they mean "I" or "me" when they say "you" or "they." Jacob repeatedly prefaced statements to me with things like "you know, you believe, I think you are angry," or "you think that …," when as best as I was aware I had no such thought or feeling, and in the case of "you know" the information was often something I had never heard before. He believed for a long time that our minds were one, and was unaware of some of his own mental content. He often assumed that he did not have to tell me his thoughts because I already knew them. Disruptions of his belief were sources of considerable anger at me for my "failure." These linguistic distinctions are not obvious as the person may be highly intelligent and fully convinced that he or she is as separate and introspecting as anyone else.

Absence of the capacity to reflect may be indicated by such unusual uses of language as the use of the first person pronoun "I" to express agency or being rather than self-awareness, and concreteness, where words are used as things of action, a kind of name calling, rather than as symbols or metaphors. The meaning of basic relational concepts including such things as caring, love, anger, separation, and the like may have been defined in a socially inverted way in the attachment phase by mothers who believe that they are caring when they are not able to be. As a result, for instance, actions that might objectively be described as hateful or rejecting are misunderstood as manifestations of love. Finally, the words used to describe images do not refer to stable continuous emotionally based mental representations, for instance fantasies or memories, but are phantasies – evanescent snapshots whose emotional and historical significance has not been processed.

President Donald Trump's peculiar use of personal pronouns bears remarkable similarity to phenomena observed in the pronouns of normal infants in the first several years of life who are negotiating the transition between the state of psychological undifferentiation and the acquisition of a separate sense of self and others. Consider his gaffe at the award ceremony for Native American code breakers. He stated "We have a representative in Congress who they say was here a long time ago. They call her Pocahontas. But you know what, I like you." As it was Trump who coined and frequently used "Pocahontas" as an epithet for Elizabeth Warren we would expect to hear a subjective "I" of acknowledgment but instead the he speaks as an undifferentiated "we" and "they." His concluding "I" contradicts his use of Pocahontas as an epithet demeaning Native Americans only seconds before. Trump uses "I" appropriately when referring concretely and operationally to denote agency – things he did or intends to do – but he does not use it to denote reflective awareness of his own problematic behavior. On other occasions when one would expect him to refer to himself as "me" or "I" he speaks as though he were another person referring to Donald Trump. On May 4, 2009, he wrote "Be sure to tune in and watch Donald Trump on Late Night with David Letterman as he presents the Top Ten List tonight!" And on May 9, 2017, he tweeted that the "Trump/Russia story was an excuse used by the Democrats as justification for losing the election. Perhaps Trump just ran a great campaign?" He regularly refers to the author of presidential actions he has taken or intends to take by fiat as "we."

I do not want the reader to leave this chapter believing that what I have proposed is merely a more benign iteration of Frieda Fromm-Reichmann's mother blaming – the so-called "schizophrenogenic mother." What I truly believe is that mothers are significantly more important than fathers in the formation of core personality, because of their physical and psychological unity and communication that commences in utero. The fact that this book is not about the positive impact of the mother on her child does not gainsay that. Fathers do have a role, but they are not as important – either for good or ill. The fact that I cannot immediately call to mind a situation where good fathering has compensated for severe pathology of attachment and separation does not mean there are no such instances. It could be they have been so successful that such persons do not seek help. But I doubt it. Among the psychotic patients I have encountered there tend to be three kinds of fathering – absent, reinforcing, and offering of psychotic alternatives. Charles and Lisabeth are examples of persons whose fathers were absent. By absent I mean not vigorously offering support for healthy separation, not necessarily physically absent. Jacob and Jane are examples of situations in which fathers reinforced the effects of pathological mothering. Jane's father was an undependable Jekyll and Hyde, mostly friendly by day but assaulting her at night. Jacob's father brutalized and assaulted him, and physically punished him at mother's whim. Caroline's father (Robbins, 2011 & 2018) is an interesting illustration of psychotic alternative in that he modelled and rewarded her remaining enmeshed with her mother, and her belief she did not have to be responsible and live by the "rules" others do.

Clinical illustrations of pathological attachment and failure to separate

Here are some comments my patients made in their essays that are relevant to problems of attachment. They reflect what was learned in the course of analytic therapy, more from a process of reconstruction based on translation of primordial conscious mentation in the context of transference than from uncovering of actual memories.

Jane writes:

> My mother routinely called me by the wrong name – generally the name of the girl who lived next door and, sometimes, by my grandmother's

name. As well, my mother at times didn't quite recognize me. For example, at one point I started wearing contact lenses after wearing glasses for over a decade. She didn't say anything. When I mentioned the change in my appearance, she exclaimed "I can't even recognize you without your glasses!" But, moments before, she hadn't recognized that I didn't have my glasses on! When I was 6 or 7 a neighbor took a photo of me and when my mother looked at it she exclaimed, "I never noticed you were so fat!" I was not fat at all. Nor ugly, as I was later called. And, later, when I had toothaches because of large cavities, having never gone to a dentist, my mother would look in my mouth (rare for her to be willing to come close to my body) and say there was no cavity and give me an aspirin. There were large black cavities in back molars that were immediately visible. Words for emotions were massively limited and it was more likely that I would be called ridiculing names than that there would be any interest in the nature and cause of my emotions. UPSET was the major category of acknowledged and self-acknowledged emotion for me. My mother was delusional/thought-disordered/mistaken/lying most of the time so anything she said was likely to be untrue. Confronting her was useless. I remember my mother worrying out loud one time about my brother because he was so happy to be so successful in his occupation. "How will he handle the inevitable failure?" she wondered. According to my mother I did not begin speaking until I was about 2½. Until then I used, she said, three names, but no other words. The names were for my father (*DaDa*), brother, (*Barbie*, which I assume was an approximation to *brother*, not to his actual name), and great-aunt (*KayKay*. Her name was *Catherine*). When I was an adult I asked my mother "No name for *you*?" and she said no; she did not indicate that she thought this remarkable. Since I wasn't given any words for external body parts, and since the message was clear that the body and body experience were not to be referred to or, better yet, even noticed, it is not surprising that I learned next to nothing about internal bodily feelings and, moreover, never learned to pay attention to them. I remember only the general designation "down there" for my body below my waist, and otherwise pretty much nothing. When I had my first menstrual period, the next day, after she found my stained underpants, she greeted me at the door by asking, "What did you do in your pants?" in a cold, rigid way. I began sobbing and apologizing and saying I didn't know and she told me to stop crying – that that was ridiculous – and to go to the bathroom and see if I "had done it again." Well, yes, of course, and I continued howling in distress, now believing that I was inadvertently soiling myself. My mother shoved a bra into my hands one day and told me I had to wear it – not that it fit.

Jacob writes about his attachment experience:

I was in a familial environment, especially shaped by my mother, where real communication and growth never took place. This milieu was totally barren of any sense of love; instead totally defined by both mental and physical abuse. At a time before I had any sense of identity, much of the abuse was magnified by a lack of boundaries between my mother and myself. Overwhelmed with no sense of individuality, I had no help in associating words with feelings. One central delusion was that my mother really loved me, with her acts of abuse perceived by me as acts of kindness. For example, my mother believed and made me, as a helpless child, believe that I was defective, plagued by all kinds of confabulated medical maladies. She believed that defective areas of my body could be reached via my rectum, which she would penetrate with her finger. In reality she was raping me. Yet I believed this was a caring act. As a young child. I would grimace in the mirror to scare myself, as my mother scared me during the day. Young and identity-less, I unconsciously joined the world of my mother thorough such facial expressions, which along with music and images served as proxies for my undeveloped feelings. To this day I still find myself using these facial images as rageful poses. Indeed this was part of my juvenile language of rage.

Lisabeth writes about her attachment experience:

Mother think is the thought process adopted full-bore from my mother's brainwashing: a mother with whom I was emotionally enmeshed as one; where the family cosmology was such that a symbiotic relationship was the only way; feelings were unacceptable; and I was no good, ugly, and worthless. People outside the family configuration were not real or trustworthy; others' perspectives (including mine) were corrected to conform to her worldview. When I began therapy I was unaware that I was inseparable from my mother and that she had used words and dogma to teach me a concealed way of thinking about relationships and attachments. Becoming attached to people outside the family was subtly discouraged. My mother was trained as a psychiatric social worker, which she touted with arrogant pride. She consistently applied a faux diagnosis to everyone (not faux to me at the time). No one was exempt. She, however, remained diagnosis free thereby making herself appear to me to be superior to others and to me. Topics of discussion were often about the troubles or "diagnoses" of others. I, too, was diagnosed: mean, hateful, uncaring, selfish, accident prone, don't like people, angry (that was the killer – oh to be angry; the worst of sins). When I expressed anger, her favorite rejoinder was "Why do you have a need to be angry?" This was not a gentle inquiry, it was a strong put-down; a diagnosis that I was "bad" or "sick" for having angry feelings. I have come to think she believed, and taught me, that the principal human afflictions were having feelings, being autonomous, thinking differently, and caring about anyone else but her. When I mentioned how much I admired a certain friend my mother said "I am watching that relationship." The implication was that the relationship bore watching because there was something wrong with my feelings about the other person, with the person herself, and with me. I was sick. Caring was forbidden. Often, when my mother met someone for the first time or when talking about a friend of mine or hers she would make a comment in a supercilious tone that so and so is "very disturbed" or "very angry" with the word "very" emphasized. I never understood what she meant by "disturbed" nor did I ask, but I think now that the categorization meant the person was a pariah. When she labeled a person as "angry" it meant that both the person and the feelings were unacceptable. She was teaching me that being angry was an intolerable human emotion yet we were tied together by anger: The idea that a person can only love one is also implicit in her comments about my father's new family: that he could not love them and me at the same time. I surmise that "why do you have a need ..." is also a statement of my mother's disapproval of basic human needs. Once I asked her if I had ever sucked my thumb. She defensively replied "absolutely not" as if the need to suck was another disease. When I began therapy with Dr. Robbins and was alone I felt the urge to suck my thumb. I tried it a couple times to see what it felt like. I speculate that when a child if I had tried to suck my thumb my mother may have pulled it out and admonished me.

And finally, here is what Charles wrote:

During the long course of my psychotherapy I have become aware of a process that has taken place in me involving the harsh emotional conditions that were an ongoing feature of my early childhood and how they became registered in me as my own experience and became part of me. I understand much of my core emotional makeup as having formed around feelings of frustration, fear, and rage. How much of these feelings I took directly from my mother as a physically dependent infant having no separate and independent self-existence, and how much of them I developed on my own as a response to having my needs neglected, is hard to say. It is clear to me that, before developing the ability to put words to the service of representing my actions and emotions, what I experienced was registered in my physical person as bodily sensations. Primary to these sensations is an idea of toxicity associated in my mind with bodily fluids: stomach juices, urine, burning tears, acidic semen, and the whiskey my mother drank to give herself permission to unleash the fury that in turn consumed her.

PART IV
Treatment of psychosis

11

THE MEDICAL TREATMENT OF PSYCHOSIS

Transforming psychosis from a socially disruptive to a socially adaptive disease

In Chapter 2 I characterized the medical treatment of psychosis as dehumanizing because it is based on the implicit assumption that psychotic mentation is a meaningless product of a brain defect or degeneracy. A close look at treatment by the medical-psychiatric model indicates that, however unwittingly, it also attempts to transform the underlying characteristics of psychosis and primordial conscious mentation into a less disruptive more socially compliant form, albeit at the expense of producing a chronically psychotic person in the process.

Consider a typical course of treatment using the medical model. Shortly after leaving home to attend university or to live and work away from his or her family for the first time, a young adult who has seemed normal to family and whose life has shown signs of being productive begins hearing voices, expressing strange ideas, and behaving in bizarre ways that are destructive to self and socially disruptive. The person is taken to a hospital, usually against his or her will because the person does not believe anything is the matter, and told that he or she has schizophrenia, an adult onset organic disease. The person is told that the delusions and hallucinations are meaningless symptoms of the disease, a kind of external affliction akin to cancer, that can be controlled and suppressed by medication but not cured. The patient is counselled to ignore or suppress the mental manifestations because they make no sense, and told "you shouldn't tell other people that you believe these ideas or are hearing these voices because they won't understand and might think something is the matter with you." Such advice promotes disintegration. The patient is encouraged to become alienated from parts of his or her own mind, and to believe that his or her thoughts are meaningless. The result is to reinforce the person's already suspicious, paranoid attitude toward the world based on undifferentiation of his or her thoughts from those of others. In other words, rather than encouraging the patient to develop reflective representational thought, such "therapy" reinforces the inappropriate use of primordial conscious mentation, albeit in this instance in a socially adaptive manner. Hopes for a normal future are dashed. The drugs "tranquilize" the person, dull what remains of the capacity for reflective thought, and have unpleasant side effects as well. He or she goes home to live with parents, or moves into a halfway house, seeing the psychiatrist regularly to monitor symptoms and adjust medication sufficiently to preserve the narcotized state. He or she becomes aimless and depressed, unable to hold a steady job or complete education. The symptoms wax and wane, other doctors may be consulted, the patient does not comply with the medication program because it doesn't make him or her feel good. Medications of various kinds in various doses are tried and re-hospitalizations may be required. Some commit suicide, others get addicted to more and more drugs, but one way or another a human life is lost and the long term drain on society is great.

Treatment with the medical model does not modify the dynamics and structure of psychosis. It merely educates the person to modify its formal content, the data the patient assimilates into the psychotic process, for example the things the person is paranoid about, in a way that is more socially acceptable and adaptable. Marginal social adaptation may be attained at the expense of solidifying the psychotic process and promoting chronicity.

This process is easiest to visualize when thinking about schizophrenia, the most severe of the psychoses. Psychotic persons are already paranoid, delusional, and hallucinating because they cannot differentiate the contents of their minds, mostly hostile, from that of others and from what is happening in the outside world, and cannot integrate aspects of themselves into a sense of personal coherence. Then, as "treatment," they are told by the doctor that they are suffering from a disease, external or alien to their person, that has attacked their minds like a cancer. They have been instructed to change the substance of their delusions. Now it is the concretely named disease, that "thing," that is dangerous, not their hostility towards other people, and certainly not unintegrated aspects of the self of which the sufferer is unaware. The underlying failure of differentiation and integration and the passivity or lack of personal agency are reinforced. Further instruction in paranoia takes the form of advising patients not to tell others about their delusions and hallucinations because others might think they are crazy, reinforcing the alienation from others that is actually based on undifferentiated and unintegrated alienation from parts of their own minds. Passivity and lack of agency are reinforced by prescription of powerful medication designed to fight, suppress, and control the disease, a term signifying the enemy alien force. The drugs are narcotizing or dulling to the affectively charged parts of the mind that, however disturbed, are active and vital. The person becomes more compliant and passive, and the interpersonal turbulence that marked the acute illness subsides. Life moves on, but human potential is lost, to say nothing of the severe side effects and long term toxicity of many anti-psychotic medications. Treatment with the medical model reinforces the characteristics of primordial consciousness that are the foundation of schizophrenia to begin with. In so doing it makes the patient easier for the environment to deal with in the short term but imposes a more subtle chronic burden on social resources.

It is interesting that over the past three decades there have been few follow-up studies of the course of schizophrenia treated by the medical model since the advent of anti-psychotic drugs. The more notable of these include studies by Strauss and Carpenter (1977); Huber et al. (1980); Harding (1987); Harding et al. (1987); McGlashan (1988); McGlashan and Keats (1989); Breier et al. (1991); Carone, Harrow, and Westermeyer (1991); and Menezes, Arenovich, and Zipursky (2006). The general conclusion of these studies is that they are chronic deteriorating conditions, with a high mortality rate, regardless of treatment.

The pharmaceutical industry drives the medical model, by a combination of powerful advertising, lavish research funding, and taking over some of the educational role formerly played by medical schools, by sponsoring the courses necessary for psychiatrists to take in order to maintain their professional licenses and by subsidizing drug research.

The journal *Current Psychiatry*, distributed without cost to all psychiatrists in the United States, exemplifies the insidious way in which the pharmaceutical industry influences psychiatry. Its articles are few and unsophisticated because its poorly concealed purpose is to advertise drugs. Its distinguished editorial board includes Jeffrey Lieberman, Chair of the Department of Psychiatry at Columbia medical school, whom I have more to say about in a moment. The fact that a number of prominent psychiatrists have agreed to be members of its editorial board is like putting lipstick on the proverbial pig, an attempt to conceal its purpose as a mouthpiece for the pharmaceutical industry. A 2015 anonymously authored article in the journal *Current Psychiatry* contained a short quiz to determine whether psychiatrists know the correct way – to use the editor's term – "manage" psychosis.

> Ms. A, age 17, and her parents are seen by you after an episode at school in which Ms. A screamed for other students to "be quiet" during a test. Ms. A complains to you that her classmates won't stop talking about her, although she never catches them doing so, and that one of her teachers laughs at her and calls her "fat and worthless." That teacher noted in the school record that Ms. A often "spaces out" and has been failing tests – uncharacteristic of a once straight-A student. Your diagnosis is first-episode psychosis; you prescribe risperidone, 3 mg/d. After 2 months of remission of symptoms, however, Ms. A relapses. Which course of treatment would you next choose for her?

The three choices all involve different anti-psychotic medications in different doses. Talking to the young woman about what might be troubling her is not listed as an option.

Since patents for prescription drugs last for 20 years from the time of first filing with the FDA, and it typically takes eight or more years of testing to obtain FDA approval, the pharmaceutical industry is in understandable haste to make a profit before the drug becomes generic. Typically there is a major advertising blitz about how the new drug is superior to existing drugs, supported by selective studies conducted by researchers whose funding has been subsidized by the drug companies themselves. The advertising shifts to newer drugs after 10 years or so when the older drug becomes generic. Over the ensuing years reports typically emerge that the drug is not as effective as was initially believed, and reports of side effects, some quite severe, emerge.

Jeffrey Lieberman, who I noted above is a member of the editorial board of the pharmaceutical industry-subsidized journal *Current Psychiatry,* is someone whose research has been subsidized by grants from major pharmaceutical companies. He is a kind of second coming of the Nobel Laureate Sir Francis Crick, mentioned earlier in the book, in that his thesis is that psychiatry has been "the black sheep of medicine" because it has believed the problems it encompasses are meaningful mental conditions rather than medical diseases. He is a scathing critic of psychoanalysis, for it epitomizes this problem. He characterizes psychoanalysts as charlatans in his recent book *Shrinks* (2015, pp. 85 & 109). Because of his stature and his unmistakable investment both professionally and financially in the psychopharmacological treatment of schizophrenia his paper commenting on the first phase of a longitudinal study (Lieberman & Stroup, 2011) is of particular interest as it would appear to cast serious doubt on the efficacy of drug treatment. It is an evaluation of the first stage of a major NIMH drug trial comparing the effects of first generation and second generation anti-psychotic drugs on 1,500 chronic schizophrenic individuals over the course of 18 months. The findings were that there was no significant difference in efficacy of the newer drugs over the old. 74% of patients discontinued their medications during the 18 months of the study. So it does not appear that drug treatment was particularly helpful. And there were numerous serious problems related to weight gain, diabetes, blood lipid pathology, and extrapyramidal symptoms. Compliance (taking prescribed drugs) is a major problem with schizophrenic patients, who tend to interpret authoritarian interventions in a paranoid manner. My patient Sara, whose story unfolds in Chapter 16, exemplifies this problem. Even in an insight-oriented therapy where her feelings about taking prescribed drugs could be examined in depth, it was difficult to ascertain when she took prescribed medication and when she did not.

Lest the reader mistakenly conclude from what I have written above that I have a black and white view of the use of medication in the treatment of schizophrenia, I want to emphasize that the problem, as I see it, is how and when drugs are used. That is, the use of drugs as part of a medical model based on assumptions of organic causality, meaningless mental processes, and symptom elimination. The judicious use of psychotropic medication is usually an indispensable adjunct to psychoanalytic therapy, especially in the early stages when it is difficult to establish a holding environment that will enable a very disturbed person to sit still and begin to talk about his or her feelings.

Problems similar to those I have described with schizophrenia, though much attenuated, are associated with the use of drugs to treat psychotic personalities, whose dissociated false selves comprise ways of concealing their distress from the world and producing a socially constructive façade.

Here is a typical unfortunate example of the results of the medical model from my own practice. Josh had a psychotic episode while in college, with hallucinations, delusions, and bizarre behavior. He was hospitalized, diagnosed with schizophrenia, and given medication. For the next 10 years he was unable to work and mostly lived at home. From time to time he would join a spiritual cult or a community that advertised itself as therapeutic. Eventually he clashed with each group and left it to go home until he became dissatisfied with that, and found another belief system group to join, only to repeat the same behavior pattern. When his hallucinations and delusions and his discomfort level worsened he would go to a psychiatrist who would prescribe drugs. Unbeknownst to them, he sometimes saw several at the same time. New medications would be added to his regimen. When he was 30 he and his parents learned that I had worked successfully with people like him by talking with them. When he came to see me I was impressed that he was very bright, but he was grandiose. He literally believed that he was having sexual intercourse with the world. He reported a complex quasi-religious hallucinatory and delusional world consisting of persecutory demons and protective archangels. He was taking three different major anti-psychotic medications, each in doses far greater than the recommended therapeutic range. He had also managed to get government disability compensation for a back problem that did not seem especially significant when I saw him, and by complaining of intolerable pain had managed to get a prescription for a fentanyl narcotic patch as well.

Despite his bizarre ideas he showed little signs of distress that might motivate him to want my help, so I made cutting down on some of his medications a condition of my agreement to work with him. As we talked over the course of a few sessions significant issues emerged such as his hostile dependency on his parents, his sexual identity confusion, and his confusion of external with internal reality, but every time we touched on painful emotions heralding the awareness of conflict he dropped the subject and insisted he wanted more medication. He told me he "just wanted to feel calm." Eventually I discovered he was simultaneously seeing two other psychiatrists, and they were giving him the medications I would not prescribe. After I confronted him with this he told me he was "taking a break from therapy." Through contacts in the community in which we both lived I discovered five years later that he was continuing to repeat the same patterns.

Treatment according to the medical model is not confined to the use of drugs and the associated chronicity promoting explanations that accompany their administration. The radical practice of treating severe mental ills as organic diseases of the brain using surgical intervention has not disappeared. In recent years a new electrical procedure known as DBS, deep brain stimulation, involving implants in the brain, has emerged. The website of Massachusetts General Hospital, a Harvard Medical School affiliate, contains the following statement: "The Stereotactic and Functional Neurosurgery Center offers a range of treatments for appropriate patients with severe and medically intractable Obsessive-compulsive disorder (OCD) and Major depression. Patients with severe and medically intractable Major depression or OCD are potential candidates for surgery" (www.massgeneral.org). The surgery includes cingulotomy, a variant of prefrontal lobotomy. While schizophrenia is not specifically mentioned I suspect that were the Kennedy family of November, 1941, teleported to the 21st century psychosurgery clinic at MGH an "appropriate" treatment would be recommended for Joe's daughter Rosemary.

Not surprisingly, doubts about the medical model have arisen in several quarters, for example Robert Whitaker's 2001 book *Mad in America* (2010). In the last decade there has been a significant reaction against the medical model of schizophrenia from among the advocates of human rights and social justice who support gender equality, racial and ethnic diversity, and freedom of sexual orientation. Many of these people feel they have been burned by the medical model and have banded together in a self-help movement that goes by many names, most frequently "service users," or "voice hearers." These persons for the most part believe they are "normal," have been discriminated against and labelled as abnormal by the medical establishment, and subjected to forced medication and hospitalization.

In the course of attending meetings of an organization that includes anyone critical of the medical approach to schizophrenia, whether professional or not, I have encountered three different classes of members in addition to persons with advanced credentials in the mental health field. The first are persons with unusual mental capacities such as synesthesia and lucid dreaming who have mistakenly been labelled psychotic rather than recognized and valued for their special abilities (Robbins, 2011). As for the others, there is an unfortunate though not obvious resonance between the harmful treatment they protest against and the effects of the remedy that they advocate. I include them in this chapter because the confusion the movement perpetuates between disease and treatment parallels the way that the medical model of treatment iterates schizophrenia. These are persons who have evident significant problems but as is characteristic of persons with paranoid delusions are convinced they are victims, normal persons unjustly imprisoned and treated as psychotic.

The third subset consists of persons who recognize they are suffering from psychosis but have been led to believe there is no such thing as mitigating their symptoms by trying to understand their psychological meaning. Both these subgroups seek or create their own alternative living centers where their behavior, however strange and destructive by common social standards, is accepted and supported; not questioned and explored as to its maladaptive significance and psychological meaning. While it may *sound* more humane and less stigmatizing to tell the psychotic person whose self-esteem is low and is experiencing significant problems in his or her life that he or she is not abnormal and give him or her a place where the thinking and behavior are accepted and not questioned, the effects can be devastating insofar as the untreated condition can lead to further destruction to self and to others.

In summary, both the medical model and the peer support model, whose advocates and practitioners are well-intentioned, alienate and dissociate the person from meaningful parts of his or her self and encourage the use of primordial conscious mentation rather than reflective representational thought, and in so doing reinforce the psychic structure and dynamics of psychosis, and promote chronicity.

12

STUDIES OF THE EFFICACY OF PSYCHOLOGICAL AND PSYCHOANALYTIC THERAPY OF PSYCHOSIS

Reports of the efficacy of psychological and psychoanalytically informed treatments of schizophrenic persons based on studies of the work of single therapists or statistical analysis adding the experience of multiple therapists are sparse in number. Moreover, they reach no consensus about whether such therapy really makes a difference. This should not surprise us considering that the severity of schizophrenia in relation to other mental ills is analogous to that of extreme medical conditions like cancer or organ failure whose outcome even given the best therapy available is in doubt. However, there may be other reasons for it as well. The limitations of traditional psychoanalytic models that I discussed in Part II may also play a part.

There are few detailed reports in the literature of single cases. Marian Milner (1969) wrote one. I am unaware of anyone other than myself (Robbins, 1993, 2011, 2018) who has written multiple lengthy reports of treatment of schizophrenic persons from start to finish. Individual therapists have made statements about their work. However, they do not contain much specificity or detail. For example Sullivan (1962) claimed that he treated 100 patients, and that 32% with insidious onset and 61% with acute onset improved, but he offers no detail. In addition, he could not have worked with any of these people longer than four years, and perhaps some of these treatments were as brief as 18 months. John Rosen (1947, 1953) claims to have cured 37 of 100 patients in two to three months, but studies of his work by Polatin, Kolb, and Hoch (Horwitz et al., 1958) and Bookhammer et al. (1966) concluded that his treatments were ineffective. In Robert Knight's preface to Harold Searles' 1965 book he reports 13 of 18 of Searles' patients were "remarkably improved." However, seven of the supposedly improved patients remained hospitalized at the time of the study, and there is no indication of how many, if any, were able to terminate treatment. In addition to lacking important detail these studies do not offer consistent and detailed criteria for judging whether treatment has been success-ful. Later in the chapter, when I describe my own work, I will try to be more specific about the criteria by which I determine what constitutes success and failure.

McGlashan (1984) conducted a follow-up study of patients treated with psy-choanalytic psychotherapy at Chestnut Lodge and concluded that two thirds were no better or were marginally improved. McGlashan and Keats (1989) did a follow-up study based on detailed hospital records of four patients treated with psychoanalytically oriented therapy at Chestnut Lodge, including Frieda Fromm-Reichmann's patient Joanne Greenberg, aka Hannah Green, author of *I Never Promised You a Rose Garden*, and concluded there were two good and two poor outcomes. A two-part prospective study of psychotherapy of schizophrenia was reported by Stanton et al. (1984). Gunderson et al. (1984) compared the out-come of 20 patients treated with supportive therapy focused on current adapta-tion and symptom management, with that of 22 patients treated with insight-oriented therapy that focused on the past as well as the present, and on the transference, over a two year period. Only one third of the patients completed the study. No great improvements were noted and there were no significant dif-ferences in outcome attributable to each approach.

Studies of psychotherapy of schizophrenia that cumulate the work of many therapists are suspect as they are based on the erroneous assumption that, like putting together the proverbial apples and oranges, the work of therapists with different personalities, levels of training, skills, and theoretical orientations, can be treated as a single variable like a dose of a particular medication, and added together. Prospective studies are flawed because in order to enable the same group of researchers to follow the patients and then write a paper the duration of therapy is usually relatively brief in relation to the severity of the illness. Long term follow-up is rarely possible. All of such studies suffer from high dropout rates.

For a more comprehensive account of studies of the outcome of psychologic-ally informed therapies the reader is referred to my 1993 book. It is significant that most of such studies were conducted prior to the turn of the millennium, at a time when psychopharmacology was still a relatively new modality and it was still "legitimate" to treat schizophrenia with dynamic psychotherapy. In the two decades since, follow-up studies of the treatment of schizophrenia, as exempli-fied by Jeffrey Lieberman's work summarized in the previous chapter, are designed to test the efficacy of various drugs, as general consensus has evolved that psychopharmacology is the treatment of choice and psychological treatment is not only ineffective and misguided, but might be a form of quackery and even malpractice.

The ascendency of psychopharmacology is not the only reason for this striking shift in therapeutic practice and research. The mental hospitals that once sup-ported psychoanalytically informed treatment and research are either gone, as is the case with Chestnut Lodge, which closed in 2008 as a consequence of the disastrous lawsuit brought by a patient who was deprived of drug treatment, or have transformed their understanding and treatment of psychosis from one that is psychoanalytically informed to one based on the medical model. This has been the case with McLean Hospital, where I spent the years in which I did much of the work reported in this and my 1993 books. During the half-century prior to 2000 there were still large numbers of schizophrenic persons in state hospitals that offered little in the way of treatment or else had been discharged and were in rehabilitation programs so it was possible to study the more or less untreated course of the illness. And there were others that had the opportunity for psychodynamically informed intervention. Since the turn of the century the acceptable treatment of schizophrenia (and severe psychotic personality disorders) is drugs to the point of behavior and mind control and then rapid discharge into the community, hence it makes a kind of sense, when asking the question about treatment efficacy, to study the relative efficacy of the various medications. Finally, as will become clearer when I describe treatment with a psychoanalytic model, the rock stars or gurus of psychoanalytic treatment, who worked within the walls of the psychoanalytically informed mental hospitals of yesteryear – persons like Frieda Fromm-Reichmann and Harold Searles at Chestnut Lodge, my mentor Elvin Semrad at the Massachusetts Mental Health Center, Otto Will at Austen Riggs, and the Menninger brothers at the old Menninger Clinic in Topeka, Alfred Stanton at McLean, and others, are dead. As I describe subsequently, much of the early work necessary to contain the acute schizophrenic experience and establish a therapeutic relationship requires a holding institution, most of the people trained by these luminaries have turned their talents to other kinds of work leaving an abandoned ship, as it were, with at best a skeleton crew.

All studies of psychoanalytically informed treatment of severe psychosis report relatively high failure rates or limited success, depending upon how you look at it. Before passing judgments on the utility of the therapy itself it is important to take into account that schizophrenia is the most severe of the mental illnesses, and if one looks at analogous medical illnesses like cancer or other severe conditions perhaps a modest success rate is the best that can realistically be expected.

In my 1993 book on schizophrenia I summarized my own experience working with schizophrenic and other psychotic persons, much of it based in my work at McLean Hospital during the last half of the 20th century. It includes lengthy detailed reports of therapy with five patients, from start to finish. Of 18 schizophrenic patients I had treated I concluded four had undergone prolonged evaluations that proved them to be unsuitable for intensive analytic treatment. Of the remaining 14 who were in treatment for more than one year, eight completed treatment with good to excellent results after an average of six years, and six were failures. The five patients whose therapies I summarized in the book at great length included two failures, and three outcomes that were in varying degrees quite positive. As an interesting footnote, the two failed cases were included in the studies by Stanton and Gunderson reported above, apparently comprising 10% of their insight-oriented (EIO) therapy group. One was Rachel, the young woman whose story I summarized in Chapter 8. The more she seemed to be making progress and showing that she had a mind and opinions of her own the more her father seemed to be threatened, and began to undercut our work. He finally persuaded her to leave the hospital and her therapy. I have written about my subsequent experience with particular patients elsewhere, for example 2003, 2011, 2012, and 2018. I summarize one of these treatments at the conclusion of this chapter and present another in detail in Chapter 16.

I have made no attempt to cumulate and report my experience working with persons with psychotic personality disorder. Some of them (Jane, Jacob, Lisabeth, and Charles) contributed essays about their experience with the language of primordial consciousness to my 2018 book, from which I have included excerpts in prior chapters. Based on their essays all of them believe that their lives are vastly improved as the consequence of treatment.

In Chapters 13 and 14 I summarize my understanding of what constitutes the psychoanalytic therapy of psychosis and I outline the criteria by which I determine success or failure. One of the most obvious of these is the capacity to terminate therapy and lead a reasonably satisfying independent life. In this regard it has been my impression, paradoxically in the light of severity of illness, that it may be more difficult to conclude treatment with persons suffering from psychotic personality disorder than with schizophrenic persons. Schizophrenic persons enter treatment after total cataclysmic failure of life adaptation, in most instances requiring hospitalization. The breakdown occurs around the second separation stage, at which time transition out of the family and construction of an adult identity usually occurs. If successful, the therapy assists them to form a self that can live independently for the first time.

In contrast, persons with psychotic personalities have often made what appears on the surface, to those who do not look deeply, to be a successful life adjustment with regard to work and relationships, albeit one based on a false-self organization. Therapy requires recognition that, however socially successful and constructive they have seemed to others, their achievements have not been rooted in a knowledge of their emotional core and an associated attention to their real human needs. Yet they have often formed a network of relationships and activities that are difficult to change, because they involve others who have no comprehension of how disturbed they have been, and see them not only as normal, but as very accomplished individuals. Family and friends often not only find it incomprehensible that the person needs therapy to begin with, but may believe the therapist is actually being destructive.

13

PSYCHOANALYTIC THERAPY OF PSYCHOSIS

Transforming primordial conscious mentation into reflective representational thought

As I described in Part II there is a disturbing similarity between the assumptions of the medical model and those of most contemporary psychoanalytic approaches to psychosis. Psychoanalytic therapy of psychosis does not have to be limited by the same flawed dehumanizing assumptions that the medical model is based upon, that psychotic persons are constitutionally different from others. This assumption is reflected in two of Freud's models, that a schizophrenic person is unable to form a meaningful relationship, and is not psychically strong enough to attain and sustain a normal/neurotic personality organization. The model I have proposed is not limited in this way. It is based on a different assumption, namely that the psychotic person has been formed by forces earlier in the developmental process and different from those that lead to neurosis, and that a therapeutic process is required that takes cognizance of this difference.

The therapeutic process

The theoretical goal of effective psychoanalytic therapy of psychosis is to promote, through analysis of transference and reconstruction of early attachment problems, differentiation of self from other and integration of externalized mental content into construction of a separate independent self that is capable of experiencing intrapsychic conflict. The object of therapy, to paraphrase Freud, is that where the undifferentiated unintegrated state of primordial consciousness was, there reflective representational thought shall be. Reflective thought implies the capacity for choice, awareness of alternatives that do not exist for the undifferentiated mind. Resolution of problems from the attachment phase leads to gradual replacement of inconstant affect-driven imagery, somatization, and impulsive action with mental representation, awareness of distinctions, and reflection about choice. The goal is to convert fragmentary contradictory mental states into intrapsychic conflict and to create a cohesive self that is able to recognize that awareness of conflict enables awareness that there are potential choices. With the ability to differentiate time past (memory), present, and future (consequences), the thoughtful mind can make choices between behavior resulting from the destructive perpetuation of primordial mentation and behavior based on caring and reflective thought. In so doing the paralysis resulting from a mind immobilized by simultaneous dissociated contradictory ideation can gradually be replaced by the sense of direction and goals that enables growth. With that comes the capacity to lead a psychologically as well as functionally separate individuated life.

The remembered and reconstructed past

Despite the fact that the repetition compulsion concept is one of Freud's signal accomplishments, the role of retrieval of actual and reconstructed memory in psychoanalytic therapy is controversial. It is even more so in the treatment of psychotic patients, for whom distinctions between memory and fantasy are even more confusing than with neurotic individuals. Of course because of irreducible subjectivity there is no such thing as veridical memory. All memories are reconstructions. However, there is a difference between what we ordinarily think of as memory, which is couched in reflective representational thought and distinguishes between times present and past, and repetition, which takes the form of mental and behavioral sequences in which the person acts in primordial conscious mentation as though he or she were in some earlier inarticulate time. In the throes of repetition the person is in a sense neither here or there. Unlike analysis with a neurotic person, uncovering salient early memories with a psychotic person is for the most part impossible because the mother tongue of primordial consciousness in which the experiences were encoded is somatic, enactive, imagistic, undifferentiated, and unintegrated. Because psychotic persons lack the capacity for reflection and representation they cannot differentiate past from present. As a result, the person cannot really tell the analyst about what happened. Indeed, he or she may literally have no idea, as witness Jane, who could not "remember" her father's repeated sexual abuse until several years into her therapy.

Retrieving thoughtful memories where possible and reconstructing ones from primordial conscious mentation where it is not are essential aspects of helping the patient to understand that the same behavior that is "unreasonable," inappropriate, and maladaptive in the present, was understandable and adaptive in the infantile and childish context in which it originated. The process of reconstruction involves psychological detective work translating diffuse poorly understood affects, body sensations, gestures, facial expressions, and enactments in the transference and outside of therapy sessions into reflective representational thought that can be talked about and communicated.

A striking example of this process can be found in my work with Jane, who was totally amnesic for key events in her childhood, such as her father's regular sexual abuse dating from when she was very small. Over the course of some years we gradually constructed, through the process I described, first the likelihood and then the certainty of these events and then used the data to comprehend the meaning of some of her peculiar behavior and delusional beliefs in the present. Vivid images that seem to be about the past that some persons may have – Jane did not – can pose a different kind of problem because they may be confused with memories, particularly when they appear to be vivid snapshots of disturbing childhood events. However, they are not associated with identifiable emotions or integrated into the patterns of thoughtful understanding that constitute true memories. One can readily be fooled as I was, in the early stages of working with Jacob. He had many images of destructive scenes from childhood involving his mother's behavior toward him. They had the vividness of photographs, and they were stereotypic in the sense he often returned to them. At first I assumed they were memories and put their obvious meaning, as examples of parental abuse, into words, and speculated that he must be angry. He would become furious at me, for not only was he unaware of having any such emotion, he actually insisted that he loved his mother and she loved him. After lengthy arduous work he eventually began to reconstruct this affectless imagery in reflective representational thought, convert his hitherto inchoate affects and somatic sensations into emotions, increasingly differentiate himself from me, and recognize more about his rage at his mother so that he could maintain a sense of self able to distinguish past from present, and self from other.

The process of therapy

The fact that the goals of treatment of a psychotic individual and the methodology necessary to achieve them are different from those with a neurotic person does not mean the treatment is not psychoanalytic, because it is incorrect to assume that psychoanalytic therapy is isomorphic with the treatment of neurosis. Psychoanalysis is a psychological theory of mind and a method of treatment based on in depth understanding of the workings of the minds of people in emotional distress. It need not be limited to the theory of neurosis or the particular methodology that has proven effective in bringing to consciousness repressed conflict. With a neurotic person one can assume the presence of unconscious conflicts whose existence can be uncovered so that they can be resolved with constructive choices through the medium of transference analysis using free association along with interpretation of defenses and resistances. The mind of a psychotic person, by contrast, is not integrated. It is dissociated, split. It is not differentiated psychologically from the mind of the therapist, so that aspects of self are perceived and responded to as though they were "out there." In other words, reality testing is impaired; not in the sense of inability to make formal distinctions, but in the psychological sense of understanding their significance. It is a mind of belief and enactment in which there are no real choices.

Some of the psychoanalytic preoccupation with proper technique is the product of the shockwaves that emanated from Freud's remarkable discoveries of the value of the arrangement whereby the analysts sits behind a couch with a supine patient, and the associated technique whereby the patient attempts to report everything that comes to mind without censorship. These arrangements are not only not suitable for work with psychotic persons, they can actually be destructive and regressive. This may be responsible for the conviction of many ego psychologists of 75 years ago that one should not take a person with "ego weakness" and psychotic vulnerability into psychoanalysis. The couch arrangement places the patient out of potentially reality-orienting sensory contact with the analyst and encourages emergence of fragmenting centrifugal internal processes. Moreover, it sets the stage for a relationship between helpless compliance and authority rather than one that encourages a kind of caring collaboration. Free association, another icon of technique with neurotic individuals, encourages the centrifugal forces that are already operative with a person whose mind is already unintegrated. The use of these techniques is a major source of the regressions the ego psychologists feared, and the stalemates, all of which have mistakenly been blamed on the illness process and the so-called "weak ego," when in fact they are at least in part iatrogenic.

In the case of psychotic personalities the results of standard technique and failure to recognize the presence and particular requirements of primordial consciousness may also support disintegration that takes the form of analysis with the false self. It is especially easy to mistake a part for the whole when dealing with a psychotic personality who presents with a history of considerable accomplishment and may have many friends and colleagues who are convinced he or she is not only normal but unusually mature. These well-meaning individuals provide reinforcement of the false self in a way that can be directly contradictory to the approach of the analyst, who sees more deeply into the dissociated "true self" and whose goal is integration. The result is a conflict in the patient's life in which these "others" express for the patient some of the hostility the patient cannot express directly to the therapist. This process may confuse the therapist as well, because real people in the patient's life, along with the patients themselves, may be convinced that therapy is not necessary and that the therapist is exploiting the patient's gullibility for purposes of his or her own. The false self is not an edifice that can be built upon, as it is not integrated with core emotional awareness but is designed to conceal emotions. Charles' considerable early success as an artist involved regression; working in a darkened studio on repetitive images that repeated disturbed mental states related to his childhood. Lisabeth's rise to prominence as organizer and leader in her field was associated with the need to conceal her belief she was worthless along with the paranoid conviction that people would soon discover what a terrible person she "really" was and reject her. The supposedly terrible part eventually turned out to be her very human emotions, caring, anger, fear, and more, which as a child she had been led to believe were unacceptable.

The transferences characteristic of the first mind of primordial consciousness are complex as they involve enactment, the belief or conviction of reality rather than that they represent thoughts or ideas to reflect about. They fail to differentiate self from other. The negative or dysphoric aspects of the patient of which the patient is unaware are believed to originate in the analyst as angry or rejecting, uncaring attitudes toward the patient. In other words, the patient does not recognize and own an integrated sense of self. The patient experiences vague dysphoric affective states such as anxiety or dread, along with somatic upset such as gastrointestinal distresss, rather than emotions of anger, fear, hopelessness, despair, and the like. The analyst is made to feel what the patient is unable to acknowledge and think about.

A simple example in a non-clinical context is how President Donald Trump characteristically accuses others of attacking and persecuting him and falsifying reality in order to do so at the same time there is abundant consensual reality these are ways in which he is behaving toward others while believing he is being caring. Kleinians call this process projective identification and consider it a defense against rage that is present at birth. However, I look upon it as part of primordial conscious mentation that interprets pathological experiences in the attachment–separation phase in an unintegrated and undifferentiated manner that is incompatible with the experience of intrapsychic conflict and the ability to initiate defensive operations.

Psychotic transferences are fraught with complexity. The misidentified aspects of the patient's self may be fragments of merged identity (not identification) made in the undifferentiated stage of infancy with a hurtful parent, and other aspects may involve infantile responses to the bad parent. Hence the therapist may find that the patient is treating him or her like the parent acted toward the patient in childhood and "making" the analyst feel the helpless, powerless feelings of despair and rage that the patient is unable to integrate and represent in thoughtful language. If some of these principles can be kept in mind during the picture-puzzle-like process of decoding the transference, what is eventually reconstructed in the course of the analysis is an integrated plausible version of the patient's painful childhood that includes both how the parents treated the child and how the child, in turn, achieved a kind of merged identity with the parent that include parental attack on and rejection of the patient's nascent self, as well as destructive enactment of parent-like behavior toward the analyst. Rage and rejection are predominant features, and I think of it as a confused survival strategy by which the patient survives what might have been lethal attacks on the self by directing aspects of parental attitudes toward others. Examples are provided in Chapter 15.

Talking to patients in the language of reflective representational (symbolic, metaphoric, analogical) thought without first recognizing and dealing with the primordial mentation is problematic. Kleinians tend to interpret *phantasies*, the equivalent of primordial mental activity, in the symbolic language of *fantasy*. They talk in the language of animated body parts, parts of objects, rage, and defense, without first recognizing that the patients are speaking in the language of primordial consciousness and teaching them to translate. This is what some critics have referred to as teaching patients a mad language. The result is like the proverbial two ships passing in the night, and as Kleinians tend to present inter-pretations with authority, the result is likely to be bafflement, anger, and a sense of being misunderstood, or worse, mindless sycophantic compliance.

The approach that leads to exploration that is every bit as deep and meaning-ful as in an "ordinary" analysis requires the use of face to face eye contact and dialectical holding through interchanges designed to track salient affective path-ways and continually clarify their meaning. In the course of this holding process, affects and somatic sensations are translated into named emotions and related thoughts, and hitherto dissociated or contradictory aspects of self can be identi-fied. This process of achieving mutual understanding needs to occur before any interpretation is possible. Examples from my patients' essays are provided in Chapter 15. Unfortunately it has been commonplace to label interpersonally active cognitively oriented methodology, such as this, used with psychotic per-sons "parameters," after Kurt Eissler. The implication is that if the classical approach, in which the analyst sits behind the patient and encourages and inter-prets "free" associations and resistances, is not enough, the result is an inferior product that is not psychoanalysis. This is yet another reflection of the con-stricted equation of psychoanalysis with neurosis.

Stages of therapy with schizophrenic persons and psychotic personalities

Freud was not entirely wrong in believing that schizophrenic persons are unable to form a working relationship with the analyst. When psychotic individuals seek out-patient therapy voluntarily, usually with the belief they are being perse-cuted by delusional and hallucinatory forces, they are usually on medication or want medication because they have been led to believe they have an organic illness and that is the correct treatment. As I described in the preceding chapter they are not emotionally motivated to form a working relationship. More com-monly, they come to attention because of acute symptoms and destructive behavior requiring institutional care. Nowadays they are likely to be hospitalized in a hospital where treatment is driven by the medical model. The most common course is described in Chapter 11 on the medical model.

What follows is the sequence of events that might have occurred in the mid-20th century in the era when there were psychoanalytically oriented hospitals such as the McLean Hospital where I worked. I have extrapolated these stages from my personal experience. Therapy commences with two solipsistic phases prior to the acquisition of sufficient representational thought to enable a mutu-ally reflective collaboration. The first solipsistic stage unfolds during the initial acutely schizophrenic break. The patient is unable to differentiate others as sep-arate individuals, so the therapist is either ignored or talked at as a non-specific element of the patient's bizarre and often dangerous mental furniture. The patient might as well be talking to him-/herself, and in the case of major delusions and hallucinations, as I describe in the case of Sara in Chapter 16, that is exactly what happens. Were it not for external containment or coercion the two would not even be sitting in the same room. As a matter of fact, if circumstances permit, the patient might not choose to remain in the room with the therapist for long.

What little motivation exists for engagement in this first phase has to do with the wish to be free of symptomatic distress – to get away from the voices and delusional and hallucinatory dangers that threaten from without, and that may not be distinguished from the person of the therapist. One common mistake of therapists is to believe that the state of acute distress in which the patient is actually trying to flee from his or her self is as emotionally terrible as it seems. It is important to realize the mental state the patient is trying to flee from is nothing more than elements of the patient's own mind too painful to thoughtfully conceptualize. On innumerable occasions patients who have graduated into more collaborative phases of treatment have told me that the psychological pain required to bear the emotions and related concerns they have come to be aware of is far worse than the pain of the acute illness. After all, the unconscious function of the symptoms is to produce a kind of narcosis by making internal distress and danger into something external that can, in a sense, be escaped from.

During this stage comprising efforts to escape from self and from the attention to self that the therapist tries to provide the patient may be overtly out of control and destructive, requiring external care, containment, and direction. In the acute stage this usually includes, in addition to hospitalization, restraints of some sort. In the days prior to medication these were physical. From that era, with rare exceptions, only seclusion in a "quiet room" remains. Modern psychiatry has substituted chemical restraint in the form of medication. If there is to be any chance for therapeutic engagement it is essential that the dose be carefully titrated so as not to "tranquillize" the person so much that all distress, and hence motivation to seek help, is removed. Then the staff needs to make clear that the route for help and change has got to be talking with the therapist.

Unfortunately most hospitals, operating according to the medical model, constrained by the cost-cutting demands of third party payers and lacking facilities for more than brief treatment, are unable to provide such care and instead rely on heavy doses of medication to tranquillize patients and render them more socially compliant so they can rapidly be discharged and returned to the community. As they have little understanding of the potential of psychotherapy they substitute "common sense" advice based on what they see as the person's coping strengths. It often takes the form of reinforcing elements of a false self and promoting further disintegration by encouraging the person to suppress and alienate his or her self from the content of delusions and hallucinations.

Difficult as it is to provide the help and containment that is the necessary foundation for building a therapy relationship in the hospital during the acute phase, it is even less likely to be possible outside, after patients in the acute stage have been tranquillized and returned to what is thought of as sustaining or rehabilitative treatment in the community. By that time schizophrenic patients are heavily medicated and not in sufficient distress to seek psychological help. Given the option of bearing and talking about emotional distress and turning to psychotropic medications, which rapidly become habituating or psychologically addicting, few are willing to make the transition, as I illustrated with the case of Josh in Chapter 11.

In the era of psychoanalytically oriented mental hospitals 50–75 years ago some patient–therapist dyads were able to make the transition from the first to the second solipsistic stage. Harold Searles, mistakenly in my opinion, believed this is the first stage and he called it ambivalent symbiosis. At this point the therapist has become an object of interest to the patient, though not one of understanding, and a relationship has begun to develop. During this second solipsistic stage the patient continues to be unable to differentiate the mind of the therapist from unintegrated aspects of self, although there are the beginnings of a sense that the therapist is in some respect different. For the most part the unintegrated undifferentiated affects, somatic sensations, and related ideas are enacted in the form of beliefs about the therapist and others in the environment. During this stage the patient attempts to coerce the therapist to acknowledge the truth of his or her beliefs and to accept ownership of "bad" characteristics as well as to collude in blaming others for similar imagined shortcomings. The therapist who resists this invitation to collude experiences a sense of identity confusion as the patient's assessment does not correspond to his or her own, as well as feelings of rejection, anger, and the urge to attack and reject back. This is what Searles meant when he wrote of being driven crazy.

The danger is that the therapist will succumb either to the urge to fight back and "rationally" reject the patient's beliefs, or else accept them, sometimes with a condescension that might be lost on the patient. The result is a state of collusion in in which the therapist avoids becoming the target of rage and perhaps risking the end of the brief relationship. Some have mis-named this collusion as maintenance of a positive transference. The result is a chronic relationship in which the therapist serves the unconscious function of a receptacle for unprocessed aspects of the patient's mind. The relationship sustains the patient in a way, but at the expense of any growth. If the therapist takes issue, however gently, with some of the patient's beliefs and does not succumb to the collusion the patient may recruit staff and others to believe that the therapist is harming him or her.

Primordial mentation based on lack of differentiation and integration does not cease with the resolution of the second solipsistic phase, but its organization may change. Patients continue to use the therapist as a psychological dumping ground or area for excretion and evacuation of unmetabolized psychological content, usually involving rage and rejection. Another form collusion may take is that the patient may tell others such as hospital staff how wonderful the therapist is, at the same time that the patient continues to be destructive and blaming of others, so that staff get the impression the patient is not changing and the therapy is not working.

I described some of these phenomena with my patient Caroline (2011, 2018). During the second solipsistic stage of her therapy in the hospital she actually told ward staff I had been hitting her, and was so convincing about this and other things she said about me that she actually turned some staff against me. As time went on and after she was discharged she repeatedly made rage-filled accusations against people in her life "out there" that were transparent examples of aspects of herself she refused to own. And while she kept telling others in her life, including family members, what a great therapist I was, she behaved in a way that made clear to them how "crazy" she was, convincing them I was a poor therapist who was not helping her and just seeing her for money. In this way she incited them to act out the rage at me she could not express directly, and she convinced others to believe that because of her presumed disability she was not responsible for her actions. The case of Sara, in Chapter 16, is a good example of the kinds of disintegrated undifferentiated confusion patients are able to induce both in the therapist and members of hospital staff.

In subsequent phases of treatment it may become evident that the patient, who has not psychologically separated from the primary caregiver and exists in a state of identity (not identification) with that person, is doing to the therapist a version of what was done to him or her during the attachment stage. It is the task of the therapist to survive these assaults, realize what they make him or her feel, and use this as a way to understand what iI must have been like for the patient to receive such treatment, especially as it occurred in a helpless state of childhood dependency. The therapist must demonstrate to the patient that it is possible to survive such attacks and metabolize them into reflective thought that involves recognizing and bearing the hitherto unbearable emotions they elicited.

During this difficult stage it is imperative that the therapist maintain as calm and exploratory attitude as possible. The therapist needs to be empathic with the patient's suffering without losing a sense of separate identity. If the therapist colludes and merges with the patient's unintegrated undifferentiated mind, either by fighting back or complying, effective therapy will end, either overtly or psychologically.

I have concentrated on work with schizophrenic persons. Work with persons with psychotic personality organization usually begins differently, when a person aware of distress and the need for help consults the therapist. In terms of the stages outlined above, the relationship begins in the second solipsistic stage, complicated or confused by the patient's efforts to engage the therapist, as he or she has done with others, with a false self, not infrequently one that is very impressive and accomplished.

If the therapy progresses and negotiates some of the pitfalls and obstacles I have enumerated, it may reach perhaps the most difficult and prolonged phase, that of choice. The patient will have achieved sufficient fluency in reflective representational thought to become aware that his or her mind can work in two different ways, and that one path involves caring and mental work whereas the other does not. It takes willingness to represent and bear the emotional pain related to childhood hurts as well as lost life consequent to the patient's adult behavior, willingness to move beyond mental passivity, endless indecision, and contradiction, and then to make choices and decisions and be prepared to live with the consequences. Although patients may become aware of the self-destruction that resulted from forced identity with destructive parents, there is an often irresistible lure to not having to work to bear emotional pain, control themselves, care, and make difficult choices in life. Some people opt not to do the work and to remain in a magical delusional world, as my patient Rachel did when confronted with the need to decide between her father's way and the highway, and others do not.

Criteria of successful treatment and outcome

The discussion of therapeutic outcome studies in Chapter 12 highlighted but did little to clarify the critical question, what are the criteria of a successful treatment outcome. Extrapolating from the preceding discussion of the process and stages of psychoanalytic therapy of psychosis I would like to summarize my own views. Success can be defined in two parts: intrapsychic change in personality structure and dynamics, and life changes as a consequence.

The intrapsychic changes can be assessed on the same axes of differentiation and integration that I have repeated throughout the book. To paraphrase Freud, where primordial conscious mentation was, reflective representational thought shall be. This requires resolution of the original inability to separate from the pathological identity with the primary parent. This involves recognition of the separateness and autonomy of self from others and the courage to acknowledge and stand up for one's emotional needs. The integrated self is capable of experiencing intrapsychic conflict and resolving it by making reasoned decisions. One of the basic conflicts of a psychotic person involves the urge to regress to the mindless narcotic state where the work of differentiation, integration, and bearing strong emotions and dealing with conflicts is avoided by compensatory delusional beliefs.

Since mind is not a disembodied entity separate from actions and their consequences, part of how the intrapsychic changes I summarized above are assessed is through related changes in the person's life. The changes, as many before me have noted, include the ability to love and to work. The development of capacity to care involves formation of relationships, both friendships and intimate family. The other pole of a meaningful life involves having satisfying goals and activities and the ability to concentrate and pursue them. In other words, if we assume the schizophrenic diathesis is not basically bio-genetic, the same criteria can be applied as one would to any psychotherapy. The differences relate mostly to inevitable losses related to the fact that the person has not been able to go through normal developmental stages at the appropriate times and needs to construct a meaningful life in a different way, including taking into account in a thoughtful way the limitations early attachment trauma may impose on such things as the development of intimacy. The patient essays that make up Chapter 15 and the case of Sara in Chapter 16 illustrate this. For example, Charles found himself in his mid-60s at a stage of development with regard to relationships analogous to adolescents beginning to explore relationships. At the same time he realized some of his vulnerabilities getting close to women. But he had a number of friends, a deep bond with his son, and he enjoyed dating.

14

QUALITIES OF A PSYCHOANALYTIC THERAPIST OF PSYCHOSIS

Freud believed that schizophrenic persons are genetically impaired in a way that renders them incapable of forming a human relationship. Beginning with Sullivan, a number of therapists with varying degrees of interest and expertise in psychoanalysis took his assertion as a challenge and set out to demonstrate it is possible to make a relationship with such persons. Out of this matrix arose the sense that such persons were performing a Herculean task. Thus arose the folklore of the super-therapist; the idea that the "average analyst" is incapable of treating a schizophrenic person, and success is an extraordinary achievement beyond the capacity of most of us.

Ironically, important as the therapist is, possibly the ingredient most essential for establishing a therapeutic relationship is not the personality of the therapist, but the provision of a supportive environment. It is the containing, holding environment that provides the care and direction the patient is unable to provide for him- or herself in the early stages of treatment until an alliance with the therapist can be established. It is also ironic that it is the very hospital settings that provided the holding environment on which the therapist depended in order to engage the patient – places like Chestnut Lodge, Massachusetts Mental Health Center, McLean Hospital, Menninger Clinic, Sheppard Pratt – that gave birth half a century ago to the myth of the super-therapist. They generated the holding environments that enabled such therapeutic engagements to develop in the first place. As these places have been either phased out of existence entirely, or transformed into hospitals that operate according to the medical model, it has become very unusual for individual therapists, however gifted, to engage in mutative treatment with schizophrenic persons on an out-patient basis. Some of the therapists who were most successful failed, in my estimation, to give due credit to the holding environment that was so critically essential to their success. During the last half of the 20th century and with the help of movies and novels there was a kind of social romance between psychoanalysis as it was publicly depicted and the severe psychoses. A generation of therapists who treated hospitalized psychotic persons achieved and in a number of instances seemed to thrive on their iconic cultural status, taking advantage of invitations that came with it to demonstrate to admiring student audiences at conferences their skill engaging schizophrenic persons. Some wrote books advertising their special status, for example the volume edited by Boyer and Giovacchini titled *Master Clinicians on Treating the Regressed Patient* (1990).

Chestnut Lodge in the era of Frieda Fromm-Reichmann and Harold Searles was the Eden that spawned these superstar fantasies. As I alluded to earlier, it closed as the consequence of a 1969 lawsuit by a former patient whose condition had progressively deteriorated as the result of the extreme psychoanalytic position of the hospital that precluded prescribing medication. Fromm-Reichmann, the luminary of the hospital, was divorced and did not have children of her own. She was very invested in her ability to provide her young patients with what, in her opinion, others whom she deemed deficient had failed to give them. She coined the unfortunate term "schizophrenogenic mother" (1948, p. 265) which launched an era of mother blaming and pathologizing of women who had been fortunate to have children but did not rear them according to her standards. But it was not just mothers toward whom she was moralistic and blaming. Comments in 1952 about therapists who cannot form relationships with schizophrenic persons are distinctly patronizing. She describes the schizophrenic as a person with very special insight into him- or herself and, without actually saying so, implies that the therapist who is mature, smart, and sensible enough to understand one is equally special. In contrast, if the relationship fails to develop, it must be because of deficiencies in the therapist. "Psychiatrists can take it for granted now that in principle a working doctor-patient relationship can be established with the schizophrenic patient. If and when this seems impossible it is due to the doctor's personal difficulties" (1952, p. 91), not to the patient's psychopathology. She lists in detail all the "problems" most psychiatrists may have that render them unsuitable to the task, and concludes "the psychiatrist should admit to himself that – in his present state of personality development – he is not equal to coping with schizophrenics, if there is a danger of his harming them with his own anxieties" (1952, p. 94). In other words, the problems are not those of the schizophrenic, but of the (other) psychiatrists who attempt to relate to them. Such views have had the unfortunate effect of intimidating persons contemplating such work to begin with, and leading others to believe they had to slavishly imitate the styles of their idols. Fromm-Reichmann was apparently a critical teacher and supervisor as well, and her own teacher, Harry Stack Sullivan, was said to be extremely caustic, at times to the point of sadism (Gibson, 1989).

What are some of the qualities that make a good therapist for psychotic individuals? I do not believe it is necessary to have extraordinary abilities in order to work productively with a schizophrenic person. Some reasonably mature and thoughtful human skills will do. For example, the therapist must be able to empathize with the patient's suffering, while maintaining a sense of personal separateness. This optimal distance protects the therapist from succumbing to an urge to feel responsible for the person that could lead to loss of boundaries, enmeshment in aspects of his or her unintegrated undifferentiated mind, and participation in destructive enactments. A sense of curiosity about the lives and worldviews of others that can be satisfied by ever growing knowledge of the depths of the patient's personality and by the increments of change that accompany it is very important as well. It is necessary to have a mind that can creatively marry one's own unique personality qualities with a knowledge of theory that is not rigid and formulaic in order to create a unique kind of relationship. Treating a schizophrenic person – for that matter anyone with significant problems – is not just a matter of common sense. Theory can be used to enrich an interaction or misused as a distracting third, a set of rules and abstractions that distance oneself from the immediacy of a human interaction.

As the purpose of therapy is to help the patient replace inappropriate use of primordial conscious mentation with reflective representational thought, it is critically important that the therapist be able to use the intense transferences and the pressures to gratify unsatisfied needs of psychotic persons as an opportunity for self-analysis and self-examination. Perhaps even more than with work with less disturbed persons the interaction with psychotic individuals can be a welcome opportunity to continue one's self-analysis at the same time that one is helping the patient to do likewise.

It is commonly supposed that because progress is slow the work is boring and requires superhuman patience. I find the work absorbing and challenging. What keeps me involved is a combination of curiosity about each person's unique worldview, how it has developed, and what it takes to help the patient to realize it is anachronistic and there is a need to change it. There is always something new, unexpected, and fascinating to be discovered. When I am not learning more about the patient I am often learning more about myself as the partner in a unique relationship. One of the reasons for the belief that the work requires extraordinary patience may be that there are often lengthy periods of silence and withholding, which usually represent the patient's way of annihilating the therapist. I have come to recognize this when I struggle in sessions to remain awake. Although it takes patience of a kind, such happenings are fruitful opportunities to learn more about the patient and about oneself.

What are some of the aspects of my own personality and style that help me do this work? For one thing, I am able to maintain a sense of personal boundaries and of who I am as a separate person in the face of intense pressure emanating from my patients' inarticulate, often bizarre, undifferentiated demands and rages. I find myself very confused at times, struggling with problems of integration and differentiation (who do I believe I am in relation to who and what the patient believes I am) and wondering what is real, as the case of Sara in Chapter 16 illustrates. However, there was only one time in my career, when I was under a great deal of personal stress, that I felt frightened when working with some of my more disturbed patients that I was losing my sense of separate identity.

Early in my career I believed that my medical training was of unique value, for it taught me a sense of life and death responsibility that my non-medical colleagues lacked. Psychotic persons, especially on the more severe end of the spectrum, are self-destructive and clearly unable to take care of themselves, unlike the "worried well" who bring their distress to the consulting room but are then able to leave at the end of an hour and take care of themselves between appointments. I have come to believe that such training has its downside as well, for in order for therapy to be successful the patient has to be able to separate from a caregiver and assume responsibility for his or her life. Establishing boundaries and setting limits in the therapeutic situation is an important part of bringing this about.

In the delimited setting of my office I am able to tolerate rage directed at me and realize that it is both real and at the same time not really about me at all. And unlike some circumstances in everyday life, when the hostile attacking patient becomes more caring in the course of the treatment I find that I can respond without a sense of holding a grudge. During the years when I was in charge of parts of McLean Hospital that housed extremely disturbed persons I can remember only two times I was actually assaulted, and one of those "only" involved having urine from a container dumped on me through an opening in a quiet room door. I have also discovered that I can sit with someone who is in a rage at me and have a kind of sixth sense about when I am actually in danger, in time to take action.

As psychotic persons lack the capacity for integration, and live in a kind of kaleidoscopic fragmentary mental state, my ability to perceive aspects of mind that are separate but from a broader perspective involve a coherent theme is very important. In other words, the capacity to synthesize is a critical part of helping the patient develop a cohesive sense of self and eventually learn to experience and resolve intrapsychic conflict. At first my patients may be upset when I point out contradictions in their thinking and the isolated fragments of ideas that bear on a common theme, and may get angry and feel that I am distracting them with things that are not important at the moment, but eventually they take this task on for themselves.

Finally, a sense of humor helps. While it is dangerous to assume that patients who are concrete and lack the capacity for symbolization and metaphor can see the humor in a shared moment, sometimes shared laughter, often ironic, is healing, and actually promotes development of the capacity to take distance from one's issues and reflect.

While I have repeatedly objected to the standard medical model practice of drugging patients in order to tranquillize them and eliminate their symptomatic complaints, I believe that medication – use of drugs – is essential in the early stages of treatment with a schizophrenic person. Its purpose is not to tranquillize them. That is the unconscious purpose of psychotic mentation. One of the rueful observations I often share with patients whose therapy is working is the realization that they have been "able" to drug themselves without using narcotics.

The therapeutic purpose of medication is to attain and sustain the optimal state in which the patient is sufficiently distressed to want to talk with a therapist but not so disturbed as to be unable to sit still and try to communicate. Drug treatment and psychoanalytic therapy need not be mutually exclusive somatic or psychological forms of intervention. In psychoanalytic treatment medication is as "psychological" an intervention as any other. Its purpose is to facilitate the treatment process by damping the intensity of painful affects not yet identified and represented, contextualized, and psychologically controlled, so that psychoanalytic exploration can continue. The risk is to over-medicate to the point of narcosis, or to medicate for too long, leading to the false sense there is no distress and nothing to work on.

A growing and I think lamentable trend among analysts is to see drug therapy and analytic therapy as parallel therapies and to believe that a psychoanalytic result can be achieved while a person also takes psychotropic medication. This occurs mostly when attempting to treat disturbed, probably psychotic, persons and is an outgrowth of the belief that psychosis represents an inherent irremediable deficiency in the capacity to attain and sustain a neurotic mental organization. This trend has spread in recent years to the analysis of non-psychotic persons as well. An outcome cannot be considered truly successful unless the patient eventually assumes the psychological role – control, regulation, modulation of affects – that the drug played. This integrative process often occurs over a lengthy period of time involving psychological work and experimentation, in the course of which medication is used, then stopped, analysis is done on the role it played, and the process continued as a learning experience until the patient can take over. It was 28 years before Caroline, who was heavily medicated when I met her and for some years subsequent, to be able to relinquish lithium, the last of her medications, and assume the self-control function it had been serving. The case of Sara, in Chapter 16, illustrates this gradual process of psychological takeover of the functions formerly performed by drugs.

15

PATIENTS WRITE ABOUT THEIR THERAPY

Although my patients whose essay excerpts illustrate preceding chapters were not asked to write about their therapy, some of the comments they made are pertinent, and I include them here. The reader might wish to return to the preface to Part III, the short biographies of the persons whose essay excerpts follow, for the context of their remarks. Following the excerpts I present a brief summary of therapy with a young man I shall call Erik.

Jane comments about her therapy:

> When we first started to meet I couldn't imagine having enough to say to fill more than an hour (if that) a week. I had virtually no experience noticing and putting into words my bodily and emotional experience, no experience talking about relationship, and no expectation that I would ever put into words the vivid daydreams (and delusions) that I held. More than not being able to express myself, I also refused to give in to the expectation that I would reveal myself clearly in language. Until you began showing interest in my gestures, I never thought of them as having meaning, only as showing my pathology which was being betrayed even as I tried so hard to pass as normal. Initially, I did not welcome your interest, since I felt like my gestures were "out of control" and I didn't want to acknowledge this. Gradually, I came to be able to receive your interest as, in fact, interest in me, and not an over-focus on an element. It took a very long time for me to come to want to understand myself and thus to tolerate your wanting to as well. I really hated the idea ("your" idea). And then I began to track when I twisted my wrists or put my hands on my neck, etc. (and also when I "froze" at home) and realized that my gestures emerged when I was particularly anxious or threatened by some mental state (whether memory and/or emotion). I began to have

a sense, or to accept your view, that different gestures had specific meanings – and so I began to have a sense that the wrist turning was related to being tied, or held down, for example and to be aware that from an early age my father was silently molesting me, and there was no language for what he was doing or for how it affected me emotionally or bodily.

Here are some of Jacob's observations about his therapy:

> It took many years of therapy before I began to develop real feelings with expressive words, evolving from these largely somatic, imagistic representations, and challenging my overwhelming belief in delusions. Over the years, Dr. Robbins provided consistent reminders about my lack of feelings and the abundance of images in their place. I remember many sessions where Dr. Robbins would say: "Do you feel any anger?" or "Are you aware of any feelings"? The bottom line was that I was unable to hold any significant feelings in my mind. This included social self-control road signs such as shame and guilt, as well as basic feelings such as caring, loving, and rage. It took repeated reminders by Dr. Robbins that I was more than bypassing these feelings. For example, Dr. Robbins again and again took great pains to show that my images of shit and killing needed to be moved up to the level of feelings, like real rage. Needless to say these reminders occurred over and over again, often unheard. Now, looking back, I can see that without feelings, any hope of integration was totally impossible. The evolution of images to feelings, and then integration is a long and arduous process. I can see that without the repeated support and reminders of Dr. Robbins to develop feelings, I would have been trapped in a mindless world of brittle images. I want to explain how Dr. Robbins and I were able to transform the image of somatic union with my mother via her breast into something positive in my development. First Dr. Robbins understood and discussed this in a very serious way. He helped me to see intellectually that this image [Jacob's somatic delusion he had a breast, associated with efforts to brush it off with his hand] was a fusion of myself and my mother. In a real sense, I began learning a new language for this image. Words were used to describe and understand this image. I'd like to say that it was the two of us, myself and Dr. Robbins, who created the goal of translating these images into real feelings. For most of my therapy, it was only Dr. Robbins, while I continued to act out the feelings with expression of primitive images. In a real sense, I am involved with Dr. Robbins in understanding my past with grief, the sadness of knowing I was not loved. It has been hard for me to drop my belief that I am a defective person. I have hung on to that belief with the image of me as a "little brown Jewish boy." Dr. Robbins and I have spent much time in understanding this image: a vulnerable (Jewish) little boy who is brown (shit). Moving from this belief to a caring

consideration of who I really am is ongoing work. Seeing the real feelings I have, like the fear of being alone (on my own), owning up to my guilt, understanding and holding the pain of my behavior in the past, taking responsibility for myself as a separate person is constant work (many times at Dr. Robbins' urging). My conversion from the language of images to one based on feelings, has provided me the real option of being loving. All of the images I have employed, the fused breast, the little brown Jewish boy, and my penis as a sword, have been shallow one dimensional views of myself. With the help of Dr. Robbins, understanding these images has provided me the opportunity to develop real feelings. As a little child, in my relationship with my mother, love was totally absent. Without the foundation of love, images had been my only mode of communication. In fact holding feelings as a separate person has been very difficult for me. But now I have the real alternative of experiencing feelings like pain, joy, guilt, and love. My work in therapy has been to take these feelings and manufacture an individual, separate, and caring self.

Here are Lisabeth's comments about her therapy:

When I told my mother that I was going to begin therapy she responded, "Don't be too dependent; remember your heritage." In retrospect a stunner, although I had no clue at the time. In that one statement she said it all: don't leave me; don't care about anyone else; remember how I have trained you. At the time I was unaware that her comment fed my tightly held mother-crafted belief system that I was never to leave her or care about anyone else. When I began therapy I transferred this way of being to the relationship with Dr. Robbins. I wanted to be his problem. I believed that the more "disturbed" I was the more he would care about me. My identity depended on it, and so did his. I would talk about "us" the patients and "them" the therapeutic community, those who had no problems and got their kicks from ours. Having problems was the ticket to this elite sanctum. If on a given day I did not feel as if I had a problem to talk about I would became intensely anxious. I feared he would kick me out. [When she began to experience caring feelings toward me she told her mother, and her mother responded "Don't worry, that's just transference."] Over time transference, of course, was key in helping Dr. Robbins and me learn about my distorted thinking. Little did my mother know that my nascent caring feelings were not transference – they were the beginnings of separate think, of breaking the destructive bond with mother. Or did she? Perhaps at some level she did know and was threatened, thereby compelling her to disparage my feelings by her comment. In the early years of therapy, my mother and I met together for three sessions with Dr. Robbins. At the beginning of the first session I started to cry. She moved to hug me, which I rejected (I never could stand to have her touch me). Dr. Robbins intervened to ask her why she thought I was crying. She opined that my tears were an expression of my upset about my troubles. On that basis, she had made a move to hug me. In fact, I cried because I was moved by my feelings of caring for Dr. R. It was a powerful moment: the first time in my life that a person was present who was an alternative voice to that of my mother's. The experience was a small lesson in how she thought she knew what I was thinking and feeling, and how I participated by never inquiring into her thought process or expressing feelings of my own. At times I behaved similarly with Dr. Robbins. I would interrupt him before he finished a thought believing I knew what he was going to say or insisting that a fantasy about him was an indisputable fact. In order to exercise on-going control over mother think I must work to bring to my awareness the mental state from which I am acting, speaking, or thinking. Am I acting from my mother's alternative delusional world of non-separateness, or from a world of separate think where people are truly individuated and can enjoy healthy intimacy?

And finally, here are Charles' comments about therapy:

> I became aware of this [that withholding was his way of psychologically annihilating me] through the course of many hours spent in therapy withholding my thoughts and feeling from my therapist, shooting him suspicious dagger glances while believing he was withholding from me. Trying to understand how my un-thought-about responses to these early experiences have entangled themselves in my adult relationships has required being able to define and identify my feelings and the beliefs I formed based on them.

Erik had a severe psychosis that I did not think justified the diagnosis of schizophrenia. He was truly a child of the contemporary drug culture and its basic assumption that whatever one's troubles, drugs, whether prescribed by the doctor or illegal, are the solution. He consulted me at age 21 at the beginning of his sophomore year of college. His destructive history showed little regard for his life, which he told me was meaningless. He was seriously contemplating suicide. He detailed a history of bizarre behavior, hanging out with serious criminals, seriously abusing drugs that he believed revealed to him the truth, and being a drug dealer, since prior to puberty. He had intermittent auditory and visual hallucinations as well as a grandiose delusion that he was the Messiah whose destiny it was to spread the LSD gospel throughout the world, and another delusion that he could actually levitate, like a hovercraft. Multiple therapies since age 10, mostly involving prescription medication, had been of no avail. For two years prior to college he had been confined in a drug detox facility. His psychosis had been partly camouflaged during his growing years by a combination of his parents' denial, even though father was a mental health professional, and belonging to peer groups consisting of kids many of whom were bizarre and antisocial themselves. Parents believed that Erik was exceptional but not that he had serious problems or that there were relevant family problems in his growing years.

When I met him Erik was disheveled and could not sit still. He seemed very intelligent but his speech was disorganized. Try as I might it was difficult to comprehend what he meant, but he assumed I did and should, and he exploded with rage at me when I indicated I didn't and asked him to explain. There were lengthy silences when he claimed to have no thoughts. When we began to discuss anything that seemed meaningful it was dismissed by disparaging laughter. He had difficulty distinguishing the contents of his mind from external reality. He was suspicious and believed that when others, including myself, acted caring, we were untrustworthy pretenders concealing our evil core, and that we were actually trying to take over and destroy his identity.

In striking contrast to how he behaved in the consulting room Erik had always done exceptionally well in school and for many years had kept a diary, played musical instruments, and written poetry. He seemed to have considerable social skills in the form of an effective false self, as well as a network of friends, most of whom were on the social fringe, used drugs heavily, and had serious problems of their own which were evident to me from his descriptions. They formed a community based on a shared belief that they were normal and it was the external world that was crazy. In his later years of college he even received high honors for a thesis on aspects of psychological theory and practice that involved caring and helping people, though he did not believe any of these ideas applied to him.

Over the course of several years we came to understand that his façade and the sense of deadness and meaninglessness that he presented protected him against awareness of an intolerable core sense of hopeless despair, rage, and hatred of people, as well as a belief that he did not deserve to be alive, which seemed to date back to earliest childhood. He repeatedly courted situations of extreme deprivation and potentially lethal consequences both because they were consistent with his self-hatred and also in an effort to break through his sense of deadness and experience being alive.

Our relationship was stormy. He made abusive verbal attacks on me for what he believed were my attacks on him and my failure to understand him. Nonetheless he gradually developed some ability to care and trust, and to bear and think reflectively about his feelings and attitudes. He became less paranoid and more able to differentiate himself from others and to integrate his issues of rage and despair into internal conflict between life and death, hatred and caring. He began to use his social networking skills, intelligence, and expansiveness in the service of constructive goals. Interestingly, one of his first jobs after college was in one of the peer self-help communities I commented on earlier. This one had attained a degree of social legitimacy by having a home and hiring help. It was based on the idea that the residents, some of whom had major psychoses and were out of control, were really normal, perhaps a bit unusual, knew best what was good for them, and only needed a safe place to "do their thing." As Erik began to change, his view of this community and the people who ran it changed from one of agreement and participation to one of criticism and opposition. He pointed out the denial of problems and their unwitting facilitation of the psychotic behavior, and began to advocate limit setting and efforts to explore the psychological meaning of their problems. As a result he became very unpopular and eventually quit the job. He proceeded to develop a longstanding literary interest and initiated a major creative enterprise that involved collaboration with others and brought him considerable recognition in academic and cultural circles. He finished college with distinction and he formed his first close caring relationship with a woman. Therapy concluded after four years because her career took her to another city and they decided to move.

16

THE 11 YEAR TREATMENT OF A CHRONIC PARANOID SCHIZOPHRENIC WOMAN

There are very few detailed reports in the psychoanalytic literature of treatments of psychotic persons from start to finish, and even fewer of failures, as for some reason analysts don't seem to want to admit publicly what is obvious and should be easy to accept, that therapy with persons with such severe conditions often does not work. I presented five such reports, two failures and three with varying degrees of success, in 1993. I am a fast typist, and at the time of the therapy I am about to report I was in the habit of taking detailed notes of sessions in the 10 minute break between patients. This report is the result of successive condensations of these detailed records.

Some years ago I was unexpectedly contacted by Sara, a former patient whose work with me had concluded more than two decades previously. She was passing through the community where I practice and she wanted to say hello and tell me about her subsequent life. Our therapy lasted more than 11 years. The treatment included intermittent hospitalizations at McLean Hospital where I was at that time a Senior Attending Psychiatrist, as well as intermittent and prolonged periods of time on phenothiazine medications. The report that follows is the condensation of detailed process notes I kept after each of our more than 1,100 sessions.

Background

Relevant elements of Sara's history will be presented chronologically as I learned them in the course of our work together. I will only sketch broad outlines here. In addition to what I learned from Sara, her history was obtained from the social worker at the hospital who worked with her mother and from the records of mother's hospitalization during Sara's pre-pubertal years, which I had the unusual opportunity to peruse with her mother's permission.

Sara was the second of four children. She had two older brothers and a sister five years her junior. Her family was wealthy, and traced its aristocratic lineage back many generations. The family prided itself on equating strength and maturity with masculinity and suppression of emotion. Except for Sara's mother there was no family history of mental illness, but given what you will learn about the family's "ability" to deny blatant problems that information may not be accurate. Sara's mother had no career other than raising her children. She was an angry, depressed woman, intermittently suicidal and prone to fits of rage and bizarre behavior, examples of which are elaborated in the pages to come. Mother had several brief mental hospitalizations in the years following Sara's birth, some following suicide attempts. Sara's father was senior partner in an international law firm and spent much of his time travelling. By accounts from Sara and later other family members he was emotionally unavailable to them, and what attention he paid to his children was directed toward doing macho activities with his sons, whereas he left his daughters to fend for themselves. Father's insensitivity was manifest in many ways. For instance Sara recalls his constructing an outdoor swing for the children hung over a large branch overlooking a steep slope. The neighbors would not permit their children to use it because it was so dangerous.

As a child Sara was obviously frightened of her mother, and did her best to be inconspicuous and hide herself from her. She never let mother know when she was hurt or in need. She spent much of her time in the basement of her house, using her father's dangerous tools without instruction or huddling next to the furnace for warmth. When Sara was nine her mother entered McLean Hospital for a two year stay that involved permanent disruption of the nuclear family. There she was diagnosed as a severe borderline personality. Following mother's hospitalization Sara developed magical ritualistic behavior, for example around the number 8, which she eventually told me represented breasts, and she began to hallucinate. Sara's father divorced Sara's mother after her hospitalization, and waged a successful legal battle to gain custody of Sara and her sibs. His attention to his career left him little time to devote to them, however, and he hired a series of caretakers. He remarried a neighbor when Sara was 12. When Sara was 14 he developed a rapidly fatal illness which the children were not told about. Sara was sent abruptly and without explanation to France to live with a male business associate, and only informed when she was summoned home for the funeral. Sara's stepmother was awarded custody, but by that time Sara had begun a regular practice of running away from home, and they had infrequent contact.

Sara would run away from home to skid row areas of cities where she would involve herself with men who abused her sexually in exchange for food and a place to sleep. At age 15 she was arrested and placed in a youth detention center. From there she was transferred to a public mental hospital where she received phenothiazine medication and unsuccessful psychotherapy for six months until she was expelled for abusing drugs. Despite this chaos Sara managed to complete high school with high grades, and over the course of years, punctuated by hospitalizations, to graduate from a good college.

Year one

Sara was 28 when she first came to see me. She was then a patient at a small private hospital in the Boston area, with which I was not affiliated, and to which she had been admitted after having been asked to take a leave of absence from graduate school. She had been told that a condition of her discharge was that she find a therapist. I do not know how she obtained my name but a friend called to make an appointment for her as Sara was too terrified to call me herself. When I met her she was drab, overweight, dressed in baggy clothing and the general impression she conveyed was one of indeterminate gender. Her gaze was vacant, she had a flat whispery voice, made no eye contact, and her discourse was vague. Although she claimed to be nervous she gave little outward evidence. I learned from the hospital psychiatrist that she spent long periods of time huddled in corners, mute and rigid except for bizarre facial expressions, but all Sara told me was that her problem was inability to concentrate and lack of a sense of personal identity. As we talked she reported a sensation that the top of her head was lifting off and she said she was hearing voices that were harassing and frightening her. She said it was difficult to think clearly since thoughts would "short-circuit" and make strange connections so that she could not understand what others were saying or express herself sequentially. After four meetings Sara expressed a wish to work with me. Other than agreeing to my suggestion we meet three times per week we did not discuss much about therapy. In retrospect and in addition to the fact she had difficulty talking with me at all, I had the sense that doing so would have been just so many meaningless words. Shortly thereafter she was discharged from the hospital, she stopped taking the medication she had been given there, and she obtained a menial job.

During our appointments Sara typically sat near the door with her head averted, often with her coat on and purse clutched to her lap; and she often bolted out the door a few minutes early. Her posture was rigid, and her gestures and facial expressions were contorted and contextually inappropriate. She was detached, her voice was flat, whispery, and without affect, and she did not make eye contact. There were long silences sometimes punctuated with sotto voce mocking laughter or muttered curses or gibberish about shapes and patterns. She had auditory and visual hallucinations. She believed bombs were planted in the walls and planes and missiles were about to attack and kill her. Our sessions consisted of a curious triadic relationship among Sara, myself, and a Greek chorus of female voices that terrorized her as they instructed her how to cope with the dangerous world she was in, including her relationship with me, and the horrible consequences that would ensue if she disobeyed them. "They" would require that she deprive herself of food and sleep and undergo various punishments in order to avoid being killed. "They" developed an immediate mistrust and dislike for me and told her they would punish her if she got involved with me because I wanted to kill her. Her thoughts often short-circuited, her sentences fragmented so that they did not make sense. My subjective sense was one of helplessness and defeat, because "they" seemed to control "her" behavior and I was unable to talk to "them" directly. Variants of this behavior recurred, waxed, and waned throughout much of the time I knew her. Occasional astute observations she made and her large vocabulary led me to believe she was unusually intelligent.

Sara was a nocturnal creature. Her admonitory voices would not let her sleep. In the middle of the night she often drove her car long distances following big trucks. She frequented bars, pool halls, and gambling casinos and involved herself in the culture of darkness, warmth, drinking, drugs, loud noise, pimps, prostitution, and abuse, sexual and otherwise. Remarkably, she never became pregnant. Her goal was to prove that no matter what was done to her it did not upset her emotionally. In that way she could believe she was in control and superior to those around her. Her self-destructiveness included depriving herself of sleep and food, smoking heavily, punishing herself, deliberately inducing accidents and injuries and then ignoring the pain and damage. Such attitudes and behaviors were not only of no concern to her, but she was thoroughly convinced that she knew how to take care of herself better than anyone else could. Such activities punctuated our work for many years.

In her previous extensive contacts with psychiatrists she believed she had acted crazy because that was what was expected of her. She was contemptuous because she believed she was successful in fooling them. She soon became frustrated because she felt that unlike others, I gave her little clue about what I wanted from her. However, most of her attention seemed directed toward what "they," her voices, were telling her, and what she was "seeing," about the dangerous world she was in and how to deal with it. Perhaps their major commandment was not to relate to me at all.

After a time there appeared transient indications of a wish to relate to me including brief eye contact and flashes of feeling, consisting of deep sadness and incipient tears, and a rage including wishes to "scream bloody murder" and kill everyone. At such times rather than maintain a continuous train of integrated emotionally based thoughts she told me that her thoughts short-circuited and she sometimes bolted from the office.

In our 14th hour she recounted her first dream: there was a cylindrical eight story building open inside and resembling a great family dining room, with tables and chairs floating around. One false move and one could take a dangerous fall. Her sister was dying. A clown began to entertain everyone and pushed her sister over the edge. At some point, probably subsequently, I learned that "8" had longstanding significance representing breasts.

She missed an appointment and I learned that she had gone to Las Vegas and put herself in dangerous situations. She admitted being angry and wanting to kill me because I had gotten her to like me despite the warning from her voices that I would kill her. Her test in a relationship was whether she thought she could shoot and kill the person; and she acknowledged with obvious reluctance that she would have trouble shooting me. She was afraid that I might die, but if

I did it would be a relief, for then she could go to a gambling establishment lose all her savings, purchase a gun, and kill herself. When she violated the commands of her voices that she was not to sleep more than four hours at night, "they" terrified her the following night with the belief that she had jumped from an airplane and her parachute would not open, and "they" regularly arranged punishments for her after any occasion in which she might be more open and communicative with me.

She had stopped taking medication before coming to see me, so during the 28th hour I prescribed anti-psychotic medication, trifluoperazine. However, it seemed to have no discernible effect. After five months we had our first substantial separation when I took a summer vacation, and despite the fact I gave her a number where she could reach me she decided I was not coming back hence she stopped the medication. She made clear her reluctance to take it and I did not insist she renew the prescription.

There ensued the first of numerous interchanges that challenged my sanity. One day she informed me that she had never really hallucinated and the stories she had been telling me were manifestations of her ability to fool and manipulate people, including "shrinks" for whom she had great contempt. She described how in the past she had played the roles of a heroin addict in withdrawal, a tough street person, a good girl, and a scholar. She seemed sincere and acted more mature and integrated. After a few sessions in which she was able to talk more directly about her struggle against feelings and dependency and there was no sign that she was hallucinating, I felt both pleased and deeply unsettled. How could I have been so gullible? I consulted informally with two colleagues in an effort to make some sense of what was happening, but it did not allay my sense of helpless confusion.

Sara visited her mother, whom she told me never made enough food for all her children, and felt jealous of the attentions mother gave to her dog, but added that her mother was planning to have the dog euthanized. Her mother had casually inquired whether Sara had stopped therapy yet, expressing her assumption that, as in the past, Sara would find it valueless. Sara imagined kidnapping Julia Child, the well-known "French Chef," and forcing her to cook lunch. She went so far as to call her but hung up when Julia answered.

But after eight months of therapy and the apparent oasis of sanity Sara became acutely paranoid. She wondered if the wiring was connected to explosives, if I had a gun in my drawer, and if I was about to strangle her. Between therapy hours she went to a bar, got drunk, and invited attack. In retrospect I believe her false-self state of "normalcy" was also a pretense based on paranoid suspicion. When she became so agitated that she paced my office and said she was going to escape to a distant city I arranged for her admission to McLean Hospital, where she remained on a locked ward for the next one-and-a-half years.

Sara immediately barricaded herself in her hospital room. In terror that staff were trying to kill her she assaulted them, and in order to contain her they had to put her in seclusion and sometimes restraints. In the quiet room she would huddle in corners, grimace and make strange body movements, bang her head against the wall, twist and smash her hands violently, glance around the room apprehensively, and pick at her face. She experienced visual projections of fragmented floating body parts, hallucinated voices either threatening her with terrifying scenarios or "protecting" her by commanding that she act in ways that were self-destructive in order to prevent terrible things from happening to her. When released from seclusion she escaped from the hospital several times and placed herself in dangerous situations.

After an evaluation in the hospital Sara was diagnosed according to the then current DSM-III standards as a chronic paranoid schizophrenic. The ward staff consisted of the administrative psychiatrist who "ran" the ward and made decisions about medication, privileges, restrictions, and the like in consultation with myself and other staff; a social worker who met periodically with mother and occasionally with Sara's siblings; and various staff nurses and occupational and rehabilitative personnel. I met with Sara in an office on the ward when necessary, in my private office in the hospital when possible, and when she needed additional external control and was placed in the quiet room I joined her there for our sessions. I attended ward rounds where staff discussed Sara on at least a weekly basis. And every several months there was a formal review and planning conference about Sara that included in addition to the ward staff a senior consultant from outside the ward.

Shortly after her admission I increased the frequency of our sessions from three to four per week, a frequency we maintained until near the conclusion of our work together. Sara remembered feigning sleep as a child so father would carry her to bed, as she knew he would not do so if she asked. She told me how she often drove off in her car in the middle of the night and followed big trucks for hundreds of miles, so as not to feel lonely. Despite her paranoid terror of me and the admonitions of her voices she admitted that she was "getting a few crumbs." Between meetings she wrote me a remarkable letter.

> I really think I am alive, and if I think about it I get so sad and I get really angry. When I sit in the room with you and I let myself believe you are there I feel so safe I just want to sit there forever. But I can't seem to be able to believe it for very long afterwards. I had no idea what I was getting into by entering therapy and I'm scared and I do hate you, but I also wish I could be with you every minute.

In apparent self-retaliation, over the ensuing weekend Sara briefly escaped from the hospital in near zero temperature without a coat.

Sara told me that her family refused to believe she had problems that justified her being in the hospital. The social worker who met with mother and other family members corroborated her impression and told me mother had almost succeeded in convincing her Sara was only pretending to be ill. Despite how bizarrely she had acted, many ward staff also apparently believed she was faking, for as Sara began to show more neediness and emotion on the ward some of the staff began to believe that her therapy was making her sicker. After one of her brothers raised questions about her need for hospitalization Sara wrote to her family:

> I am not dependent on the hospital, in fact I have trouble even asking staff for a towel or for change. I have been operating under the delusion that I am very confident in taking care of myself and trying to persuade everyone as well as me that this is the case, but it is not. Hanging out on skid row, getting beaten up, putting myself in very dangerous situations wandering around the streets of the big city in the middle of the night totally paranoid, in my apartment all day in what my therapist calls psychotic terror, alone and pretty nuts. My ability to come off as rational, functioning, jobs, school. talk to people etc. is an integral part of the craziness. When I sit with another person I focus on them entirely, try to figure them out and organize my own self around information I can pick up. It could be described as human Saran wrap, weak ego boundaries. The day I arrived in the hospital I thought the staff was going to kill me. I ended up in four-point restraints flat on the mattress with my arms and legs strapped down. I am struggling for my life here because I have gotten crazier as the years go by. I am fighting myself, the part that hates the whole goddamn world and doesn't want anything to do with anyone, that part is supported by my saying shit to me like "I hate Dr. Robbins," and I tell myself to get the hell out of the hospital. Part of the treatment is forming a real human relationship with him, telling him I hate him for exposing me to all the rage, sadness, feelings, and that I like him. I have to practice asking for things and saying no to people. I need a safe place to take risks.

This lucid insightful letter about her capacity to be fraudulent was, among other things, yet another example of the utter confusion transferences based on a mind that is unintegrated and undifferentiated elicit. Subsequent events show how little of what she wrote she really meant.

Year two

Preceding a short separation Sara became more detached and I commented that she was trying to leave before I did. That night she escaped from the hospital into a cold rainy night. She returned for our final meeting before my absence and I pointed out that she was creating a world of rejection, misery, and abuse and trying to believe that she could control it by not acknowledging how much it disturbed her. On my return she remarked to me sheepishly "I'm addicted to you; a Robbins addict." It was a cold and wintry day and shortly after telling me of her wish that I would surround her, she said she had an urge to go out into the woods and lie in the snow were she was convinced it would feel warm and secure. I wondered if she was trying to make me feel responsible for the distress she felt when I was gone, and her laughter confirmed the accuracy of my speculation. She told me how as a child she spent much time in the basement of her house, hiding from her mother, snuggling up to the furnace for warmth, and how she taught herself to use dangerous power tools without any sense of fear even though on more than one occasion she had come close to electrocuting herself. Then she remarked that she had been using power tools in the hospital shop and had told the supervisor that she was frightened. She was stunned when he responded that he was glad to hear it, and if she were not afraid he would not allow her to use the tools. As she seemed to regain some control she was allowed for the first time to visit me in my office in Cambridge. However she immediately became terrified of me and of her voices and said she wanted to split my skull with an ax. She talked of her wish for a womblike world where it would not matter what she thought because I would take care of everything.

We resumed meeting in the hospital where she seemed almost catatonic. I talked with her about how her delusions and hallucinations were external reflections of her own mental state of fear and rage but this confused her and made her hate and fear me and wonder if I was driving her crazy. She gave me a self-portrait. In addition to revealing her considerable artistic ability what was striking was that it looked like an aerial view of a landscape consisting of geometric plots each filled with busy designs and a large empty space in the middle. She was aware of urges to do violence to me, and her paranoid-determined violent behavior often required ward staff to place her in restraints and seclusion. Her trifluoperazine dosage was gradually increased, and when there was no discernible improvement chlorpromazine was added. Because she was convinced that the staff had gone crazy and attacked her I asked a staff nurse to join a session. Sara was confused when told that her assaultive destructive behavior could evoke powerful responses from others, because her family "normally" seemed unaware of her presence. For the first time she felt rage at her family for their failure to appreciate her needs and she began to raise objections when her mother and brother ridiculed psychiatrists and mental hospitals and said she had no need to be in a mental hospital, but she also expressed rage at me for making her know this.

Remarkably, considering her out of control states, Sara's capacity to seem rational and logical were once again very effective convincing hospital staff that she was normal and simply feigning illness, and that it was me and my "therapy" that were driving her crazy. Her family was insistent about this to the social worker, who vacillated in her own belief. Over the course of the second year on several occasions the ward psychiatrist and staff raised serious questions about whether therapy was harming her and whether I should stop seeing her. The staff acted out their belief in various ways including waiting for two days after one of Sara's escapes from the hospital before notifying me. Because of her repeated paranoid destructive episodes her medication dosage was again increased. There were several formal conferences during these months, and fortunately for Sara and our work the outside consultant consistently, repeatedly, and strongly supported her therapy.

Sara was beginning for the first time to note the passage of time in relation to the rhythm of our appointments. She worried about my forthcoming summer vacation. She recalled how father abruptly sent her to live with an acquaintance in France without explaining that he was dying. She was contemptuous of my "weakness" for continuing to care about her. But she admitted having feelings of caring about me and when I asked her what they were she pointed mutely to her heart. She was able to acknowledge that the hospital was her home for now and decided to keep a diary when I was away.

When I left she escaped and bought a plane ticket to France but she changed her mind and returned to the hospital where she involved herself with a male patient who was known for his violent behavior. She sent a letter to me that said, in part,

> I am really lost; I am 1,000,000 miles away and I don't know where that is. I have all these fantasies about taking off with him, staying stoned, drunk, getting pimped out, beaten up. I want to cry and scream and hit people and I am so angry. You know I am really smart. I am creative and imaginative. I could've done a hell of a lot with myself, and here I am coming up on 30 and I am sitting in a nut house kissing a fucking psychopath. I am so angry at you. I want to scream, tear the room apart.

When I returned from my summer vacation Sara said that she was enraged that I had left her but that it had not been safe for her to leave me until I returned. She then lost control and when restrained and placed in the quiet room she giggled, hallucinated, and banged her head against the wall. Yet again I experienced a sense of helplessness and hopelessness similar to what she seemed to feel about relating to another person. I believe that a critical therapeutic element in her treatment was my sense of personal boundaries that enabled me to experience the kinds of confusion about reality and helplessness and hopelessness she seemed to feel without rejecting her and running away as she had done.

The administrative psychiatrist increased her dose of chlorpromazine again. Sara learned that yet again the staff had serious doubts about her therapy and that our relationship might be in jeopardy. She was very distressed and correctly surmised that she was setting others up to enact her hatred of me and her confusion of sanity and craziness, the part of herself she now associated with the attitudes of her parents.

During one of mother's hospital visits Sara tried to talk to her about her feelings of having been neglected, and she told me matter-of-factly that in response mother became enraged, called Sara a bitch, threw an ashtray against the wall, and resisted efforts of staff to calm her. Our responses to her story were curiously congruent; I wondered if Sara had imagined the incident and it was an example of her lack of differentiation from her mother. Sara herself did not find anything remarkable about her description of mother's behavior. Interestingly, mother's behavior was subsequently confirmed in its particulars by a staff member who had been present. Thus commenced a series of visits between Sara and mother in the presence of the social worker, after which Sara regularly expected the social worker to conclude that mother's behavior was unremarkable and was amazed to discover that the social worker was impressed by mother's caged pacing around the room during their interviews and her threats to leave. This led to Sara's recollection of an incident from early childhood when mother, in a rage, had literally thrown Sara and her siblings around the room. After telling me this Sara experienced herself fragmented in pieces sitting in several different areas of the room, one part running away from me, and another feeling attached to me and sitting near me as protection against mother.

We had another review conference in which the nursing staff voiced their near unanimous belief that therapy was not working and that my treatment was making Sara regress, but the consultant supported continued hospitalization and therapy. When Sara next escaped from the hospital I was not notified by the staff, although it was customary hospital procedure. I first learned about it more than a day later when I found a message from her on my answering machine telling me she had "split" and assuring me she was safe and would return. Sara had gone to Las Vegas but resisted the prompting of her hallucinations to walk the streets late at night. She had also resisted calling me for fear it would make her have feelings and hence "fall apart." On return she talked of her urge to "split" again and we realized that splitting was both literal and psychological, and signified cutting herself off from her feelings. When she observed herself hallucinating she asked the staff to put her in the quiet room where she felt safe. Sara was genuinely confused about whether medication was making her better or, as she put it, "driving her crazy," and she was aware of a belief that her food was being poisoned. I was similarly and reciprocally confused and regularly questioned my own sense of reality. Often I did not know what to believe.

Sadness, anger, and related childhood memories began to surface more regularly. Sara looked forward to her hours with me and reported a feeling of security she claimed was entirely novel in her life. Yet she told me she was much more comfortable relating to an assaultive patient on the ward than she was to me. I responded that while she longed for caring, the only treatment she seemed able to tolerate was a reflection of her own hateful uncaring attitudes. Her condition improved and she was allowed to leave the hospital and come to my private office for therapy appointments. She adopted a motherly role toward an adolescent female patient who repeatedly ran away and got herself into destructive predicaments. It was around this time, late in the second year of therapy, that a mature integrated sense of identity began to emerge.

But yet again she became paranoid and assaultive, and fought off all efforts to help her. Her privileges to leave the hospital were curtailed, and she required restraint and seclusion in the quiet room. Then she was able to talk about her rageful fantasies of ripping herself apart and blowing up the hospital and me. She felt her head swelling and occupying all corners of the room.

I remarked that she did not seem to be attending to anything I said. She laughed and tried to convince me that my perceptions were not accurate. I suggested she might tape-record her sessions to help her determine who was accurate (Robbins, 1988), a modality I had used with others, and she agreed to do so. Sara was responsible for the taping and the tapes were in her possession to use as she chose. Once again I had to deal with my helplessness and uncertainty about what use she might make of the recordings. However she soon informed me that she was learning how little she actually listened to me. She told me this was the first experience in her life of a caring relationship with another person in which her needs were satisfied and the realization made her depressed and enraged. Caring was a chink in her armor and a threat to her "independence." She remembered an incident in which mother took her and her siblings sailing and threw them in the ocean in order to teach them not to be frightened and prove to herself that she could rescue them if need be. Soon afterward Sara again escaped from the hospital, went to a bar, got drunk, and had casual sex. When she literally tried to tear her face off she was put back in restraints. There she told me "you can only destroy what you have."

Year three

Sara was again confined to the quiet room because she had begun to tear at the skin on her face in what she admitted was an effort to tear her face off. I shared with her my feelings of powerlessness to help her and we both marveled at the power of her hatred. She regained some self-control and became very sad as she realized her drive to destroy what was important to her. She realized that she was trying to drive me crazy. Paranoid terrors that her mother would kill her, and episodes when she shouted at the ward staff and had urges to blow up the world were followed by memories of having been attacked by her mother as a child.

Sara gradually regained more consistent self-control, and discharge planning began. She began to drive to her therapy appointments at my office which was now in my home some distance from the hospital grounds. When her car would not start after an appointment she frantically pushed it away from my house and down a nearby hill and almost into a main street full of rush-hour traffic, so terrified was she that I might notice her predicament and she might have to ask for help.

After 26 months and 355 hours of therapy and one-and-a-half years of hospitalization Sara moved to a halfway house. She realized the hospital had become a kind of home and family. In the new setting she felt her mother was omnipresent in other women, the sense there was a lion outside her bedroom at night, and a presence hiding behind my office plants.

She anticipated my summer vacation with terror and articulated her fear that I was abandoning her to the clutches of a crazy woman. We agreed that the woman was no longer her mother but part of herself. She realized how unaware she tended to be of injury, illness, fatigue, hunger, and sexual feelings and for the first time was frighteningly aware that her self-protective instincts were deficient, that the things that upset most people did not bother her. I added that the things that signified home to most people such as intimacy terrified her. Finally Sara concluded that she might need to return to the hospital while I was gone, and immediately she felt better. She said she loved me and she gave me a gift of a lovely ceramic car she had made, which she called her "getaway" car. She remembered swimming much too far out in the ocean until she was no longer certain she could get back, only to realize that the prospect of trying to return was so terrifying she did not know whether she wanted to try. Turning off her feelings was a form of triumph; it meant no one could hurt her. Episodes of caring, work, and insight were small oases in a desert of paranoid detachment and lengthy silence, and I found myself responding with sleepiness and boredom to the rhythmic alternation. When she noticed this Sara articulated wishes to tease and torture me and put me in a dark place so that I would feel trapped and alone, give up hope as she had done, detach myself from my body and feelings and go crazy. She was relieved next hour to find I was still intact. These ideas alternated with memories of having such things done to her, first by mother, then brother, and ultimately some of the sadistic men she had apprenticed herself to.

When we separated for my month-long vacation Sara reentered the hospital as planned, but she quickly realized she no longer knew anyone there. She escaped and went to London where in fact she knew no one, but she called to reassure me that she was well and taking care of herself and she sent me a card from Freud's house.

She was pleased to see me on my return and seemed positive about our relationship and aware of her problems with self-care, but her characteristic paranoid withdrawal and muteness followed. I responded with interpretation of my countertransference drowsiness and detachment as a response to her wishes to drive me crazy as had been done to her. When a destructive act was committed at the halfway house, although the perpetrator was known, Sara was almost convinced she had done it. It seemed that we were immobilized in the throes of a mutual struggle between gaining sanity in her case and retaining it in mine on the one hand, and a powerful pull toward a state of hopelessness and resignation to losing our minds on the other. I told her I was thinking about recommending re-hospitalization and to my surprise she cried, felt closer to me. She construed my setting limits on her as the actions of a good parent. She felt pleasure when a policeman stopped her for speeding. She dreamed chickens had escaped the coop and a raccoon was about to kill them. She recalled unsuccessfully concealing from her mother the fact that she had cut her finger rather badly. When she and her mother arrived at the hospital the doctor wanted to suture the wound but mother objected and would not permit it. She told me that mother never made enough food for her and forced her to eat things she did not want, and associated to how she performed fellatio on abusive men in the belief she was controlling them.

In the fall Sara began constructive planning and returned to graduate school. But once again she pulled the rug of sanity and reality out from under me. She said, very convincingly, that she was upset because she had been untruthful with me and that she really did not hallucinate, and the stories of abuse and skid row were fabrications. She said when she was in London and had wanted attention and sympathy she went to a restaurant and convinced the waiter that she was a bereaved widow revisiting the scene of her marriage. I felt shocked and a bit sick to my stomach and I wondered aloud whether I could trust my senses about what was real. Sara tried to convince me that she was telling me these "truths" because our relationship was deepening and she cared, but I felt suspicious, a bit paranoid myself as I struggled with what was real. Fortunately I observed and I pointed out that she was sitting in the farthest corner of the room and showing no emotion. In response she reported that the room was becoming animated in sinister and threatening ways, and she feared that I was going crazy.

She told me life was becoming meaningful to her, that she was taking better care of herself, and she expressed gratitude. She had felt pain immediately when she accidentally jabbed her hand on a nail head. For the first time in her life she took a stuffed animal to bed with her. She attended a family dinner and recounted that mother had called her infant granddaughter "hysterical" when she fell downstairs and cried, and called her daughter-in-law overprotective for comforting her.

She asked mother for permission to see mother's hospital records and to talk with her mother's former therapist so she might find out what had really happened to her as a child. To her surprise mother agreed. But mother did not follow through. After dreaming she was in a world of seductive vampires and had to decide whether to swallow a concoction and become like them Sara again asked her mother. This time mother got angry and accused Sara of trying to persecute her. Sara began to express rage at her mother and a wish to kill or drive her crazy, but her talk was punctuated by disruptions, self-derision, and the sensation of choking and suffocating. She wrote me a letter that included:

> I hate the whole fucking world. Not only does my head get splintered up but the room goes to pieces and words get blasted into meaningless letters. So the four walls of the room no longer join and I don't feel safe here. Everything gets unglued. I get so angry I just want to blow up the world. Where the hell are you?

She seemed more aware of how identical her own attitudes and behaviors were to those of her mother and how unreliable and inconsistent both of them were.

Sara then revealed that she did not believe mother had been in a mental hospital or had been mentally ill. She subscribed to the family belief that mother had been hospitalized for a physical problem. Nonetheless I received detailed records of mother's hospitalization along with her permission to share what I thought appropriate. Sara wondered whether they contained information about whether mother cared about her. After reading the notes I responded that there was little concern about her marriage or her children. Sara told me she was chopping up her thoughts and physically choking back massive rage and that she might kill me. When Sara reported delusions of a terrifying woman in the doorway of her room at night I read her a nursing report that mentioned mother's abusiveness, threats of violence and suicide, running away, periods of disorientation and immobility lasting for hours, and mother's terrifying hallucinations of a persecutory old woman. We realized how similar she and her mother were and how much she had been invested in her efforts to control mother's behavior by invisibility, compliance, and identity merger.

Year four

For the first time she shared fantasies of having a home and husband of her own but then she withdrew, told me that she was crazy and that there was a bomb bursting in her head. Around the time of her birthday Sara struggled with feelings of homelessness and wishes to be my little child on the one hand, and terror of me because I looked crazy, which she associated with the urge to speed, get picked up by the police, attack them, and get killed. Eventually she sought help of the staff at the halfway house and was briefly and constructively re-hospitalized. She said "if I'm going to feel all this stuff then I want to have people around all the time to share it with."

After a conversation in which mother told her how hard she had tried to select a birthday gift for her that Sara would not interpret as a rejection, Sara came away with a more balanced view of a mother who was making an effort. She went to a family gathering at her mother's house and told one of her brothers how important he was to her and how angry she was at some of the ways he treated her. He became angry, withdrew, and uttered a mocking laugh she was very familiar with. To Sara's surprise mother empathized with her and attempted to stop the quarrel.

When she talked about how the bar room atmosphere of darkness, drunkenness, and abuse was a "home" of deadness where she felt no one could touch her I asked her to agree not to go to a bar again. She did so reluctantly and was overwhelmed with feelings of homelessness and rage. Sara moved out of the halfway house and into a house she rented jointly with several women. At night when she began to be terrified and paranoid she hugged her stuffed animal.

Once again my summer vacation approached. After another episode of rage and fantasies of bombing and destroying the entire East Coast Sara laughed and told me that she had fooled me yet again, this time into believing that we were getting closer. When she observed my drowsiness in response to her detached silence she vehemently asserted that it was because she didn't want me near her. Seemingly oblivious to what she was doing she tracked mud over my office rug with dirty sneakers. She wished to go to a foreign country where she did not speak the language so there could be no communication. I commented that that country was called the land of backward schizophrenia.

Nonetheless she managed our separation well, obtained a job as a preschool teacher's aide and undertook more course work. Her teaching experience exposed her to scenarios of infants crying for their mothers and mothers claiming them. She felt overwhelming sadness and rage, associated her feelings to my vacation, and voiced confusion about whether she was a small child and I had in fact abandoned her. She reported that at the end of the previous hour she had stood outside the office door wanting to knock and tell me she needed a hug for security. Instead she went to a bar and got drunk. The theme was that an abandoned child feels so overwhelmed with pain that eventually she no longer wants anyone to come back and make her aware of it.

After another period of paranoid detachment she remarked that going crazy was a terrible price to pay for not being able to say no to her mother, and the nature of the current conflict emerged. Mother had recently had surgery, and Sara had been driving mother to the hospital for her treatments. She recalled a childhood incident where she had hidden from mother but mother had found her, hit her, and told her that if she saw her again she would cook her in the oven and eat her for dinner. She was able to tell mother that she could not see her for the foreseeable future and mother was surprisingly accepting. This too enraged Sara, for she felt that it came much too late and she had no forgiveness in her heart, only hatred.

She began to keep a diary between sessions in the in the form of letters to me. She wrote:

> I would like to kill a lot of people and they don't know it but really I don't want to kill you. I wish I could give you a big hug and tell you how I feel, that I am so lonely and so tired and so scared and I can't sleep. I know it won't be you that kills me, it is my feelings that I think will kill me; feeling good, safe, loving you, wanting to hug you and never leave. I think of you sitting in your chair and I feel warm inside and safe and so sad I can hardly bear it, like I could cry forever.

She told me about the summer that she was sent abroad when her father was dying and she remembered visiting an old baker to whom she became very attached. He had an endearing pet name for her and she recalled wishing that he would adopt her. I had a familiar sense of surprise and disorientation learning of this hitherto unmentioned oasis of caring in her life. But the very next hour Sara informed me that she had listened to her tape-recording and realized that what she told me was what she had wanted to believe whereas in fact she had only run errands for the baker. She described her terrifying mother, tall and wiry, "wired up" all the time. I recalled some of her delusional preoccupations with electricity and some of the near serious mishaps she had made when she did electrical wiring; she laughed and related this to her wish and fear to hold on, adding: "if the voltage is high and you hold on with both hands the current will go through your heart and kill you."

She learned mother was planning to move to another state. Sara rapidly oscillated between pleasure in seeing me and wishes to hug me and wishes to hit me which were associated with reflexive fist clenching and demonstrations of her right cross. She said "the biggest mistake I ever made was to start seeing you." She literally made fists at me which meant "touch me emotionally and I'll clobber you." She started to pick up a small statue and throw it at me and when I moved it away from her she became confused; for a time she could not "locate" her anger.

When mother moved Sara felt sad and alone. She had derived a perverse sense of security and predictability from being able to anticipate and cope with mother's disturbances by being invisible, elusive, and inconsistent, and now she felt exposed and vulnerable and did not know how to be in a situation that required direct emotional expression and assertion.

She decided she needed to talk with me about sex since she wanted to have children of her own, and she was beginning to show some interest in men. She remembered the experiences she had when she performed fellatio, and how she transformed her feelings of helplessness and the wish to vomit, to hit, and to bite off the penis, into a sense of mastery and control in which she felt superior, in control, and belittling of the man for being so insanely excited. I suggested that real control was based on consistency, knowledge of her emotions, and selective action based on that knowledge. She responded that for the first time in her life she felt listened to and attended to, and she realized that the more she accepted her upset feelings the less she hallucinated, and she was sleeping better at night.

Year five

Another birthday approached. Sara imagined that I came over to her and removed a tiny baby from within her and nurtured it. She recalled that her mother was unable to remember any of the children's birthdays. I gave her a birthday card and wrote "we all deserve the opportunity to be special to someone. I hope you won't let the misfortunes of your past imprison you so that you won't have yours." Her response was a fragmented combination of tense laughter, sadness, anger, and flat words of thanks. I had upset her expectation that I would not remember.

Again her sense of time expanded, and she began to envision a future and for the first time feel hopeful. She was doing very well at school and would become a full-fledged teacher the following year. But she fought with me over everything, remained withdrawn, and would allow a bit of contact only just before the end of an hour. We began to wonder whether the best she could do was to be like a squirrel that gets its nut and then runs. She reported a nightmare in which she was with a former patient who was wheelchair-bound, her hands and feet amputated, and Sara was hugging her and trying to estimate just how much she was capable of learning to do. We talked about her chronically hunched-over posture in the office which was an effort to deny the existence of her body and sexuality. She was literally unable to sit back. When she tried she felt dizzy and nauseated with powerful sensations of terror that she would be attacked, ripped apart, and annihilated. She told me this is why she had never felt safe enough to wear a skirt.

She received her master's degree and at graduation fellow students and teachers expressed caring for her and described her as gifted and creative. She told me that for the first time in her life she felt optimistic and excited and had even purchased a dress to wear to a job interview. She was certain she now had enough control so that she would not become psychotic during the upcoming summer separation. At the conclusion of the last hour she shook my hand, expressed her gratitude to me for having "put up" with her, and said she would miss me. I remarked that she had had to put up with me as well and that it hadn't been easy and with a brief burst of sadistic laughter she departed.

When we resumed she had begun a full-time teaching position. She dreamed she was observing a person of indeterminate gender who was wearing a plastic raincoat and who set her- or himself on fire. No one paid attention. The victim was amazed to find out that he or she had not died but the coat had melted into the person's body. After this she recalled a childhood incident when mother's sailboat tipped over throwing Sara into the water with the sail on top of her. Because she had followed mother's instructions and had worn a life preserver she was trapped beneath the sail and could not get out.

Sara was less rigid physically and emotionally, and more spontaneous. She was more sensitive to temperature and pain. She sat a bit closer to me in the room, spontaneously clapped her hands when she said something, and wanted to examine an object of interest in my office. At times she sat back and relaxed, and once yelled in an angry voice, "fuck you." These gestures and spontaneous expressions of emotion terrified her. She feared she would be attacked but she realized it was she who had been attacking everything both of us did or said.

For the first time she began to worry about real problems of her life like finding a caring husband rather than about her hallucinations and delusions. She realized that she wanted to have children and that there were now men she liked, and she would be forced to talk to me about sex if she wanted a man in her life. We concluded that this idea was a concrete way of expressing her belief that in order to get any semblance of attention or affection she was forced to perform oral sex. She perceived me as a crazy man, out of control of my sexuality and sadism, and she concluded I had been trying to disrupt our relationship by prematurely forcing the subject of sex on her. Nonetheless she took the unprecedented step of telling her oldest and perhaps only male friend that she cared about him. He responded that he did not reciprocate her feelings. She fled to a pool hall where she proceeded to take out her pool stick and defeat every man who would play with her.

Despite her concern I would not want her to do it, Sara planned a holiday trip abroad with a friend. She gave me a small gift before leaving and shook my hand, demonstrating a violent physical oscillation I now associated with alternating holding on and breaking off. At the beginning of our separation Sara had the first dream that she could recall in which I figured, which she told me on her return. She was in my office and there was a big window against which lay a monstrous dead whale. It seemed normal to her that it be there, until my teenage daughter came along and Sara asked her what the whale looked like from the outside. Sara saw me approach from another building and feared I would get angry at my daughter for talking to her. She related the dream to her deadness identity and to a childhood memory of seeing people pick apart a dead whale that washed up on the beach. "Dead whale" became an important therapy metaphor for the state of being she continued to strive to achieve.

Year six

Sara uncharacteristically showed emotional upset at a family dinner and when she tried to leave, one of her brothers followed her. She burst into tears as they shared their mutual mistrust of others and the belief that the ability to be detached and unfeeling represented control, and her brother hugged her. Sara angrily blamed me for this. Soon thereafter she reported a nightmare in which she had entrusted the care of her students to someone else and went off and forgot their existence. When she remembered and returned it was evident that something terrible had happened to one of the students. I told Sara that I knew what had happened, that it had been unbearable for the student to be left alone so she had gotten herself beaten into unconsciousness. I commented that Sara had to make a choice between the mother of caring and attention to thoughts and feelings and the mother of rage, destruction of her mind, and deadness.

When her first teaching year ended, students, their parents, and faculty expressed praise and gratitude to her. Once again our relationship seemed stalemated, and when our summer vacation separation approached she wrote me a letter:

> you shouldn't bother with me and should take a painkiller and sleep. You know I do hear you and I feel I am being attacked because it is not too pleasant what you're saying. I just want to tell you to go to hell and take your damn caring with you because I want to blast everyone to hell especially someone who cares. It is becoming clear what I want and what I don't want and I didn't get and that clarity makes me so angry it scares the hell out of me.

She then dreamed that someone killed her brother, cooked his appendix, and gave it to her to eat as though this were normal. In the dream she was terribly upset, screamed, and then awoke. It turned out that the brother image represented things she liked and valued in her life, whereas her cannibalism represented the killing of caring. As my summer vacation approached Sara reproached me for leaving, saying "look who you're leaving me with!"

When we met in the fall Sara told me how constructive her month had been. She had purchased a house of her own in a safe neighborhood, was being assertive and creative at work, and had maintained a sense of me within her that helped her make good decisions. As usual there was another side. She began to miss appointments and then reported a dream in which she had spilled coffee on the lovely dining table she had purchased for her new home, and in order to avoid awareness of the contrast between the marred area and the rest of the tabletop she hacked it to pieces.

Sara told me she said she was afraid she might wear two mismatched shoes to a forthcoming parents' meeting, and she realized this represented how little dialogue there was between the caring and hating parts of herself. I suggested that she try to find names for each one and that she sit in different chairs in the office when talking from each position. She called the two parts "black" and "red" and over the next five weeks we elaborated the characteristics of each. Ms. Black turned away from me and muttered curses. When expressing Ms. Red she told me that Ms. Black was thoughtless, ignorant, rigid, hateful, and destructive, and possessed a vocabulary limited to name calling. She began to panic and said that I did not understand that she would punish herself for this conversation once she got herself alone.

She reported a nightmare: her house was burning down, she walked down a dark, empty street with burns on her feet, but she did not seem to care. She told me how she had burned some food and burned her hands removing it from the oven and she twisted her fingers violently. At the same time she began to express horror at the Ms. Black part of herself, calling it mean and "Neanderthal." But she felt frightened and told me that her mind was exploding and her thoughts flying apart, and she was barely able to speak.

When Sara told me how she had cared for two children at school who had been injured I contrasted her capacity to care with her refusal to take care of herself. She responded by telling me how she was walking around with a hole in her shoe, that she habitually drove without a seatbelt, that she allowed her house to remain a mess, did not allow herself sleep, and physically tortured her hands so badly when expressing her caring for me that she worried that she might break her fingers. After sharing her impulse to travel to a nearby city where the news media reported a mass murderer had been killing women. Sara reported a nightmare. She had cancer and was being her own doctor. She took slices of herself and put them in the oven to incubate, and they grew to be monstrous, black, gross, and disgusting. She said "if I lock up this Neanderthal part then I will have lost the only part that has ever taken care of me and I will feel intolerably alone."

We began to talk about her broken heart and she remembered sitting immobilized after mother was hospitalized when she was nine. In our last hour before a separation she admonished me to take care of myself so that nothing would happen to me and she would not be heartbroken. I responded that she needed to take care of herself which meant bearing her feelings. She struggled against the urge to cry. She imagined having me sit next to her and put my arm around her so that she would feel secure and be able to fall sleep. But she panicked until she realized that it was because her image of me had changed into that of her mother, with long fingernails, ready to strangle her.

Year seven

After reiterating her belief that she had to perform oral sex in order to have a relationship Sara realized that it was after mother's hospitalization that she began to run away and get men to abuse her and force her to do that even though it made her choke and want to vomit. She began to cry. She knew she had been breast-fed and began to wonder what it had been like. She became terrified of me.

On Sara's birthday, our 998th hour, I gave her another card on which I wrote:

> I am sorry I can't be the loving mother you never had. And I can't take away your memories and feelings about never having had one. But I would like to help you put these things where they belong so that you can get some love in the future.

Sara clutched it for the entire hour, interrupted at times by the feeling that mother was about to take it from her, and at other times by her own wish to get away. She told me that she had kept on her person for half a year the other card I had given her. At the conclusion of this hour she said, quite unaware, "I'm going to take care of myself even if it kills me!"

After another deadening stalemate I remarked somewhat facetiously that I needed a consultation from her. Little did I know I was mobilizing her ability to write, think, reflect, and be artistically creative, presaging some of her later accomplishments. In response she began to bring me a series of documents, beautifully illustrated as though they were children's stories, with the theme that holding on to mother was a barrier between us and that she needed to face her rage and tears over having had no mother. She wrote about how she had been destroying her life and our relationship, adding:

> I don't want to spend my life doing a Woody Allen impersonation. The pendulum has been swinging for 35 years, without any joy, love, sadness, company. I want more with you and I want the rest of my life also. I want lots of things but the minute you show up I don't want anything but to drive you nuts and run.

There followed a section written in red ink to indicate the thoughts of Ms. Red which concluded with "so I waste my time getting revenge on you who has never hurt me in any way and in reality getting revenge on myself, carrying out my mother's misdirected revenge on me." After a sentence in black starting with "this is a bunch of bullshit" she concluded in red that she was taking courses with me, "feelings 101" and "elementary language."

Year eight

Preceding my summer vacation the stalemate between the two sides of Sara intensified along with her anger at me no matter what I did, and I struggled during her hours with the urge to lose consciousness and fall asleep. Sara commented that she wanted me to experience what had been forced on her: a terrified state of helplessness, hopelessness, futility, and paralysis. Then she spontaneously decided to tell me a story. It was about a little donkey and his caring mother. The mother was shot by a bad boy, leaving the little donkey all alone, staring into the mud and rain. I commented that this was a story about heartbreak and the end of the world. There ensued more self-destructive behaviors and grisly fantasies and we realized that the "crazy" part of herself not only did not think but had no words. She began to use words more to describe this part and I felt relief, and told her that when she put it into words and talked about it I felt less crazy because her words made sense in relation to my experience of her.

During our summer separation she enrolled in a program abroad, and when we resumed in the fall she was tanned, well dressed, and had lost weight. She talked enthusiastically about her adventures, new relationships, and the future.

She was distressed that she had a dream in which I appeared because it indicated my importance. We were sleeping in separate sleeping bags, entirely zipped up, on a beach on the northern coast. We had been there a long time, there was water and a line of seaweed over much of us, and she was half awake. This clear illustration of our disengagement, the deadness and endlessness, was most troubling to Sara. She admitted that she missed me and had pretended the teddy bear she now used for comfort represented me, but then she called herself a "stupid jerk."

She said with regret that despite her love of children she would probably never be able to have any of her own because she was now in her mid-thirties. I likened the way she led her life to how she customarily waited until the end of therapy hours to get anything from our relationship and wondered if she might be inventing a new form of self-punishment by making herself wait until it was too late in life to get what she wanted. As she struggled over her heartbroken childlike longing to cry, be comforted, and fall asleep, she tried to cover herself with the blanket on my couch but her striking motor inability to hold it enacted her difficulty holding on to caring feelings.

Sara told me she had gotten drunk and had slept with a "loser" who lived in her neighborhood. She began to hallucinate cursing commentary on her relationship with me. She told me that over the holiday she had felt rejected and excluded from my family. I suggested and she agreed that she resume trifluoperazine. For perhaps the first time she allowed medication to help her and to think and talk about what was happening. Almost immediately her hallucinations diminished and she became calmer and better able to sleep, to focus attention and concentrate and organize her life. She recalled her struggles in the hospital to fight off the effects of medication and felt terrified that she was allowing someone to get into her mouth and influence her. She tried to sit closer to me and had a fantasy of being dragged back into the corner by her hair. I encouraged her to identify the parts of herself by moving from one chair to another again. In the "black" chair she talked about her contempt for human beings, relationships, and her own well-being. In the "red" chair she told me she had made a new female friend, had joined a health club and was expressing anger more appropriately when people mistreated her. At the end of this hour she reported "a splitting headache."

Disturbing memories of performing fellatio made her consider whether this had been a repetition of her breast-feeding experiences. She talked about being force-fed and having to pretend that she enjoyed it while experiencing sensations of suffocation, gagging, and wishes to bite. She remembered it was after mother was hospitalized that she began to run away and engage in the enslavement relationships that involved sucking the penis to ejaculation. She had a sudden urge to suck her thumb. She dreamed she and her brother were attempting to escape from her home of origin through an underground garage but mother came along in the car and flattened them. In another dream she came to my house for an appointment but there was a party and she could find no place to park. She dreamed of travelling down a jungle river with a guide. On the last part of the journey they went over rapids and she fell overboard, swallowed water, and drowned. She felt certain that the dream and memory of almost drowning under the sail when mother's boat capsized related to her breast-feeding experience. She recalled mother in the kitchen, cursing, threatening, throwing things, baking a cake, and making the children sit in a circle on the floor and one by one lick the remains of the batter from her finger.

She recalled her terror watching mother shaving her legs, and watching her newborn sister lose a piece of umbilical cord. Perhaps mother had done something to her. She had the urge to sleep with a man and I wondered if this was her way of assuaging doubts about her gender. To my surprise Sara agreed and began to talk about the feeling that she had been "ripped off" and forced to be a girl in a world where boys got everything. She recalled childhood activities using a blowtorch in her basement which she now believed were efforts to construct a penis. She was apprehensive that I might want "a blow job" from her.

She wrote me a letter in which she described a dream:

> I was searching for something but there was this demon following me around in the shadows killing people. It was like some robot that ripped the tops of people's heads off and ate their brains and hands. It killed everyone that I saw or talked to. What a vivid picture of what I am doing! The monster is

obviously me and I can't kill it and you can't kill it because all it does is constantly try to kill you. I don't think you really understand what a monster I am. I get you where it hurts. I get you to care about me and try to help and then kick you in the head over and over.

We returned to the subject of castration and discovered that she believed all children are initially male. Males have power and control but they are "pricks, have brains in their crotch." Some children get "ripped off" and become eunuchs. In my notes subsequent to this session I subsequently realized I had written "it is like pulling teeth to get her to continue to think about this." She realized that getting beaten up and "ripped off" and trying to control the penis and get it inside her was re-enacting her struggle to get a penis as well as the feeding struggle with her mother. She realized that she tried to control me by withholding her thoughts and feelings, withdrawing and "ripping me off."

Year nine

She reported a "splitting headache" as she contemplated the part of her that wanted to be close to people and the part that was enraged at human beings. She missed hours and made the tape recorder malfunction. She picked fights with me over everything and wanted to "kick my balls." She resumed sleeping with an old boyfriend and hallucinating. She insisted on stopping the trifluoperazine because it made her feel drunk. I suggested it was helping her wake up, but she was adamant, and I decided she needed to bear the consequences of her decisions. The thoughtful work that had characterized recent sessions stopped as well. She walked in front of her car after parking it on a hill without setting the brake and nearly succeeded in running herself over. When she said that I looked like I felt helpless I readily assented. She felt as though we were saying goodbye and she were attending her own funeral. After a long silence she said that it was pointless, that she was not going to change, and that although she would miss me, tomorrow would be our last hour. Perhaps she was right, I thought, and in any case I felt I needed to accept her right to control her life, so I shared my concern for her and my sadness.

Sara called me soon thereafter to say she had reconsidered and she told me her fantasy had been to quit therapy, stop caring, quit her job, and drive off. We agreed that she wanted to take a trip from the city of caring and loving to one of hatred, insanity, and perhaps suicide. She talked about how little it would disturb her family if this were to happen, and I responded that I cared and it would distress me deeply. She was touched and cried. When she left the session she discovered that she had locked herself out of her car and had to return to the office for help. The next hour, after preliminary curses, she said she had been relieved to find herself locked out of her car because she was certain that had been her unconscious effort to keep herself from driving off and quitting, and this was the first instance she could recall in which her unconscious motivation had been constructive!

Unlike other positive moments in our work this incident heralded a permanent change. Sara no longer seemed psychotic. She told me that to her surprise she had never been this depressed before without having delusions and hallucinations. She decided to cut back to once weekly therapy. We met for another year and a half prior to terminating, and although our relationship remained stalemated there was no recurrence of hallucinations or delusions. Sara reported progressive expansion in the areas of close friendships and work. She began to develop an identity as an educational crusader as evidenced by meteoric career advancement and the high esteem in which she was held by other educators, parents, and most of all the children she taught. It became clear that the extent of her professional ambition and effort would be the only limiting factor in the success of her career.

About seven months after we decreased the frequency of her appointments Sara gave me another one of her illustrated letters as a kind of Christmas gift. After summarizing her accomplishments she concluded:

> from the quiet room to this. That is saying a lot. For a huge chunk of each day I am happy, enjoying myself, challenged. You stuck by me. Thank you for your amazing patience and caring. I did everything I could to drive you away, and I continue to keep you at a distance with all the ways I have worked out over the years. But at the same time I take little pieces of our friendship and use them to patch my broken heart. You have given me a good life with friends and a satisfying job. You have also, like you said a long time ago, given me choices. My happiness with what I have now fuels my rage and urge to destroy you and my feelings, destroy myself. But much of me wants more and thinks that I can go further.

Although she realized it was unlikely that she could attain her goal of intimacy with a man without further intensive work with me, each gesture in that direction was regularly followed by some form of destructiveness. She seemed to be saying "I won't" to the prospect of more intensive emotional involvement with me. Finally I suggested that she was saying by her angry negative behavior what she was unable to say in words, namely that she did not wish to go further in therapy. Then it turned out that Sara did not want to experience the intense sadness of termination, either. She seemed to want to continue our ambivalent contact endlessly without movement. She seemed no more capable of saying goodbye than she was of continuing our work. We agreed to her wish to visit and report to me every half year or so, in the hope that eventually she might be able to reach a more definitive decision of one kind or another. During one such interval she wrote me:

> There are nights when I get so depressed and feel helpless and angry and want to die, but I can survive them, I have control and know more clearly that the feelings will not kill me. I do not take drastic action anymore.

Often I don't pay attention to my feelings and it is only when I get very close to being psychotic that I force myself to figure out what is going on. You helped me to do this many, many times. I can do it myself now. Thank you for your patience and caring. Thank you for giving me choices. You sat there for years waiting for me to show up. You ran the risk of holding out your caring and being rejected over and over and over. I know that I didn't entirely arrive, but I am happy. I know that it is not ideal that I carry you around in my head as a watchdog. Ideally it should be me that does this but the part of me that wants to destroy all caring and all life is very powerful and I need you there in my mind as a third-party.

After another hiatus in our sessions Sara returned and informed me that she had made a very satisfying relationship with a man she described as kind and intelligent. She shared the surprising news that they had a good sexual relationship. Part of the reason was her realization that in order to retain her sanity during sex she had to reserve the right to ask him to stop lovemaking at any time, a condition he was willing to honor. He lived in a distant city and they had concluded that in order to decide whether they wanted to make a commitment to one another they would first need to live together. This awareness coincided fortuitously with Sara's conclusion that in order to advance her career she needed to change jobs and get a Ph.D., and this might just as well be done in the city where he lived. She knew I would be pleased and she had come to say goodbye. She expressed moving tears of farewell and gratitude.

Epilogue

More than 20 years elapsed before Sara unexpectedly contacted me and came to visit. I felt I was in the presence of an impressively mature woman with a solid sense of self who made direct eye and emotional contact with me, had a sense of values and purpose, and was highly intelligent and articulate. She described a very satisfying marriage to the man she had told me about in that final session. She and her husband had adopted a very disturbed adolescent boy and raised him to a constructive and mature manhood. In her career as teacher and educational innovator she was greatly valued by colleagues and by the community. She had resigned her position some years previously after a dispute with authorities in which she had the backing of her colleagues and the community, and obtained a master's degree in creative writing. She had written and illustrated a coming of age novel for 9–12 year olds which had been published and very favorably reviewed. She had never again sought or required therapy or medication. Remarkably what she recalled most about our work was not things I had said to her, but my unwavering patience and caring during her long periods of silence and disengagement.

Discussion

Confusing as our relationship seemed during much of the treatment, in retrospect the transference and my reciprocal countertransference were simple in outline. They involved Sara's undifferentiated relationship with her mother and with me and her lack of an integrated separate self. She attempted to make me the object of the kind of annihilating rage, mind-bending distortions of reality, and disruptions of continuity and trust that had become her own identity as a result of having been subject to them in the earliest undifferentiated unintegrated attachment phase. She had been unable to separate from mother and instead formed an identity with her that she enacted in an undifferentiated relationship with me. In so doing she induced in me reciprocal feelings of confusion about reality as well as hopelessness, helplessness, and at times anger, and she pushed me toward a mind-numbing paranoid psychosis such as she experienced. It was my task to demonstrate to her that one could not only survive such assaults, but learn to deal with them in a more constructive effective way by thinking, representing her emotions, and remembering. I was gradually able to help her to substitute reflective representational thought for primordial conscious mentation and language.

In the course of our work Sara underwent a fundamental personality transformation. She developed the capacity to care, to reflect, to represent emotions, and to integrate the disparate elements in her personality so as to become capable of experiencing and resolving internal conflict, and to form a coherent cohesive sense of self. As a result she became capable of experiencing and resolving oral and phallic/gender conflicts. As a consequence she underwent significant psychosexual development from a dissociated sadistic/masochistic oral relationship with her mother and the belief she was a castrated male, to establishment of a mature gender role identity, and she achieved the capacity for intimacy, motherhood, and a successful career.

17
CONCLUSION

Psychoanalysis and psychosis are two entities that have passed in the night, so to speak, but have never met. They have co-existed in a state of mutual alienation. In fact, psychiatrists were once known as alienists, suggesting an attitude toward their patients. Psychosis can be viewed as the successive iteration of human alienation at human phenomenological systems levels – intrapsychic, interpersonal, social, and cultural. From the perspective of human development over the course of a single generation it begins with the alienation of mother from infant. It is reiterated within the undifferentiated unintegrated psyche of the growing child, then expressed at the social level as the alienation the psychotic person experiences from a world populated with his or her inner demons, and reciprocally, the alienation so-called "normal" people have for bizarre psychotic persons. Finally there are the cultural attitudes toward psychosis that have been codified for generations. Socio-cultural alienation is rooted in widespread unconscious acceptance of the biases of the dehumanizing organic medical model on the one hand, and those of a psychoanalysis that looks upon psychotic persons as constitutionally unable to become normal or neurotic on the other. As a result psychoanalysis has rejected psychosis as beyond its scope and abandoned it to a medical society that conceives of it in a way that alienates the subject from his or her own mind. This social alienation has been rationalized as scientific.

Our journey began by tracing the history of conceptualizations of psychosis starting with the medieval belief that it is a bizarre degenerative expression of a constitutional defect that renders afflicted persons less than fully human. We examined its evolution in the early days of medical science through the work of Kraepelin and Bleuler, to the current reductionist belief promulgated by DSM psychiatry that holds it is a genetically based neurological disease despite the absence of research evidence.

Psychoanalysis first encountered psychosis at the time Kraepelin and Freud's friend and colleague Bleuler were proposing that it is a degenerative neurological illness of late adolescent onset (dementia praecox). Freud did not knowingly work with psychotic individuals, and it is not surprising that he seems to have been influenced by the psychiatric beliefs then in vogue. His relatively sparse writings on the subject mostly reflect his belief that psychotic persons are unable to form normal relationships and to develop and sustain a normal/neurotic mental organization. Instead he was busy formulating his basic theory of mind and its development around neurosis, an affliction he looked upon as a variant of normal personality based on the faulty resolution of intrapsychic conflicts over infantile sexuality and authority. As he minimized the importance of mothers in development he did not consider the possibility that the psychotic difficulty forming a relationship might be a result of disturbance in mother–infant bonding rather than a constitutional defect.

Freud set out to create a scientific psychology whose concepts could ultimately be reduced to their biological origins. However, rather than situating his field within a scientific context like academic psychology or medicine he chose to create his own organization or movement. As a result psychoanalysis has qualities of a religion or a cult of personality. The pressure toward conformity and perpetuation of Freud's beliefs has interfered with a science-like accretion of knowledge. The efforts of his successors to meet with psychosis from within their own clinical experience and psychoanalytic theory have been compromised by an unconscious acceptance of Freud's basic belief that its organic origins places it beyond the scope of psychoanalysis. Many of the interesting and thought-provoking attempts to view the psychotic mind as meaningful such as those of Klein and Bion have been couched in the context of his pessimistic conclusions. The result is that the old wines of Bleuler and Freud have been marketed with new personal brand names, and psychoanalysis and psychosis have remained fundamentally alienated from one another.

The effective psychological treatment of psychosis is impossible in a culture that supports human alienation and has not separated itself from the primitive belief that psychotic individuals are constitutionally inferior specimens. The psychological introspection and work required to effect truly mutative treatment is not compatible with the values of our society. Our mental health system is increasingly oriented toward externalization of problems and minimizing personal responsibility and accountability for one's mind. Instead the system prescribes mind-altering substances to transform dysphoric states of mind into more acceptable ones.

As a result of the unfortunate confluence of belief between psychiatry and psychoanalysis our understanding of psychosis is almost entirely based upon the medical model. Its treatment is consigned to the pharmaceutical industry and the quest for new and lucrative drugs that are effective in mitigating symptoms. The medical model unwittingly promotes the very alienation that characterizes psychosis. It alienates the afflicted person from the meaningfulness of his or her mental symptoms and instead attempts to suppress them so that the person will seem less bizarre and more socially acceptable. It normalizes the surface manifestations of the illness but reinforces alienation by promoting disintegration of the disparate meaningful aspects of the sufferer's mind from one another. The combination of disintegration with undifferentiation causes the psychotic person to be alienated from others. Other persons are experienced not as separate selves but as unintegrated or repudiated aspects of the psychotic person's mind, in ways ranging from simple undifferentiation to more blatant hallucinations and delusions.

Fortunately Freud did leave an opening for subsequent development of a psychoanalytic theory of psychosis. In the process of trying to understand dreaming he discovered that mind works in two equally important but qualitatively different ways: the primary and secondary processes. He speculated in passing that the primary process, which he believed was unconscious and which does not support intrapsychic conflict, is the basis of psychosis as well as dreaming. Unfortunately he failed to pursue this line of speculation. Furthermore, the primary process concept is flawed by his confusion about whether it is normal or abnormal, whether it is truly different from symbolic thought or simply an arcane variant of thought, and most importantly, his confusion about the nature of conscious and unconscious mental processes.

I have followed the road Freud and his followers did not take. Psychosis originates from a severe disturbance or alienation in the mother–infant bond in the attachment–separation phase of development. The attachment–separation phase is negotiated by primordial conscious mentation, the first expression of mind, which is related to Freud's primary process. Failure to separate from the primary relationship leads to inappropriate and maladaptive persistence of primordial conscious mentation in contexts where reflective representational thought would be appropriate and adaptive.

Psychosis manifests itself as a spectrum of conditions of varying degrees of severity. These disturbances emerge at stages in the life cycle that call for maturational steps in the separation–individuation process leading to gradual formation of a secure cohesive self that is differentiated from other selves. This cohesive self is able to bear and represent emotions and the ideas related to them, to experience and resolve intrapsychic conflicts, and to make constructive decisions and growth-promoting choices. The most severe of the psychoses manifests itself in early childhood in the form of unrelatedness to others and inability to separate from home sufficiently to begin school. This condition or conditions are beyond my experience and beyond the scope of the book. Schizophrenia manifests itself in young adulthood around the second stage of separation from home at the time it is appropriate to begin a work life and form sustaining relationships and family of one's own.

Schizophrenia, incidentally, is an unfortunate label because the social stigma attached promotes alienation. Nonetheless, the meaning of the term, split mind, does capture one of the major features of the illness, lack of integration.

Hopefully over time, if some of the humanizing ideas I have put forward gain social acceptance, nomenclature may change.

Perhaps the largest group of psychotic individuals are those with psychotic personality disorders. This condition afflicts many of society's most interesting and productive persons. On the surface they seem able to negotiate life's first two separations and are generally viewed as normal and not infrequently exceptional, because their socially effective functioning is based on a façade designed to conceal their distress and maladaptation from the world at large. But their apparent success at separation and individuation is illusory. Their psychosis becomes evident when they seek help because of suffering they have tried to keep secret from others including difficulties in relationships and work, or when they collide with social agencies because of their actions. These people go under many different names – narcissistic, sociopathic, borderline, addictive, severely obsessional/phobic, and schizoid.

Psychosis and neurosis can both be conceptualized under the umbrella of psychoanalysis as its two major pathologies, each with its own separate line of development, and each based on a qualitatively distinctive but conscious mental process. Neurotic pathology is based on a self that has negotiated the initial differentiation–integration phase and is capable of experiencing intrapsychic conflict and utilizing defense mechanisms to try to resolve it. Psychotic pathology is based on failure to separate from primary caregivers and others and to integrate a cohesive self. This pre-self is incapable of experiencing and resolving intrapsychic conflict. It follows that there are different requirements and models of therapy that are suitable for each, ones that take into account an understanding of their unique developmental origins and mental processes. However, different as they are, each clinical approach and technique is equally psychoanalytic.

Even if social attitudes toward psychosis and its treatment were different, there are two stark realities. One is that schizophrenia is the most severe of the mental ills, and like its analogous severe organic illnesses, bears an uncertain prognosis under the best of circumstances. The other is that the human knowledge, skill, and labor-intensive dedication necessary to treat a single person is a scarce resource that cannot be made available to everyone. Ironically, in the long run the cost to society and the individual treated by the medical model may be far greater than the cost of providing the resources necessary for intensive psychoanalytic therapy, if they are available. Persons treated by the medical model for the most part are marginal contributors to society and require chronic support from their communities in one form or another. A meaningful autonomous human life usually has positive effects on other lives and on society whereas a disabled one is a chronic social drain. The case of Sara, in Chapter 16, illustrates the "ripple effect" mutative therapy can have.

A psychoanalytic model of mind that has a place for a theory of neurosis and a theory of psychosis under the same conceptual umbrella enables psychoanalysis to expand its scope and become more socially relevant. It offers the possibility of mutative treatment to at least some individuals who would otherwise have been consigned to a less than fully human existence.

Such a model also opens the way for a new look at the endless debate about the very nature of psychoanalysis itself. The debate traditionally centers around an implicit equation of psychoanalysis with the clinical technique traditionally used to treat neurotic individuals and the assumption that the only mental organization is that which underlies neurosis. From this perspective work such as I have described is dismissed as "not psychoanalysis." The neurotic model assumes a mind capable of experiencing intrapsychic conflict and utilizing defense mechanisms, principally repression, splitting, and projection. It emphasizes the essential importance of concrete aspects of the clinical situation such as the office arrangements that separate analyst from analysand (couch with chair behind), and on frequency and length of sessions. These are deemed essential in order to access and make conscious the analysand's defenses against mental content. The model is implemented by a standard technique in which the analyst encourages the patient's free, unchecked expression of mind. It assumes the development of a transference. The analyst more or less restricts him- or herself to making periodic observations and interpretations designed to make the unconscious nature of this emerging mental content conscious. Work with psychotic patients not only has no place in such a technical system, but if attempted it is actually harmful rather than helpful. The harm has mistakenly been attributed to the inherent nature of the illness rather than to mistaken theory and technique.

I propose a more encompassing definition of psychoanalysis, not as the clinical technique used with neurotic persons, but as a theory or set of theories about the structural and dynamic nature of mind as it expresses itself in relation to others. Such a theory encompasses both the neuroses and the psychoses. The traditional definition of psychoanalysis as the clinical treatment of neurosis need not be discarded, but can be subsumed under technology or technique. As with any discipline that aspires to be scientific, various technologies spin off from it. In the case of psychoanalysis these include techniques of therapy with neurotic and psychotic patients, as well as other applications like literary criticism, social commentary, and biography.

Scientia est potentia. Knowledge is power. The knowledge that psychosis is the understandable human outcome of a developmental pathway different from but not inferior to the pathways that lead to the neuroses has the potential to bring about a major change in social attitudes. Unfortunately the prejudices that alienate society – at least western society, for many tribal cultures are different – from psychotic individuals, and the societal repudiation of psychoanalysis as a discipline relevant to it are deeply and historically ingrained. Changing words and changing attitudes are two different things. The name of the institution in which I did my psychiatric residency was changed in the 1950s from Boston Psychopathic Hospital to Massachusetts Mental Health Center, but the basic attitude toward the patients it housed remained the same. The attitude of human inclusion rather than alienation offers hope to afflicted persons through psycho-analytically informed intervention that society more or less extends to persons with less severe afflictions. It brings psychoanalysis in from the cold as well, and makes it more socially relevant.

If psychoanalysis can truly meet psychosis so that condition assumes a place within psychoanalytic theory and clinical practice that is independent from but at least equally important as that of neurosis, then the wall of alienation can be breached, and psychosis can be embraced, as Sullivan advocated, as a human condition. It is my fervent hope that this book becomes part of the education of a new generation of mental health professionals, and that the ideas I have put forth in it might help to humanize the attitudes toward psychosis of the public with whom they interact.

REFERENCES

Ainsworth, M. (1982). Attachment: Retrospect and prospect. In: Parkes, C. & Stevenson-Hinde, J. (Eds.). *The Place of Attachment in Human Behavior*. New York: Basic Books, 3–30.

Ainsworth, M.D.S., Blehar, M.C., Waters, E., & Wall, S. (1978). *Patterns of Attachment: A Psychological Study of the Strange Situation*. Hillsdale, NJ: Lawrence Erlbaum.

Alexander, F., & Selesnick, F. (1965). Freud–Bleuler correspondence. *Archives of General Psychiatry*, 12: 1–9.

Arieti, S. (1955). *Interpretation of Schizophrenia*. New York: Basic Books.

Arieti, S. (1967). *The Intrapsychic Self*. New York: Basic Books.

Arlow, J., & Brenner, C. (1964). *Psychoanalytic Concepts and the Structural Theory*. New York: International Universities Press.

Arlow, J., & Brenner, C. (1969). The psychopathology of the psychoses: A proposed revision. *International Journal of Psycho-Analysis*, 50: 5–14.

Balint, M. (1937). Early developmental states of the ego: Primary object love. *Imago*, 23: 270–288.

Balint, M. (1958). The three areas of the mind: Theoretical considerations. *International Journal of Psycho-Analysis*, 39: 328–340.

Balint, M. (1968). *The Basic Fault: Therapeutic Aspects of Regression*. New York: Brunner/Mazel.

Best, C., & McRoberts, G. (2003). Infant perception of non-native consonant contrasts that adults assimilate in different ways. *Language and Speech*, 46: 183–216.

Bion, W. (1957). Differentiation of the psychotic from the non-psychotic personalities. *International Journal of Psycho-Analysis*, 38: 266–275.

Bion, W. (1959). Attacks on linking. *International Journal of Psycho-Analysis*, 40: 308–315.

Bion, W. (1962). *Learning from Experience*. London: Tavistock.

Bleuler, E. (1896). Review of Breuer & Freud, *Studien über Hysterie*. *Münchener Medizinische Wochenschrift*, 43: 524–525.

Bleuler, E. (1906). Freud'sche Mechanismen in der Symptomatologie von Psychosen. *Psychiatrisch-Neurologische Wochenschrift*, 34: 316–318;, 35: 323–325; 36: 338–340.

Bleuler, E. (1911a). *Textbook of Psychiatry*. New York: Macmillan (1924).

Bleuler, E. (1911b). *Dementia Praecox or the Group of Schizophrenias*. New York: International Universities Press (1950).

Bleuler, E. (1912). Review of Freud (1911). *Zentralblatt für Psychoanalyse und Psychotherapie*, 2: 343–348.

Bookhammer, R., Meyers, R., Shober, C., & Piotrowsky, Z. (1966). A five-year follow-up study of schizophrenics treated by Rosen's "direct analysis": Compared with controls. *American Journal of Psychiatry*, 123: 602–604.

Boston Change Process Study Group (BCPSG). (2007). The foundational level of psychodynamic meaning: Implicit process in relation to conflict, defense and the dynamic unconscious. *International Journal of Psycho-Analysis*, 88: 843–860.

Bowlby, J. (1969). *Attachment and Loss*, Vol. 1: *Attachment*. London: Hogarth Press and the Institute of Psycho-Analysis.

Boyer, L.B., & Giovacchini, P. (1990). *Master Clinicians on Treating the Regressed Patient*. Northvale, NJ: Jason Aronson.

Breier, A., Schreiber, J., Dyer, J., & Pickar, D. (1991). National Institute of Mental Health longitudinal study of chronic schizophrenia. *Archives of General Psychiatry*, 48: 239–246.

Brill, A. (1944). *Freud's Contribution to Psychiatry*. New York: Norton.

Brunswick, R. (1928). A supplement to Freud's "history of an infantile neurosis". *International Journal of Psychoanalysis*, 9: 439–476.

Carone, B., Harrow, M., & Westermeyer, J. (1991). Posthospital course and outcome in schizophrenia. *Archives of General Psychiatry*, 48: 247–253.

Chassell, J. (1962). Schizophrenia as a human process. *Psychoanaytic Quarterly*, 31: 556–559.

Choi, J., Cutler, A., & Broersma, M. (2017). Early development of abstract language knowledge: Evidence from perception-production transfer of birth-language memory. *Royal Society Open Science*, 4: 160–166.

Church, J. (1966). *Language and the Discovery of Reality*. New York: Vintage Books.

Condon, W., & Sander, L. (1974). Neonate movement is synchronized with adult speech: Interactional participation and language acquisition. *Science*, 183: 99–101.

Crick, F. (1994). *The Astonishing Hypothesis: The Scientific Search for the Soul*. New York: Charles Scribner's Sons.

Deutsch, H. (1942). Some forms of emotional disturbance and their relationship to schizophrenia. *Psychoanalytic Quarterly*, 11: 301–321.

Durkin, K., Rutter, D., & Tucker, H. (1982). Social interaction and language acquisition: Motherese help you. *First Language*, 3: 107–120.

Eissler, K. (1951). Remarks on the psycho-analysis of schizophrenia. *International Journal of Psycho-Analysis*, 32: 139–156.

Fairbairn, W. R. (1940). Schizoid factors in the personality. In: Fairbairn, R. (Ed.). *Psychoanalytic Studies of the Personality*. London: Routledge & Kegan Paul (1952), 3–27.

Fairbairn, W.R. (1941). A revised psychopathology of the psychoses and psychoneuroses. *International Journal of Psycho-Analysis*, 22: 250–279.

Fairbairn, W.R. (1943). The repression and the return of bad objects (with special reference to the "war neuroses"). In: Fairbairn, W.R (Ed.). *Psychoanalytic Studies of the Personality*. London: Tavistock (1952), 59–81.

Fairbairn, W.R. (1944). Endopsychic structure considered in terms of object-relationships. *International Journal of Psycho-Analysis*, 25: 70–92.

Fairbairn, W.R. (1952). *Psychoanalytic Studies of the Personality*. London: Tavistock.

Fairbairn, W.R. (1963). Synopsis of an object-relations theory of the personality. *International Journal of Psycho-Analysis*, 44: 224–225.

Falzeder, E. (2003). Sigmund Freud and Eugen Bleuler: The history of an ambivalent relationship. *Psychotherapies*, 23: 31–47.

Federn, P. (1952). *Ego Psychology and the Psychoses*. New York: Basic Books.

Ferenczi, S. (1924). *Thalassa: A Theory of Genitality*, H. Bunker (Trans.). New York: Norton (1968).

Ferenczi, S. (1932). The confusion of tongues between adults and children: The language of tenderness and of passion. *International Journal of Psycho-Analysis*, 30: 225–230

Fernald, A., & Kuhl, P. (1987). Acoustic determinants of infant preference for motherese speech. *Infant Behavior & Development*, 10: 279–293.

Fernald, A., & Simon, T. (1984). Expanded intonation contours in mothers' speech to newborns. *Developmental Psychology*, 20: 104–113.

Frances, A. (2014). *Saving Normal: An Insider's Revolt against Out-of-Control Psychiatric Diagnosis, DSM-5, Big Pharma, and the Medicalization of Ordinary Life*. New York: William Morrow.

Freud, S. (1895). Project for a scientific psychology. In: Strachey, J. et al. (Ed. and Trans.). *The Standard Edition of the Complete Psychological Works of Sigmund Freud*, Vol. 1, 295–397.

Freud, S. (1900). The interpretation of dreams. In: Strachey, J. et al. (Ed. and Trans.). *The Standard Edition of the Complete Psychological Works of Sigmund Freud*, Vols. 4–5.

Freud, S. (1907). Delusions and dreams in Jensen's *Gradiva*. In: Strachey, J. et al. (Ed. and Trans.). *The Standard Edition of the Complete Psychological Works of Sigmund Freud*, Vol. 9, 1–96.

Freud, S. (1909). Notes upon a case of obsessional neurosis. In: Strachey, J. et al. (Ed. and Trans.). *The Standard Edition of the Complete Psychological Works of Sigmund Freud*, Vol. 10, 151–220.

Freud, S. (1911). Psycho-analytic notes on an autobiographical account of a case of paranoia (dementia paranoides). In: Strachey, J. et al. (Ed. and Trans.). *The Standard Edition of the Complete Psychological Works of Sigmund Freud*, Vol. 12, 9–82.

Freud, S. (1914). On narcissism. In: Strachey, J. et al. (Ed. and Trans.). *The Standard Edition of the Complete Psychological Works of Sigmund Freud*, Vol. 14, 73–102.

Freud, S. (1915). The unconscious. In: Strachey, J. et al. (Ed. and Trans.). *The Standard Edition of the Complete Psychological Works of Sigmund Freud*, Vol. 14, 159–216.

Freud, S. (1916–1917). Introductory lectures on psycho-analysis. In: Strachey, J. et al. (Ed. and Trans.). *The Standard Edition of the Complete Psychological Works of Sigmund Freud*, Vols. 15–16.

Freud, S. (1920). Beyond the pleasure principle. In: Strachey, J. et al. (Ed. and Trans.). *The Standard Edition of the Complete Psychological Works of Sigmund Freud*, Vol. 18, 3–64.

Freud, S. (1924). The loss of reality in neurosis and psychosis. In: Strachey, J. et al. (Ed. and Trans.). *The Standard Edition of the Complete Psychological Works of Sigmund Freud*, Vol. 19, 183–190.

Freud, S. (1940). Outline of psychoanalysis. In: Strachey, J. et al. (Ed. and Trans.). *The Standard Edition of the Complete Psychological Works of Sigmund Freud*, Vol. 23, 141–208.

Freud, S., & Jung, C. (1994). *The Freud–Jung Letters*. Princeton, NJ: Princeton University Press.

Fromm-Reichmann, F. (1939). Transference problems in schizophrenics. *Psychoanalytic Quarterly*, 8: 412–426.

Fromm-Reichmann, F. (1948). Notes on the development of treatment of schizophrenics by psychoanalytic psychotherapy. *Psychiatry*, 11: 265–273.

Fromm-Reichmann, F. (1950). *Principles of Intensive Psychotherapy*. Chicago, IL: University of Chicago Press.

Fromm-Reichmann, F. (1952). Some aspects of psychoanalytic psychotherapy with schizophrenics. In: Brody, E. & Redlich, F. (Eds.). *Psychotherapy with Schizophrenics*. New York: International Universities Press, 89–111.

Fromm-Reichmann, F. (1954a). Psychotherapy of schizophrenia. *American Journal of Psychiatry*, 111: 410–419.

Fromm-Reichmann, F. (1954b). Psychoanalytic and general dynamic conceptions of theory and of therapy: Differences and similarities. *Journal of the American Psychoanalytic Association*, 2: 711–721.

Gibson, R. (1989). The application of psychoanalytic principles to the hospitalized patient. In: Silver, A. (Ed.). *Psychoanalysis and Psychosis*. Madison, CT: International Universities Press, 183–206.

Glover, E. (1943). The concept of dissociation. In: Glover, E. (Ed.). *On the Early Development of Mind: Selected Papers*. New York: International Universities Press (1956), 307–323.

Green, H. (1964). *I Never Promised You a Rose Garden*. New York: Holt, Rinehart & Winston.

Greenspan, S., & Shanker, S. (2005). *The First Idea: How Symbols, Language and Intelligence Evolved from our Primate Ancestors to Modern Humans*. Cambridge, MA: Da Capo Press.

Grieser, D., & Kuhl, P. (1988). Maternal speech to infants in a tonal language: Support for universal prosodic features in motherese. *Developmental Psychology*, 24: 14–20.

Groddeck, G. (1923). *The Book of the It*. New York: Nervous and Mental Disease Publishing Company (1928).

Groddeck, G. (1977). *The Meaning of Illness, Selected Psychoanalytic Writings of Georg Groddeck*, Schacht, L. (Ed.) & G. Mander (Trans.). New York: International Universities Press.

Gunderson, J., Frank, A., Katz, H., Vanicelli, M., Frosch, J., & Knapp, P. (1984). Effects of psychotherapy in schizophrenia: II. Comparative outcome of two forms of treatment. *Schizophrenia Bulletin*, 10: 564–598.

Harding, C. (1987). Chronicity in schizophrenia: Fact, partial fact, or artifact? *Hospital and Community Psychiatry*, 38: 477–491.

Harding, C., Brooks, D., Ashikaga, T., Strauss, T., & Brier, A. (1987). The Vermont longitudinal study of persons with severe mental illness, II: Long-term outcome of subjects who retrospectively met DSM-III criteria for schizophrenia. *American Journal of Psychiatry*, 144: 727–735.

Hartmann, H. (1953). Contribution to the metapsychology of schizophrenia. *Psychoanalytic Study of the Child*, 8: 177–198.

Hesse, E., & Main, M. (2000). Disorganized infant, child, and adult attachment. *Journal of the American Psychoanalytic Association*, 48: 1097–1127.

Horwitz, W., Polatin, P., Kolb, L., & Hoch, P. (1958). A study of cases of schizophrenia treated by direct analysis. *American Journal of Psychiatry*, 114: 780–783.

Huber, G., Gross, G., Schuttler, R., & Linz, M. (1980). Longitudinal studies of schizophrenic patients. *Schizophrenia Bulletin*, 6: 592–605.

Isaacs, S. (1948). The nature and function of phantasy. *International Journal of Psycho-Analysis*, 29: 73–97.

Jones, E. (1916). The theory of symbolism. In: Jones, E. (Ed.). *Papers on Psychoanalysis*. London: Bailliere, Tindall & Cox (1948), 87–144.

Joseph, J. (2003). *The Gene Illusion: Genetic Research in Psychiatry and Psychology under the Microscope*. Ross-on-Wye: PCCS Books.

Jung, C. (1906). *The Psychology of Dementia Praecox*. New York & Washington, DC: Nervous and Mental Disease Publishing Company (1936).

Jung, C. (1909). Letter from C.G. Jung to Sigmund Freud, November 8, 1909. In: McGuire, W. (Ed.). *The Freud/Jung Letters: The Correspondence between Sigmund Freud and C.G. Jung*. Princeton, NJ: Princeton University Press (1994), 256–258.

Jung, C. (1939). On the psychogenesis of schizophrenia. *Journal of Mental Science*, 85: 999–1011.

Kernberg, O. (1966). Structural derivatives of object relationships. *International Journal of Psycho-Analysis*, 47: 236–253.

Kernberg, O. (1967). Borderline personality organization. *Journal of the American Psychoanalytic Association*, 15: 641–685.

King, P., & Steiner, R. (1991). *The Freud–Klein Controversies 1941–1945*. London: Tavistock & Routledge.

Klein, M. (1932). *The Psychoanalysis of Children*. New York: Free Press (1975).

Klein, M. (1935). A contribution to the psychogenesis of manic-depressive states. In: Klein, M. (Ed.). *Love, Guilt and Reparation and Other Works 1921–1945*. London: Hogarth Press (1975), 262–289.

Klein, M. (1937). Love, guilt and reparation. In: Klein, M. (Ed.). *Love, Guilt and Reparation and Other Works 1921–1945*. New York: Free Press (1975), 306–343.

Klein, M. (1946). Notes on some schizoid mechanisms. *International Journal of Psycho-Analysis*, 27: 99–110.

Knight, R. (1953). Borderline states. *Bulletin of the Menninger Clinic*, 17: 1–12.

Kohut, H. (1971). *The Analysis of the Self*. New York: International Universities Press.

Kohut, H. (1977). *The Restoration of the Self*. New York: International Universities Press.

Kolata, G. (1984). Studying learning in the womb. *Science*, 225: 302–303.

Kraepelin, E. (1919). *Dementia Praecox and Paraphrenia*. Chicago, IL: Chicago Medical Book Company.

Lieberman, J. (2015). *Shrinks*. New York: Little, Brown & Co.

Lieberman, J., & Stroup, S. (2011). The NIMH-CATIE schizophrenia study: What did we learn? *American Journal of Psychiatry*, 168: 770–775.

Lindner, R. (1966). *The Fifty-Minute Hour*. New York: Bantam Books.

Lombardi, R. (2015). *Formless Infinity: Clinical Explorations of Matte Blanco and Bion*. London and New York: Routledge.

Lyons-Ruth, K. (2003). Dissociation and the parent–infant dialogue. *Journal of the American Psychoanalytic Association*, 51: 883–911.

Mahler, M. (1952). On child psychosis and schizophrenia: Autistic and symbiotic infantile psychoses. *Psychoanalytic Study of the Child*, 7: 286–305.

Mahler, M. (1968). *On Human Symbiosis and the Vicissitudes of Individuation*, Vol. 1: *Infantile Psychosis*. New York: International Universities Press.

Mahler, M., Bergman, A., & Pine, F. (1975). *The Psychological Birth of the Human Infant: Symbiosis and Individuation*. New York: Basic Books.

Matte-Blanco, I. (1959). Expression in symbolic logic of the characteristics of the system Unconscious. *International Journal of Psycho-Analysis*, 40: 1–5.

Matte-Blanco, I. (1975). *The Unconscious as Infinite Sets*. London: Karnac.

Matte-Blanco, I. (1988). *Thinking, Feeling, and Being: Clinical Reflections on the Fundamental Antinomy of Human Beings and World*. London: Routledge.

McGlashan, T. (1984). The Chestnut Lodge follow-up study. II: Long-term outcome of schizophrenia and the affective disorders. *Archives of General Psychiatry*, 41: 586–601.

McGlashan, T. (1988). A selective review of recent North American long-term follow-up studies of schizophrenia. *Schizophrenia Bulletin*, 14: 515–542.

McGlashan, T., & Keats, C. (1989). *Schizophrenia: Treatment Process and Outcome*. Washington, DC: American Psychiatric Press.

Mehler, J., & Christophe, A. (2000). Acquisition of languages: Infant and adult data. In: Gazzaniga, M. (Ed.). *The New Cognitive Neurosciences*. Cambridge, MA: MIT Press, 897–908.

Menezes, N., Arenovich, T., & Zipursky, R. (2006). A systematic review of longitudinal outcome studies of first-episode psychosis. *Psychological Medicine*, 36: 1349–1362.

Milner, M. (1969). *The Hands of the Living God*. London: Routledge (2010).

Morel, B. (1851). *Etudes cliniques*, Vol. 1. Paris: Grimblot, Raybois, & Victor Masson.

Morel, B. (1860). *Traité des maladies mentales*. Paris: J.B. Baillière.

Okasha, A., & Madkour, O. (1982). Cortical and central atrophy in chronic schizophrenia. *Acta Psychiatrica Scandinavia*, 65: 29–34.

Partanen, E., Kujala, T., Naatanin, R., Liitola, A., Sambeth, A., & Huotilainen, N. (2013). Learning-induced neural plasticity of speech before birth. *Proceedings of the American Academy of Sciences*, 110: 15145–15150.

Paus, T., Zijdembos, A., Worsele, K., Collins, L., Blumenthal, J., Geidd, J., Rapoport, J., Evans, A., et al. (1999). Structural maturation of neural pathways in children and adolescents: In vivo study. *Science*, 283: 1908–1911.

Poster, M.F. (2009). Ferenczi and Groddeck: Simpatico. *American Journal of Psychoanalysis*, 69: 195–206.

Rank, O. (1924). *The Trauma of Birth*. London: Dover Press (1994).

Rank, O. (1926). The genesis of the object relation. In: Kramer, R. (Ed.). *A Psychology of Difference: The American Lectures*. Princeton, NJ: Princeton University Press (1996), 140–149.

Rank, O. (1938). Modern psychology and social change. In: Kramer, R. (Ed.). *A Psychology of Difference: The American Lectures*. Princeton, NJ: Princeton University Press (1996), 264–276.

Reichard, S. (1956). A re-examination of "Studies in Hysteria". *Psychoanalytic Quarterly*, 25: 155–177.

Rivera-Gaxiola, M., Silvia-Pereyra, J., & Kuhl, P. (2005). Brain potentials to native and non-native speech: Contrasts in 7- and 11-month-old American infants. *Developmental Science*, 8: 162–172.

Robbins, M. (1988). Use of audiotape recording in impasses with severely disturbed personalities. *Journal of the American Psychoanalytic Association*, 36: 61–75.

Robbins, M. (1993). *Experiences of Schizophrenia*. New York: Guilford.

Robbins, M. (2008). Primary mental expression: Freud, Klein and beyond. *Journal of the American Psychoanalytic Association*, 56: 177–202.

Robbins, M. (2011). *The Primordial Mind in Health and Illness: A Cross-Cultural Perspective*. London and New York: Routledge.

Robbins, M. (2012). The successful psychoanalytic therapy of a schizophrenic woman. *Psychodynamic Psychiatry*, 40: 575–608.

Robbins, M. (2013). Affect, emotion and the psychotic mind. In: Gumley, A., Gillham, A., Taylor, K., & Schwannauer, M. (Eds.). *Psychosis and Emotion: The Role of Emotions in Understanding Psychosis, Therapy and Recovery*. London and New York: Routledge, 149–163.

Robbins, M. (2015). The "royal road" – To what? *Annual of Psychoanalysis*, 38: 196–214.

Robbins, M. (2018). The primary process: Freud's profound yet neglected contribution to the psychology of consciousness. *Psychoanalytic Inquiry*, 38: 186–197.

Robertson, J. (1971). Young children in brief separation: A fresh look. *Psychoanalytic Study of the Child*, 26: 264–315.

Rosen, J. (1947). The treatment of schizophrenic psychosis by direct analytic therapy. *Psychoanalytic Quarterly*, 21: 3–25.

Rosen, J. (1953). *Direct Analysis: Selected Papers*. New York: Grune & Stratton.

Rudnytsky, P. (2002). *Reading Psychoanalysis: Freud, Rank, Ferenczi, Groddeck*. Cornell, NY: Cornell University Press.

Schwab, K., Groh, T., Schwab, M., & Witte, H. (2009). Nonlinear analysis and modeling of cortical activation and deactivation patterns in the immature fetal electrocorticogram. *Chaos. An Interdisciplinary Journal of Nonlinear Science*, 19. Retrieved from www.ncbi.nlm.nih.gov/pubmed/19335015

Schwing, G. (1940). *Ein Weg zur Seele der Geisteskranken*. Zürich: Rascher. Trans. Ekstein, R. & Hall, B., *A Way to the Soul of the Mentally Ill*. New York: International Universities Press (1954).

Searles, H. (1965). *Collected Papers on Schizophrenia and Related Subjects*. New York: International Universities Press.

Searles, H. (1986). *My Work with Borderline Patients*. Northvale, NJ and London: Jason Aronson.

Sechehaye, M. (1951a). *Autobiography of a Schizophrenic Girl*. New York: Grune & Stratton.

Sechehaye, M. (1951b). *Symbolic Realization*. New York: International Universities Press.

Sechehaye, M. (1956). The transference in symbolic realization. *International Journal of Psycho-Analysis*, 37: 270–277.

Sharpless, E. (1985). Identity formation as reflected in the acquisition of personal pronouns. *Journal of the American Psychoanalytic Association*, 71: 861–885.

Stanton, A., Gunderson, J., Knapp, P., Vanicelli, M., Schnitzer, R., & Rosenthal, R. (1984). Effects of therapy in schizophrenia: I. Design and implementation of a controlled study. *Schizophrenia Bulletin*, 10: 520–563.

Stanton, A., & Schwartz, M. (1954). *The Mental Hospital*. New York: Basic Books.

Strauss, J., & Carpenter, W. (1977). Prediction of outcome in schizophrenia. III: Five-year outcome and its predictors. *Archives of General Psychiatry*, 34: 159–163.

Sullivan, H.S. (1931). The modified psychoanalytic treatment of schizophrenia. *American Journal of Psychiatry*, 88: 519–540. Reprinted in: Sullivan, H.S., *The Collected Works of Harry Stack Sullivan, M.D.*, Vol 2: *Schizophrenia as a Human Process*. New York: Norton (1956), 272–294.

Sullivan, H.S. (1933). Mental disorders. *Encyclopedia of Social Sciences*, 10: 313–319. Reprinted in: Sullivan, H.S., *The Collected Works of Harry Stack Sullivan, M.D.*, Vol. 2: *Schizophrenia as a Human Process*. New York: Norton (1956), 297–307.

Sullivan, H.S. (1940). *Conceptions of Modern Psychiatry: The First William Alanson White Memorial Lectures*. New York: Norton (1966).

Sullivan, H.S. (1953). *The Interpersonal Theory of Psychiatry*. New York: Norton.

Sullivan, H.S. (1954). The psychiatric interview. In: Sullivan, H.S. (Ed.). *The Collected Works of Harry Stack Sullivan, M.D.*, Vol. 1. New York: Norton, 3–246.

Sullivan, H.S. (1962). *Schizophrenia as a Human Process*. New York: Norton.

Swados, E. (1991). *The Four of Us: The Story of a Family*. New York: Farrar, Straus & Giroux.

Tsao, F., Liu, H., & Kuhl, P. (2006). Perception of native and non-native affricate–fricative contrasts: Cross-language tests on adults and infants. *Journal of the Acoustical Society of America*, 120: 2285–2294.

Vita, A., Sacchetti, F., Calzroni, A., & Cazzuto, C. (1988). Cortical atrophy in schizophrenia: Prevalence and associated features. *Schizophrenia Research*, 1: 129–137.

Von Domarus, E. (1925), Über die Beziehung des normalen zum schizophrenen Denken [On the relationship between normal and schizophrenic thought], *Archiv für Psychiatrie und Nervenkrankheiten*, 74: 641–646.

Von Domarus, E. (1944). The specific laws of logic in schizophrenia. In: Kasanin, J. (Ed.). *Language and thought in Schizophrenia*. Berkeley, CA: University of California Press, 104–114.

Walker, E., & Lewine, R. (1990). Prediction of adult-onset schizophrenia from childhood home movies of the patient. *American Journal of Psychiatry*, 147: 1052–1056.

Wallace, C., Mullen, P., & Burgess, P. (2004). Criminal offending in schizophrenia over a 25-year period marked by deinstitutionalization and increasing prevalence of comorbid substance abuse disorders. *American Journal of Psychiatry*, 161: 716–727.

Werker, J., & Tees, R. (1984). Cross-language speech perception: Evidence for perceptual reorganization during the first year of life. *Infant Behavior & Development*, 7: 49–63.

Werner, H., & Kaplan, B. (1963). *Symbol Formation: An Organismic-Developmental Approach to Language and the Expression of Thought*. New York: Wiley.

Whitaker, R. (2010). *Mad in America*. New York: Basic Books.

Winnicott, D.W. (1945). Primitive emotional development. *International Journal of Psycho-Analysis*, 26: 137–143.

Winnicott, D.W. (1951). Transitional objects and transitional phenomena. In: Winnicott, W.D. (Ed.). *Collected Papers*. London: Tavistock (1958), 229–242.

Winnicott, D.W. (1960). Ego distortion in terms of true and false self. In: Winnicott, D.W., *The Maturational Processes and the Facilitating Environment*. London: Hogarth (1965), 140–152.

INDEX